Damned Facts

Fortean Essays on Religion, Folklore and the Paranormal

Edited by

Jack Hunter

αporetic press

This edition first published 2016 by

αporetic press
Registered Office: Samou 4, Konia, 8300, Paphos, Cyprus

http://aporeticpress.wordpress.com
Email: aporeticpress@gmail.com

ISBN 978-9963-2214-2-4 (paperback)
ISBN 978-9963-2214-3-1 (ebook)

A copy of this book has been deposited at the Cyprus Library

For Rosie and the Mystery Someone.

Illustrations

Cover Image taken from page 301 'Ghosts: being the experiences of Flaxman Low ... With twelve illustrations by B. E. Minns', Kate O' Brien Prichard (London: C. A. Pearson, 1899). The British Library.

Decoration 1, Foreword, p. xiii
Image taken from page 116 of 'The Old World in its New Face: Impressions of Europe in 1867-1868,' Vol. 1, Henry Whitney Bellows (New York: Harper & Bros, 1868). The British Library.

Decoration 2, Introduction, p. 1
Image taken from page 400 of '[Death's Doings; ... illustrations of twenty-four plates designed and etched by Richard Dagley.]' (London: J. Andrews; W. Cole, 1827), Second edition, with considerable additions. The British Library.

Decoration 3, Chapter 1, p. 15
Image taken from page 41 of 'Real Sailor-Songs. Collected and edited by John Ashton. Two hundred illustrations.' (London: Leadenhall Press, 1891). The British Library.

Decoration 4, Chapter 2, p. 28
Image taken from page 285 of 'The Death Shot. A romance of forest and prairie, etc', Vol. 2, Mayne Reid (London, 1873). The British Library.

Decoration 5, Chapter 3, p. 41
Image taken from page 63 of '[Bachelor to the Rescue. [A novel.]]' Anne Florence Louisa Mary Patton Bethune (London Remington & Co., 1894), Second edition. The British Library.

Decoration 6, Chapter 4, p. 54
Image taken from page 115 of 'A Day of Fate', Edward Payson Roe, Vol. 1 (London: Ward& Lock, 1880). The British Library.

Decoration 7, Chapter 5, p. 68
Image taken from page 239 of 'The Death Shot. A romance of forest and prairie, etc', Vol. 1, Mayne Reid (London, 1873). The British Library.

Decoration 8, Chapter 6, p. 81
Image taken from page 264 of 'The Death Shot. A romance of forest and prairie, etc', Vol. 3, Mayne Reid (London 1873). The British Library.

Decoration 9, Chapter 7, p. 97
Image taken from page 63 of '[Appleton's European Guide Book illustrated.... Containing ... maps, etc.]', Vol. 1, Daniel Appleton (New York; Longmans & Co, 1879); (D. Appleton & Co., Spring edition, 1879, revised). The British Library.

Decoration 10, Chapter 8, p. 113
Image taken from page 236 of 'Reprints of Rare Tracts, Imprints of Ancient Manuscripts ... chiefly illustrative of the history of the Northern Counties: and printed at the press of M. A. Richardson, Newcastle', 1847. The British Library.

Decoration 11, Chapter 9, p. 130
Image taken from page 89 of 'The Death Shot. A romance of forest and prairie, etc.', Vol. 1, Mayne Reid (London, 1873). The British Library.

Contents

ix

Acknowledgements

The editor would like to thank everyone who has contributed to this volume, without whom, naturally, it would not exist. Big thanks go to Aspasia Stephanou and Amba J. Sepie for vital assistance with proof-reading and editing. Thanks also to Gary Lachman, Bernardo Kastrup and Jeffrey J. Kripal for useful comments on this book.

Foreword

Damned Comparisons and the Real

Jeffrey J. Kripal

The scholar of religion Walter Capps once asked his readers to imagine what the study of religion would look like today if its past practitioners would have followed the erotic illuminations and channelled poetry of the British visionary William Blake instead of the Enlightenment rationalisms and neat reductionisms of our present canon.

> Consider...what turmoil William Blake's insights would create for the methodological conceptualization of standard religious studies. How could any of them be fitted to any coherent scheme, or, if they were, would they remain what they were originally? Why is the mentality of the technician sanctioned in religious studies while the attitude of the artist is treated with suspicion?[1]

I have often wondered myself what our shared fields would look like if we would have followed the damned comparisons and irreverent deconstructions of science and religion of Charles Fort. Much weirder and funnier, no doubt. And, I dare add, way more interesting.

I remember the day I first encountered Fort. Or almost encountered him. I was at an Esalen symposium with David Hufford, the folklorist, medical humanist, and scholar of spirituality and health who wrote *The Terror That Comes in the Night* (1982) and has since done so much to challenge the erasure of 'spirit' from our academic vocabulary and methods. David said something to me to the effect, 'Gee, Jeff, you sound a lot like Charles Fort.' 'Who the heck is Charles Fort?' I asked (maybe not quite like that). David educated me. I went home and ordered the standard green Dover edition of his collected work; you know, the one with the falling fish on the cover. I was simply blown away, and delighted, and bedazzled. I was also immensely entertained. I laughed all the way through, from the opening oracular pages of *The Book of the Damned* to the bubble-gum chewing 'poltergeist girls' of *Wild Talents*. If you

---

1. Walter H. Capps, *Religious Studies: The Making of a Discipline* (Philadelphia: Fortress Press, 2000), 342.

have read him, you know the feeling. You know what I mean.

I have spent the last ten years or so exploring what the study of religion would look like if we were to put Charles Fort in our canon. I then put my tentative conclusions into a series of books, all of which are cited in the following essays in some abundance. Thank you, each of you, for reading me. It is a pleasure and a joy to see one's writing taken so seriously and fairly and, most of all, to see it put to work in the work of others. Personally speaking, I am so heartened.

Alas, this has not always been my experience. Writing and publishing books in the humanities often feels like a thankless task, if not a hopeless one. In a world that thinks everything that is real is quantifiable, a number, trying to make sense of non-quantifiable realities like meaning and consciousness, much less 'something' as real-unreal as the paranormal, is as countercultural as it gets these days. The image that comes to my mind when I think about writing in what Fort calls the 'philosophy of the hyphen,' is throwing a Kleenex off the Grand Canyon. The result? Nothing. Absolutely nothing.

And then, suddenly, something happens. Someone actually reads a book (instead of endless text messages and social media posts). Someone actually writes a book (instead of endless text messages and social media posts). Someone gets up the courage not to be bullied into silence by some invisible cultural norm. And as more people read and write, the invisible cultural norm weakens and begins to waver. Actually, it was always weak and wavy.

I felt this with the present volume, from Jack's powerful Introduction, through Eden and Christopher's binary-collapsing transmediumizers, to Roberta's beautiful reflection on her own massive precognitive experience and her subsequent struggle to come to terms with it, to accept it, to authorize it.

I don't know what I can say here that the essayists have not said more fully and much better. But toward some sort of attempt, let me offer three conclusions that I have gathered from Fort and that are certainly reflected here. The first involves comparison. The second involves the fetishization of the past in the study of religion. The third involves—forgive me—reality.

The first conclusion involves the practice of comparison, about which I care a great deal and think we must renew and revision now. Comparison 2.0. I took such hope, such satisfaction, from the essayists here, so many of whom are young intellectuals just beginning their professional careers. May you change the field. May you change us.

Please never forget that Charles Fort was first and foremost a comparativist. Without comparison, there is no Charles Fort, no *The Book of the Damned*, no *Wild Talents*. Indeed, in all four of his books, he sought to awaken us to the questions of what we compare and why, and most of all why we keep so much material off of our comparative tables. Our conclusions about both 'science' and 'religion,' he taught us, are largely a function of what we do not allow on those tables. Science and religion only work by deciding what to ignore. What they allow are generally those things, with respect to science now, that we can explain with our rationalisms, materialisms and reductionisms or, in the case of religion, with our established faiths. With respect to our religious traditions, we look at all of that stuff and declare: 'Oh, that is an angel, and that is a demon, and that is nothing at all.' With respect to our science, or social science, we look at all of the same stuff and declare: 'There is nothing truly strange or mysterious here. It is all just math. Or matter. Or code for something else, something bad no doubt—like ideology, colonialism, or the denial of death.' Such conclusions, of course, carry their own truths, but they only work so far, and then they don't.

Put most simply, our methods of comparison determine our conclusions, which are more often than not at once predictable, depressing and, quite frankly, often more than a little boring.

I think this is one reason we should read Charles Fort again. So that we can read and think our way out of our predictability, depression and boredom. The truth is not depressing in Fort, after all. It might be super weird, or insane, or giggling, but it is seldom depressing, and it is never ever boring. I mean, really, things are falling out of the sky or popping into or out of existence everywhere in his books. Reading Fort is sort of like reading Mark Twain, Mircea Eliade and Philip K. Dick, but all at once.

So that's the first thing. Those damned comparisons that still might awaken us out of our materialist and religious sleep.

The second thing involves what we think of as the past. As a historian of religions who works primarily in the nineteenth and twentieth centuries, I have long been disturbed by my discipline's overwhelming (and basically conservative) tendency to fetishize the premodern past, as if we can only be profound speaking and thinking in Hebrew, Greek, Latin, Arabic, Sanskrit, or classical Chinese. That assumption is complete nonsense, and dangerous nonsense at that. Extraordinary religious experience-events (and these are historical events) as mind-blowing as anything that happened in the past are as common as water, if only we knew where to look and could abandon our easy intellectual derisions and, deeper still, the ancient biblical condemnations of the monotheistic imagination, which has long hated anything smacking of 'magic' or 'witchcraft,' which is what the 'paranormal' is at the end of the day. Fort knew that. He playfully called his own hoped for future, or Third Dominant, the Era of Witches and Wizards, among whom he playfully counted himself, on his better days, at least. He wasn't so sure on his bad days.

After reading Fort, we can easily see that underlying assumptions like 'all religious profundity is in the past,' or 'all forms of consciousness are historically constructed'—regardless of their intentions—function as ideological fire-walls to protect the past revelations and enlightenments (read: the religions and their scriptures) from robust critical analysis. I can easily understand why religious authorities want to do this: they are 'disciplining' the present to protect the past (and, of course, their own authority and worldview). I cannot understand why scholars of religion want to do this.

Fort would have none of this, of course. He in fact did the exact opposite. He just stopped at 1800 and focused on English and French newspapers and journals. It's sort of funny, if you think about it. And it is truly arbitrary, if you think about it again. But it works just as well as any other arbitrary slice through human culture and history, which is what every history or ethnography is at the end of the day.

So there's the second thing. Damning the present to protect the past. Please don't.

The third thing is the strangest thing of all. It involves how our comparative practices and historical slicing might actually contribute to the shifting of the real, by which I mean the human experience of reality, whatever (or whoever) that is. This is where things get a bit megalomaniacal. But so what? We're talking about Charles Fort, aren't we?

Fort taught us that paranormal events are as common as water, but that they are ruthlessly repressed, or just ignored, by our scientific and religious filters and their own magical practices. Today the magic word that people use to whisk the wonderful and terrible away is 'anecdotal.' Oddly, it works. The results are fascinating to think about.

There are really two options here, both of which Fort was fully aware of and entertained in different ways. Delightfully, both of these options very recently appeared, of all places, in the *New York Times*. In 'Ghosts in a Secular Age,' columnist Ross Douthat began by invoking a report of a widow encountering her discarnate husband. The significant thing here was not so much the discarnate husband (again, we are veritable experts at ignoring the marvelous), but the fact that the couple hailed from the hyper-secular world of the New York literary establishment. The widow was Lisa Chase, and the husband, Peter Kaplan, was editor of the *New York Observer*. Douthat goes on to reference another essay he had written earlier about an outbreak of ghosts after the recent Japanese tsunami. There he invoked the Canadian philosopher Charles Taylor to ask the question of why ghosts no longer appear in the present to the same extent that they seemed to appear in the past.

The first possibility is that modern peoples experience the mystical and the ghostly as much as premodern peoples, but their secular culture or 'immanent frame' encourages them to privatize these and keep them out of the public culture. Hence the illusion that these experiences are uncommon or anecdotal flukes, statistical blips, as it were. The second possibility is that what Taylor calls the 'immanent frame' somehow 'buffers' the self and prevents the numinous from reaching us to the same extent. As Douthat explains, 'the secular frame somehow changes the very nature of numinous experience, so that it feels more attenuated and unreal, and the human self is more 'buffered' against its enchantments, terrors, and pull.'[2] Here, religious experiences are actually being repressed and made less possible, even impossible, by the cultural filter and subsequent heavily buffered self.

In *Authors of the Impossible*, I lean heavily toward this latter hypothesis, partly through reading Fort, partly through the 'filter thesis' of consciousness (which sees the body-brain, in effect, as a kind of buffering or stepping down of consciousness as such), but mostly through the work of the French sociologist and philosopher Bertrand Méheust, whose two-volume history of animal magnetism and psychical research in eighteenth-, nineteenth-, and early twentieth-century France demonstrates the same thesis in rich and erudite detail.[3] Following Bertrand, I suggest that we have literally made the once possible impossible. We have changed the texture and reach of the real, even if its potential spectrum remains the same as it always was (or is).

Jack explores a similar notion in his Introduction through his concept of 'ontological flooding,' and many of the essayists return to the same tantalizing idea in their essays. Of course, we cannot prove this notion of a 'culturally conditioned nature,' as the Italian anthropologist Ernesto de Martino had it, but we can certainly think with it and see where it leads.

Somewhere strange, no doubt. I think, with Jack, that paranormal phenomena are the real 'X-Files of the humanities.' One of my colleagues likes to call the study of religion the 'Area 51 of the university' in a similar Fortean spirit. Both playful descriptions capture something important (including the way that popular culture has become a major locus of inspiration for academics). What would our disciplines look like if we embraced the anomalous and integrated the phenomena directly into our theories and research agendas? What would our intellectual practices and our forms of knowledge look like if we opened the X-Files and just walked right into Area 51? Well, it would look something like these wonderful essays.

2. Ross Douthat, 'Ghosts in a Secular Age,' *New York Times*, October 7, 2015, http://douthat.blogs.nytimes.com/2015/10/07/ghosts-in-a-secular-age/
3. Bertrand Méheust, *Somnambulisme et médiumnité (1784-1930)*, two volumes (Le Plessis-Robinson: Institut Synthélabo Pour Le Progrés de la Connaissance, 1999).

Introduction

Intermediatism and the Study of Religion

Jack Hunter

Over the course of four groundbreaking books published between 1919-1932,[4] Charles Hoy Fort (1874-1932) meticulously presented thousands of accounts of anomalous events that he found documented in scientific journals, newspapers and books at the New York Public Library and the British Museum. In conducting his wide-ranging textual excavations, Fort uncovered impossible numbers of extraordinary reports of fish and frogs falling from the sky, poltergeists wreaking havoc on unexpecting families, spontaneous human combustion, unidentified flying objects, levitations of people and things, mysterious disappearances, apparitions, and so on.[5]

All of these strange events, according to Fort, had been brushed under the carpet by mainstream science,[6] indeed his books were deliberately intended as an out-and-out affront to the scientific establishment, and in particular to the idea that science has essentially 'sorted it all out' already. Fort was not at all convinced by this, and his collections of 'Damned Facts,' as he called them, served as evidence in support of his suspicions and speculations. Fort obsessively catalogued these 'Damned Facts' on small pieces of card, which he stored in hundreds of shoe boxes in his New York apartment, ready to be unleashed in the wild processions of his books.[7]

Fort's books would go on to become classics of 'paranormal' literature, and inspired others to employ a similarly 'Fortean' approach in their own work, notably including writers such as John A. Keel (1930-2009), Colin

---

4. *The Book of the Damned* (1919), *New Lands* (1925), *Lo!* (1931), and *Wild Talents* (1932).

5. In the introduction to *The Directory of Possibilities* (1981), Colin Wilson criticises Fort's scatter-gun approach to presenting his 'procession of Damned Facts.' Wilson writes 'He jumbles up all kinds of weird occurrences...as if all were on the same level, and he fails to make the slightest attempt to explain them.' To Fort, as we will see, however, all phenomena *are* on the same level, and this, in a sense, works towards his explanation for them.

6. Perhaps 'scientism' would be a better term.

7. Jim Steinmeyer, *Charles Fort: The Man Who Invented the Supernatural* (London: Heinnemann, 2008).

Wilson (1931-2013), Robert Anton Wilson (1932-2007), and Jacques Vallée, amongst others (some of whose work will be discussed in later chapters of this book). Fort's books and approach were also the inspiration behind the founding of the famous magazine *Fortean Times*, which, since it was first published in 1973, has helped to keep Fort's eclectic legacy alive.[8]

The original goal of *this* book was to explore what a Fortean approach to the study of religion might look like, with all of its associated anomalous events and enigmatic experiences. The book you hold in your hands, however, became something much more diverse. Indeed, as we shall see, the writers collected here each offer their own unique perspectives and insights, and take us to places that we might not immediately associate with 'religion.' With this eclecticism in mind, then, what I would like to do in this introduction is to give a basic overview of some of Fort's philosophical speculations on the nature of science, religion and reality more generally, and then to outline some of my own ideas concerning what a Fortean approach to religion might entail.

Intermediatism

Throughout all of his published works on the anomalous, Fort employed a philosophy that he called 'Intermediatism,' the basic tenet of which suggests 'that nothing is real, but that nothing is unreal,' and 'that all phenomena are approximations in one way between realness and unrealness,'[9] a kind of ontological indeterminacy. He writes:

> ...in general metaphysical terms, our expression is that, like a purgatory, all that is commonly called 'existence,' which we call Intermediateness, is quasi-existence, neither real nor unreal, but the expression of attempt to become real...[10]

Through the lens of this ontologically agnostic perspective, in which all phenomena take place somewhere along a spectrum between the real and the unreal, Fort was able to explore some exceedingly strange territory, unearthing phenomena that mainstream science had either refused to comment on or had rejected outright. In the process, Fort (often half-jokingly) postulated some intriguing hypotheses to account for his damned data, including, for example, the frightening idea that human beings are, in some undefined way, 'property,' and the equally bizarre notion of a 'Super-Sargasso Sea,' a mysterious place to

---

8. Paul Sieveking and Bob Rickard 'Introduction by the Editors of *Fortean Times*,' in *The World's Most Incredible Stories: The Best of Fortean Times*, ed. Adam Sisman (London: Warner Books, 1996), 10-14.
9. Charles Fort, *The Book of the Damned: The Collected Works of Charles Fort* (New York: Jeremy P. Tarcher, 2008), 15.
10. Ibid.

which objects are teleported.[11] Fort, however, often immediately contradicted and discredited his own theories, and is famous for announcing that: 'I believe nothing of my own that I have ever written. I cannot accept that the products of minds are subject-matter for beliefs.'[12] His agnosticism extended even to his own theories and ideas.

By approaching *all* phenomena as equally real/unreal, from the common-place and everyday to the most exceptional and far-out, Fort was essentially proposing a Monistic metaphysics, according to which all events, in all their varied manifestations, are, in some sense, fundamentally connected to one another. All are part of the same process of 'becoming real,' of moving toward 'positiveness,' and all give equal insight into the 'underlying oneness.'[13] Fort suggests that this oneness might best be thought of as a living system, perhaps as a cosmic 'organism,' maybe even possessing some form of purposive intelligence and agency.[14] This idea was later taken up by John Keel, who suggests the possibility that 'the earth is really a living organism, and that it in turn is part of an even larger organism.'[15] For Fort, the strange phenomena he collected provided glimpses into the underlying nature of this system. He writes:

> We shall pick up an existence by its frogs...if there is an underlying oneness of all things, it does not matter where we begin, whether with stars, or laws of supply and demand, or frogs, or Napoleon Bonaparte. One measures a circle, beginning anywhere.[16]

To the Intermediatist, then, all phenomena, from the most mundane to the most extraordinary, provide gateways through which we can approach the structures and processes of the 'underlying oneness.' Perhaps strange events are something akin to 'phantoms in a super-mind in a dreaming state.'[17] Maybe these 'phantoms' reveal the working structural mechanisms of the super-mind itself.

The implication is, then, that the extraordinary phenomena and experiences reported by humankind, throughout history and across continents, may well prove fertile ground for investigating not only the nature of religion, culture, and human consciousness, but also of 'reality' itself, and should not be brushed under the carpet because they don't yet make sense, nor because they

---

11. A term that Fort coined in *Lo!*
12. Fort, *The Book of the Damned*, 555-556.
13. Here, Fort's perspective seems to resemble the Process Philosophy of Alfred North Whitehead (1861-1947). Whitehead suggested that 'the actual world is a process, and that the process is the becoming of actual entities,' *Process and Reality* (New York: Macmillan, 1979), 22.
14. Fort, *The Book of the Damned*, 556.
15. John A. Keel, *The Eighth Tower: On Ultraterrestrials and the Superspectrum* (Charlottesville: Anomalist Books, 2013), 248.
16. Ibid., 544.
17. Ibid., 258.

contradict our currently dominant models of reality. Fort's philosophical approach emphasises wholeness, and cautions us away from ignoring any aspect of existence, no matter how bizarre or disconcerting.[18] There is much to be learned from the anomalous, and Fortean Intermediatism provides us with a useful framework through which to approach it.

Dominants

Writing some forty-three years before the publication of Thomas Kuhn's (1922-1996) famous *The Structure of Scientific Revolutions*,[19] which emphasises the role of successive 'Paradigms' in the development of science,[20] Fort was already keenly aware of the influence of what he called 'Dominants' on the interpretation of phenomena and events: 'All phenomena,' he writes, 'are "explained" in the terms of the Dominant of their era.'[21]

Much like the anthropologist James Frazer (1854-1941), whose book *The Golden Bough* proposed an evolutionary model of the development of modern rationalism (from magic, to religion, to science),[22] Fort proposed a three-tiered model of successive 'Dominants.' While Frazer's stages culminate with 'science' as the pinnacle of human intellectual development, however, Fort's model projects forward to a future state: Frazer stops at science, but Fort pushes on. Fort's model moves from the old Dominant of religion, through the scientific Dominant (which we still seemingly inhabit early in the twenty-first century), through to the so-called 'New Dominant,' a state of intermediatism.[23] He writes:

> In our acceptance, Dominants, in their succession, displace preceding dominants not only because they are more nearly positive, but because the old Dominants, as recruiting mediums, play out. Our expression is that the New Dominant, of Wider Inclusions, is now manifesting throughout the world, and that the old Exclusionism is everywhere

18. Fort's yearning for greater holism brings to mind William James' (1842-1910) comments on the importance of incorporating the full range of altered states of consciousness into our models and conceptions of reality: 'No account of the Universe in its totality can be final which leaves these other forms of consciousness quite disregarded,' *The Varieties of Religious Experience* (New York: Barnes and Noble, 2004), 355.
19. Thomas Kuhn, *The Structure of Scientific Revolutions* (Chicago: University of Chicago Press, 1970).
20. Kuhn defines a paradigm, very simply, as 'universally recognized scientific achievements that, for a time, provide model problems and solutions for a community of practitioners' (1970, 11).
21. Fort, *The Book of the Damned*, 306. See also Colin Bennett, *Politics of the Imagination: The Life, Work and Ideas of Charles Fort* (Manchester: Headpress, 2002).
22. J.G. Frazer, *The Golden Bough: A Study of Magic and Religion* (Ware, Hertfordshire: Wordsworth Editions, 1993).
23. Jeffrey J. Kripal, *Mutants and Mystics: Science Fiction, Superhero Comics and the Paranormal* (Chicago: University of Chicago Press, 2011), 87.

breaking down.[24]

Fort's use of the terms 'Exclusionism' and 'Inclusionism' here refer to each Dominant's attitude towards 'Damned Facts.' The old Dominants of religion and science are both *exclusionist* in Fort's view, rejecting the anomalous in favour of their long established models of an ordered reality. The New Dominant, by contrast, would be *inclusive* of damned facts, no longer rejecting them, but embracing them, taking them seriously as part of the nature and process of reality.

Unlike Frazer, again, who held 'science' up as the final point of human intellectual development, Fort was of the opinion that the 'New Dominant' too would one day become rigid, stagnant and fixed, at which point another Dominant would emerge to build on and succeed it, moving humankind further towards greater inclusivity and an appreciation of *all parts* of the 'whole.'

Natural and Supernatural

For a student of extraordinary phenomena it might come as something of a surprise to learn that Fort was not at all interested in the 'supernatural,' at least not as the term is classically defined. The supernatural, he writes:

> ...has no place in my vocabulary. In my view, it has no meaning, or distinguishment. If there never has been, finally, a natural explanation of anything, everything is supernatural.[25]

Here Fort's approach echoes the efforts of Psychical Researchers in the late nineteenth century to escape from the religious connotations of the 'supernatural' in their investigations of strange and anomalous experiences (apparitions, extrasensory perception, telepathy, psychokinesis, and so on). Frederic Myers (1843-1901), a founding member of the Society for Psychical Research in 1882, for example, proposed the term 'supernormal' (later becoming 'paranormal'), as a means of indicating that extraordinary experiences and phenomena are not in any sense *un-natural*, abnormal, or beyond the scope of rational investigation, but are, in actuality, natural and suprisingly common.[26] The Fortean rejection of the 'supernatural' also

---

24. Fort, *The Book of the Damned*, 249.
25. Ibid., 655.
26. '[Supernormal refers to] a faculty or phenomenon which goes beyond the level of ordinary experience, in the direction of evolution, or as pertaining to a transcendental world. The word supernatural is open to grave objections; it assumes that there is something outside nature, and it has become associated with arbitrary inference with law. Now there is no reason to suppose that the psychical phenomena with which we deal are less a part of nature, or less subject to fixed and definite law, than any other phenomena' Myers, 1902, in Kripal, *Mutants*, 67.

resonates with Émile Durkheim's recognition that the category of the 'supernatural' itself is a distinctly 'modern' one, and that:

> In order to call certain phenomena supernatural, one must already have the sense that there is a natural order of things, in other words, that the phenomena of the universe are connected to one another according to certain necessary relationships called laws.[27]

Fort rejects the label 'supernatural,' precisely because he remains unconvinced of the 'natural' laws proposed by mainstream science. Fort's notion of the 'natural order of things,' is significantly different to the dominant cosmology of materialist science.

Fort's philosophical perspective, then, which is founded upon a radical skepticism regarding the authority of cultural 'dominants' (both religion and science included), questions the solidity of science's underlying assumptions (that there are natural physical laws, that matter is inert, and so on) and, as such, he remains open to the possibility of extraordinary events - they are no less possible than anything else. Fort argues that his procession of 'Damned Facts' actually challenges the established 'natural' laws of science (as well as those of religion), and actively push us towards adopting an intermediatist position,[28] according to which all things are understood to partake of a 'quasi existence, neither real nor unreal,'[29] and all events are connected by an 'underlying oneness.' In Bernardo Kastrup's words anomalous phenomena are 'calls to the absurd,'[30] while for Peter Berger, they are 'signals of transcendence,'[31] hinting that there is *something more going on, just below the surface.*

Witchcraft, Psi and Faculty-X

> Religion is belief in a supreme being. Science is belief in a supreme generalization. Essentially they are the same. Both are the suppressors of witchcraft.[32]

Fort's use of the term 'witchcraft' here refers to unusual human capacities and experiences,[33] such as the ostensible ability to predict future events, the

---

27. Émile Durkheim, *The Elementary Forms of Religious Life* (Oxford: Oxford University Press, 2008), 28.
28. Which could, perhaps, be understood as a form of 'magical consciousness.' In which case, Fort's model of development through Dominants is a virtual reversal of Frazer's.
29. Fort, *The Book of the Damned*, 15.
30. Bernardo Kastrup, *Meaning in Absurdity: What Bizarre Phenomena Can Tell Us About the Nature of Reality* (Winchester: Iff Books, 2011)
31. Peter Berger, *A Rumour of Angels: Modern Society and the Rediscovery of the Supernatural* (Harmondsworth: Penguin, 1971).
32. Fort, *The Book of the Damned*, 999.

strange manifestations that seem to occur around 'poltergeist girls,' and the morbid wounds of Stigmatics. From a Fortean perspective, then, the term 'witchcraft' is much like Colin Wilson's 'Faculty X,'[34] or the term 'psi,' as employed in the parapsychological literature, which refers to such phenomena as 'anomalous processes of information or energy transfer that are not currently explainable in terms of known physical or biological mechanisms.'[35] Psi, Faculty-X, witchcraft and magic are natural, not supernatural.

Again, Fort's understanding of witchcraft is prescient of the writings of anthropologist E.E. Evans-Pritchard, whose 1937 book (published 5 years after Fort's final publication), *Witchcraft, Oracles and Magic Among the Azande* suggested that the Azande of Northern Sudan:

> ...have no conception of 'natural' as we understand it, and therefore neither of the 'supernatural' as we understand it. Witchcraft is to Azande an ordinary and not an extraordinary...event. It is a normal, and not an abnormal happening.[36]

So, just as witchcraft is a normal, taken for granted, component of Azande life and cosmology, so it is also to be expected in Fort's metaphysics and philosophy, where it is viewed as a natural human capacity.

In *Lo!* Fort explores the idea that the manifestation of 'witchcraft' is significantly influenced by the psychological, social and cultural factors that surround the agent or experient. In the context of religious revivals, for example, Fort writes:

> ...when a whole nation, or hosts of its people, goes primitive, or gives in to atavism, or reverts religiously, it may be that conditions arise that are susceptible to phenomena that are repelled by matured mentality.[37]

Here Fort preempts the theories of the Italian anthropologist Ernesto de Martino (1908-1965), whose book *Magic: Primitive and Modern*[38] suggests that

---

33. Because, in Fort's view, Religion (with a capital 'R'), acts as a suppressor or witchcraft, I feel that a Fortean approach to religion (with a little 'r'), would be primarily concerned with what Rudolf Otto calls 'the numinous,' defined as the 'non-rational' experiential component of religion, *The Idea of the Holy* (Oxford: Oxford University Press, 1958). Witchcraft and the numinous are equivalent. A Fortean approach to religion might also intersect nicely with 'ordinary theology' and 'vernacular religion' approaches in Religious Studies.

34. Wilson writes: 'If by "normal" we mean something that tells us the truth, then Faculty X is far more normal than our everyday awareness, and the reality seen by the mystics is the most normal of all.' *Beyond the Occult* (London: Corgi, 1989), 123.

35. Daryl Bem, 'Feeling The Future: Experimental Evidence for Anomalous Retroactive Influences on Cognition and Affect,' *Journal of Personality and Social Psychology*, 100 (2011): 407.

36. E. E. Evans-Pritchard, *Witchcraft, Oracles and Magic Among the Azande* (Oxford: Oxford University Press, 1976), 30.

37. Fort, *The Book of the Damned*, 666.

paranormal experiences and phenomena are embedded in broader networks of psychological, social and cultural influence: 'culturally conditioned nature.' The idea is that psychical phenomena manifest more readily in socio-cultural conditions that are open to their existence, while conditions that are 'actively anti-magic' will repel or inhibit them.[39] According to this view, culture, or a Fortean Dominant, serves as a sort of lens or filter for what is deemed possible, and this, in turn, filters what is actually able manifest as 'real,' or, in Fort's terminology, to 'become positive.'

It is also clear that Fort recognised the centrality of human consciousness, and especially altered states of consciousness, in the mediation of psychic experiences, suggesting that mind can be trained (consciously through the practice of meditation, for example, or unconsciously through the influence of cultural Dominants), to manifest in fantastic ways. This notion is further elaborated in Fort's final book *Wild Talents*, published in 1932, where he examines the influence of conditions of religious belief on the manifestation of certain psychical phenomena. In discussing the apparitions witnessed at Lourdes, the apparent miraculous curing of a young boy's paralysis 'by the touch of a bit of bone of St. Anne,' and recent cases of Stigmata, for example, Fort suggests that:

> The function of God is the focus. An intense mental state is impossible, unless there be something, or the illusion of something, to center upon. Given any other equally serviceable concentration-device, prayers are unnecessary. I conceive of the magic of prayers. I conceive of the magic of blasphemies. There is witchcraft in religion: there may be witchcraft in atheism.[40]

Fort's idea of witchcraft is not bound by any particular ideology, but is instead a natural function of the 'underlying oneness' of our 'quasi-reality,' ready and waiting for a gap in our 'matured mentality,' or for just the right socio-cultural conditions, to allow it to filter through us and manifest.[41]

'The realization of the imaginary'

Fort's notion of witchcraft also includes extraordinary mind-body processes within the human organism. He asks:

---

38. Ernesto de Martino, *Magic: Primitive and Modern* (London: Tom Stacey, 1972).
39. Ibid., 58.
40. Fort, *The Book of the Damned*, 1001.
41. Sociologist Eric Ouellet, taking inspiration from parapsycholgist Walter von Lucadou's model of RSPK (poltergeist) cases, has proposed a social-psi explanation for the UFO phenomenon. According to Ouellet's model, waves of UFO slighting can be understood as collective psi events, expressive of underlying social, cultural and political tensions. Eric Ouellet, *Illuminations: The UFO Experience as Parapsychogical Event* (Charlottesville: Anomalist Books, 2015).

Can one's mind, as I shall call it, affect one's own body, as I shall call it? If so, that is personal witchcraft, or internal witchcraft. Can one's mind affect the bodies of other persons and other things outside? If so, that is what I call external witchcraft.[42]

Fort's notion of 'internal witchcraft' sounds a lot like certain theories put forward in discussions of Stigmata, which appears to represent a highly culturally specific (usually, though not always, Catholic),[43] manifestation of the influence of consciousness and culture on the physical body. Researcher of Stigmata Ian Wilson suggests that in such cases 'the flesh really does change, in an extraordinarily dramatic way, in response to mental activity,'[44] which he takes as indicative of the notion that Stigmata is a psycho-physiological phenomenon related to social and cultural expectation. He notes, for example, that the particularly dramatic symptoms of Stigmata (gorey, bleeding wounds, and so on), only appear in the historical record following an aesthetic cultural shift in depictions of the crucifixion. It was only *after* artists began depicting the crucifixion in vivid, life-like, detail that Stigmatics began to manifest their own graphic wounds.[45]

We also see similarities here with the 'psychosomatic,' or 'psychogenic' disorders, which appear to manifest physical symptoms that are shaped by cultural expectation,[46] and with the field of psychoneuroimmunology, which emphasises the role of psychosocial influences on bodily healing processes.[47] The veil between the 'ordinary' and the 'extraordinary' feels especially thin here, as do the boundaries between the 'mental' and the 'physical,' the 'internal' and the 'external,' and the 'cultural' and the 'natural.' Fort captures this break-down of dichotomies in his concept of transmediumization:

> ...meaning the passage of phenomena from one medium of existence to another...I mean the imposition of the imaginary upon the physical. I mean not the action of mind upon matter, but the action of mind-matter upon matter-mind.[48]

Here Fort seems to be talking about some form of panpsychism, or the notion

---

42. Fort, *The Book of the Damned*, 1014.
43. Parapsychologist Stanley Krippner has written on Stigmatic phenomena occurring with the Brazilian medium Amyr Amiden, who was brought up in the Islamic faith.
44. Ian Wilson, *The Bleeding Mind: An Investigation into the Mysterious Phenomenon of Stigmata* (London: Weidenfeld & Nicolson, 1988), 100.
45. Ibid., 80-81.
46. Edward Shorter, *From the Mind into the Body: The Cultural Origins of Psychosomatic Symptoms* (New York: The Free Press, 1994).
47. Michael Winkelman, *Shamanism: The Neural Ecology of Consciousness and Healing* (London: Bergin & Garvey), 209.
48. Ibid.

that mind and matter have co-evolved and are fundamental to one another,[49] in other words, that both matter and consciousness 'are two aspects of a single system.'[50] What if, then, the very foundations of the dominant materialist perspective (upon which most 'Western' academic theorising is tacitly based), are misguided, or incomplete? What if all matter is, in some sense, conscious, or at least has the *potential* to become conscious? And what if we, as consciousness-matter ourselves, can interact with the matter-consciousness surrounding us in subtle, and less subtle, ways? *If this is the case*, does it mean that we will have to reconsider some of our dominant explanatory models and theories? Whether we like them or not, these are important questions.

Fort's intermediatist approach raises fundamental questions about the limitations of our understanding of the world around us,[51] and totally destabilises the metaphysical assumptions and ontological certainty inherent in positivist-materialism, which dominates scholarly discourse and the cosmological models it constructs.[52] This destabilisation of ontolgical certainty, I suggest, is a useful starting point for exploring the extraordinary, religious and paranormal dimensions of human experience.

The X-Files of the Humanities

As an academic discipline concerned, in the first instance, with 'belief,' Religious Studies frequently assumes an agnostic framework that allows exploration without the need to commit to a single interpretation. This is one of the ways in which Religious Studies has sought to distance itself from Theology. Often, however, this agnostic stance does not extend beyond the 'beliefs' of our informants. When discussing beliefs, things are easy enough to deal with: we do not have to share those beliefs, and we embrace a relativist position.[53] But what about experiences and events? What about when our informants tell us that something highly unusual happened to them, or what if (heaven forbid), something extraordinary happens to the researcher in the field?[54] The standard approach has been to 'bracket' the phenomenon/experience, to demarcate it as beyond the realms of acceptable

---

49. Max Velmans, 'The Co-Evolution of Matter and Consciousness,' *Synthesis Philosophica* 22.44 (2007): 273-282.
50. Kastrup, *Meaning in Absurdity*, 105.
51. Rupert Sheldrake, *The Science Delusion: Freeing the Spirit of Enquiry* (London: Coronet, 2012).
52. Other recent writers have come to similar conclusions. See Thomas Nagel, *Mind and Cosmos* (Oxford: Oxford University Press, 2012), for example.
53. E. E. Evans-Pritchard, *Theories of Primitive Religion* (Oxford: Oxford University Press, 1972), 17.
54. See David E. Young and Jean-Guy Goulet (eds.) *Being Changed by Cross-Cultural Encounters: The Anthropology of Extraordinary Experience* (Ontario: Broadview Press, 1994); Jack Hunter, 'The Anthropology of the Weird,' in *Darklore VI,* ed. Greg Taylor (Brisbane: Daily Grail, 2010).

scholarly contemplation, to move on, and look at something else instead.[55] In Fort's view this would be a deliberate exclusion of an essential part of the whole.

Miraculous events, strange powers and supernatural beings are fundamental components of many (if not most) of the world's religions, and yet, for some reason, their relevance and implications have been somewhat downplayed in the scholarly discourse. Folklorist David J. Hufford, following Max Weber's (1864-1920) similar observations, has identified a process of disenchantment within Western scholarly discourse, whereby the 'modern' rational and scientific worldview emerged in opposition to traditional, magical and mythic modes of understanding the world. Indeed, this modern worldview actively constructs itself in opposition to what it deems 'unreal' and 'irrational.'[56] This is the underlying framework that supports much of the theorising in the humanities.

I am of the opinion that Religious Studies and other allied disciplines such as anthropology, folklore, and so on, have the potential to become the *X-Files* of the humanities. A safe place to catalogue, compare and analyse the anomalous and extraordinary experiences and capacities of human kind, and to critically engage with their implications. What I mean to say is that Religious Studies is already ideally suited to the exploration of a wide range of extraordinary phenomena while still maintaining its academic respectability as a discipline. Jeffrey Kripal's recent textbook *Comparing Religions* (2014), gives a good example of how one such approach to Religious Studies might look. Kripal explains that he is

> sceptical of models of religion that focus on the normal, on the everyday, and on the ways these events are domesticated, rationalized, and institutionalized. All that, too, is 'religion' - of course. Maybe it is most of religion. But, if we only focus on these social processes, we will get a very flat view of religion, which is exactly what we have today in much of the field.[57]

In essence, what we have here is a more inclusive Religious Studies, an Intermediatist Religious Studies, that does not exclude the extraordinary, but rather understands it as an essential part of the system under study. Kripal is not the only voice calling for a more inclusive Religious Studies, however. Other scholars have also been exploring the possibilities inherent in this kind of open-minded approach to the study of religion. See, for example, the work

---

55. Jeremy Northcote, 'Objectivity and the Supernormal: The Limitations of Bracketing Approaches in Providing Neutral Accounts of Supernormal Claims,' *Journal of Contemporary Religion* 19.1 (2004): 85-98.
56. David J. Hufford, 'Modernity's Defenses,' Paper presented at Symposium on *The Anthropology of the Paranormal*, Esalen Institute, Big Sur, California, Oct. 2013.
57. Jeffrey J. Kripal, *Comparing Religion: Coming to Terms* (Oxford: Wiley-Blackwell, 2014), xiv.

of anthropologist Edith Turner in regard to experiencing the reality of spirits, and on the efficacy of ritual,[58] Geoffrey Samuel and Jay Johnston's recent edited book on the significance of 'subtle bodies' in religious practices,[59] Ruy Blanes and Diana Espírito Santo's volume examining spirits as agents rather than symbols,[60] and Fiona Bowie's efforts to investigate afterlife beliefs through the lens of 'cognitive empathetic engagement,'[61] amongst others.[62] All of these researchers are pushing the study of religion further toward greater inclusivity.

Ontological Flooding

In a nutshell, then, what I am suggesting is that we extend Fortean agnosticism[63] into the domains of ontology,[64] and question the very foundations of what we understand as 'real.' In other words, we should not assume that we already know what is *really* real. Fort's intermediatist philosophy goes some way towards achieving this kind of ontological destabilisation. According to this perspective nothing can be said to be wholly real, just as nothing can be said to be wholly unreal. This opens up the ontological flood barriers, a process I have referred to elsewhere as 'ontological flooding.'[65]

But what is the point?

The point has to do with admitting the limitations (or at least the possibility of limitations), inherent in the dominant explanatory models of the social sciences, and with embracing the *possibility* that there may be more going on in the things that we study than the established models can adequately account for. This does not mean that we have to become believers in 'the

---

58. Edith Turner 'The Reality of Spirits: A Tabooed or Permitted Field of Study,' *Anthropology of Consciousness* 4.1 (1993): 9-12.

59. Geoffrey Samuel and Jay Johnston, *Religion and the Subtle Body in Asia and the West* (Oxford: Routledge, 2013).

60. Ruy Blanes and Diana Espírito Santo, *The Social Life of Spirits* (Chicago: University of Chicago Press, 2013).

61. Fiona Bowie 'Building Bridges, Dissolving Boundaries: Towards a Methodology for the Ethnographic Study of the Afterlife, Mediumship and Spiritual Beings,' *Journal of the American Academy of Religion* 81.3 (2013): 698-733.

62. See also Jack Hunter and David Luke (eds.) *Talking With the Spirits, Ethnographies from Between the Worlds* (Brisbane: Daily Grail, 2014), Jack Hunter (ed.) *Paranthropology: Anthropological Approaches to the Paranormal* (Bristol: Paranthropology, 2012), and Jack Hunter (ed.) *Strange Dimensions: A Paranthropology Anthology* (Llanrhaeadr-ym-Mochnant: Psychoid Books, 2015).

63. Robert Anton Wilson, *The New Inquisition: Irrational Rationalism and the Citadel of Science* (Phoenix: Falcon Press, 1987).

64. In this context, the term 'ontology' is taken as referring to 'the philosophical study of the nature of being, becoming, existence, or reality.'

65. Jack Hunter, "'Between Realness and Unrealness": Anthropology, Parapsychology and the Ontology of Non-Ordinary Realities.' *Diskus: Journal of the British Association for the Study of Religion* 17.2 (2015): 4-20.

supernatural' (Fort certainly did not), but just that we need to be aware of the fact that our models are more than likely incomplete. There may well, for example, be more going on than social functional processes, cognitive processes, power struggles, economic struggles, politics, doctrines or ideologies (of course, that is not to say that such factors are not involved, just that they are not necessarily *all* that is going on).

What if religious rituals and collective worship are at least attempting to tap into psi, Fort's 'witchcraft,' or Wilson's 'Faculty-X,' for their efficacy? What if prayer really is effective in some way? What is going on in cases of Stigmata or physical mediumship? Is it all fraud, or are such cases hints of 'internal witchcraft'? Is spirit possession purely a social-functional phenomenon, or a cognitive phenomenon, or something more? What if there is a God, or gods, or some God-like thing(s)? Some kind of intelligence(s) perhaps? Or spirits? Might matter possess consciousness? Do shamanic practitioners enter into other worlds during their rituals and trance states? The dominant approach, grounded in the established materialist metaphysics, says 'No,' but, like Fort, I remain unconvinced that we have worked it all out, and so, for this author at least (and, no doubt, for Fort as well), the possibility that there is 'something more' going on remains open (whatever that 'something more' might be).

Fortean Approaches

In keeping with the agnostic nature of Fort's philosophy, the chapters gathered in this collection each approach their subject matter in different ways. There is, then, no defining stance or conclusion that unites the essays that follow, nor was this ever the intention in putting this book together. Instead, the chapters are united by an open-minded willingness to consider the implications of Fort's procession of Damned Facts.

In 'No Limestone in the Sky,' Amba J. Sepie introduces us to the politics of Damned Facts, especially in the context of anthropology, an academic discipline in which encounters with 'spirits' in the field are not an uncommon occurrence. Timothy Grieve-Carlson's paper then looks at the similarities between Charles Fort's philosophy of Intermediatism and William James' philosophy of radical empiricism. Although it is unclear whether Fort read James, Grieve-Carlson suggests that much of Fort's philosophical perspective is pre-empted in James' writings on radical empiricism.

Next, Wellington Zangari and colleagues from the University of São Paulo give an overview of extraordinary and religious phenomena from Brazil, which include everything from encounters with apparent alien entities, to cases of physical mediumship and poltergeist manifestations. Their chapter summarises religious, folkloric, scientific and Fortean interpretations of such experiences. In 'A New Demonology: John Keel and the Mothman Prophecies,' folklorist and journalist David Clarke examines John Keel's ultraterrestrial hypothesis and its impact on the 'Occult Revival' of the 1960s and 1970s. Clarke's paper is then aptly followed by Robin Jarrell's chapter on 'UFO Abductions as Mystical Encounter,' in which she draws on Jacques Vallée's famous research linking contemporary UFO and abduction experiences to traditional faerie folklore motifs. Jarrell's paper pays particular attention to the extensive abduction experiences described by the horror author Whitley Strieber, and links them back to the writings of Vallée, the seventeenth century Scottish priest Robert Kirk (1644-1692), and the early twentieth century ethnographer W.Y. Evans-Wentz (1878-1965).

David V. Barrett's contribution takes a slightly different Fortean approach to religion, leaving behind the UFOs, poltergeists and Stigmatics to focus on British-Israelism, the belief that the British people are descended from the Ten Lost Tribes of Israel. Not only is this chapter fascinating for its exploration of the ways in which such beliefs are supported by the misunderstanding of myth as historical truth, it is also frightening to see how these beliefs can come to be used in the promotion of particular (often far-right) political ideologies and agendas.

Next, in 'The Transmediumizers,' Eden S. French and Christopher Laursen take Fort's concept of 'transmediumization' as their starting point, and look forward to the dawning of the New Dominant, when binary oppositions of 'man/woman, black/white, human/beast, life/death, human/God, organic/artificial' break down to reveal 'a larger, more complex, networked ecology of materiality and immateriality.'

Interestingly, the two final chapters in this collection both draw on the labyrinth as a model for exploring the nature of mind and reality. In 'The Mirror Maze,' James Harris takes us on a kaleidoscopic journey through art, revelation and neuroscience in an effort to make sense of a psychedelic vision he had under the influence of Psilocybin mushrooms. Harris argues that we must come to accept 'that it is puzzles all the way down.' In the final chapter, Roberta Harris Short gives a very personal account of an experience she had following a premonitory dream about her mother. When the dream apparently came true her understanding of the nature of reality shifted considerably, leading her, like James Harris, to ponder its labyrinthine qualities.

This is an eclectic book, which, I hope, captures something of the essence of Fort's Intermediatist approach, so why not let down your ontological flood barriers, and go with the flow...

1

No Limestone in the Sky:
The Politics of Damned Facts

Amba J. Sepie

Any question becomes unanswerable if one does not permit oneself a large enough universe to deal with the question.[66]

~Aloisius H. Louie, 'Essays on More Than Life Itself'

All of our unconscious assumptions—our 'hidden shackles' and a priori biases—could be said to have been inherited from the past: but, not just any version of the past, in case it is presumed that this is some sort of benign reference to an actual, fixed history. The past to which I refer, which is the common metaphysical inheritance of the modern, Westernized mind, is a specifically cultural version of a past that is so ingrained that it is not only generally invisible and unquestionable to any person who does not deeply contemplate its contradictions, but has become the hero (or villain?) in a great number of tales that masquerade as serious academic non-fiction. Spirits, for instance, being generally conceived of as the shadows of religious beliefs that are not-quite-dead, impossibilities, flights of fancy, or perhaps even evidence of delusion, are generally left out of such stories and relegated to the artsy world of science fiction, in novels, or as quirky anecdotes in biographies. Gillian Bennett, a folklorist studying the borderlands of afterlife beliefs, writes that (in academia): 'No-one will tackle the subject because it is disreputable,

---

66. Aloisius H. Louie, 'Essays on More Than Life Itself,' *Axiomathes* 21.3 (2011): 474.
Note that the title of this paper is derived from an example given by Charles Fort: 'In *Science*, March 9, 1888, we read of a block of limestone, said to have fallen near Middleburgh, Florida. It was exhibited at the Sub-tropical Exposition, at Jacksonville. The writer, in *Science*, denies that it fell from the sky. His reasoning is: 'There is no limestone in the sky; Therefore this limestone did not fall from the sky.' Charles Fort, *The Book of the Damned* (New York: Book Tree, 2006).

and it remains disreputable because no one will tackle it.'[67] Part of this inheritance is the methodological atheism that is required and, yet, is mostly denied under the auspices of intellectual inquiry, freedom, and the like, as if to prove, over and over again, that the Enlightenment was a roaring success.[68] I am always quite suspicious when such things are overstated; or, for that matter, glossed over so casually. As Serres notes, science 'doesn't ask the question; it considers the question as resolved, no doubt since the Age of Enlightenment.'[69]

According to Stengers, we shall not regress, nor betray hard truths, nor acknowledge the 'smoke of the burning witches' still lingering in our nostrils.[70] Neo-pagan feminist Starhawk is her provocateur, awakening in Stengers a profound awareness of what has been lost, hunted down, and eliminated from her own socio-cultural milieu.[71] As Stengers writes, 'Learning to smell the smoke is to acknowledge that we have learned the codes of our respective milieus: derisive remarks, knowing smiles, offhand judgments...'[72] Charles Fort ignored these rules regarding how to be taken seriously; in fact, by all accounts, he seemed to flaunt his reasoned disrespect for the established conventions of intellectualism at every opportunity. Fort's damned facts have gone on to have a modest second life in scholarship,[73] although not much has changed in terms of the reception of such ideas. The proliferation of disciplinary silos, in which a group of experts who, according to Bauman, 'must know best the things on which they are experts,'[74] seem to ensure that the processes of knowledge production remain ouroborically contrived, with each generation perpetuating the output of the next, in accordance with

---

67. Gillian Bennett, *Traditions of Belief: Women and the Supernatural* (Harmondsworth, England: Penguin, 1987). Cited in David Hufford, 'Beings without Bodies: An Experience-Centred Theory of the Belief in Spirits,' in *Out of the Ordinary: Folklore and the Supernatural*, ed. Barbara Walker (Logan, Utah: Utah State University Press, 1995), 17.

68. For a compelling argument regarding the requirement that scholars research in accordance with methodological atheism, see Douglas Ezzy, 'Religious Ethnography: Practicing the Witch's Craft,' in *Researching Paganisms*, ed. Jenny Blain, Douglas Ezzy, and Graham Harvey (New York: Altamira, 2004). The term itself originates with Peter Berger.

69. Michel Serres and Bruno Latour, *Conversations on Science, Culture, and Time, Studies in Literature and Science* (Ann Arbor, Michigan: University of Michigan Press, 1995), 128.

70. Isabelle Stengers, 'Reclaiming Animism,' *e-flux* 36 (2012): 1-10 (http://worker01.e-flux.com/pdf/article_8955850.pdf).

71. Isabelle Stengers, 'Experimenting with Refrains: Subjectivity and the Challenge of Escaping Modern Dualism,' *Subjectivity* 22.1 (2008): 48-49.

72. Stengers, 'Reclaiming Animism,' 6.

73. See Mary Daly, *Beyond God the Father: Toward a Philosophy of Women's Liberation* (Boston: Beacon Press, 1973), 11; Michel Foucault and Colin Gordon, *Power/Knowledge: Selected Interviews and Other Writings, 1972-1977* (Brighton: Harvester Press, 1980), 81-82; Liz Stanley, ed. *Feminist Praxis: Research, Theory, and Epistemology in Feminist Sociology* (London; New York: Routledge, 1990), 11; Richard Green, *The Thwarting of Laplace's Demon: Arguments against the Mechanistic World-View* (New York: St. Martin's Press, 1995); John Law, After Method: Mess in Social Science Research, International Library of Sociology (London; New York: Routledge, 2004).

74. Zygmunt Bauman, *Liquid Fear* (Cambridge; Malden, Mass.: Polity Press, 2006), 23.

prescribed limits, methods, and agreed upon parameters. Daly wrote that method subjected thought to 'an invisible tyranny...[which] prevents us from raising questions never asked before and from being illumined by ideas that do not fit pre-established boxes and forms. The worshippers of Method have an effective way of handling data that does not fit into the Respectable Categories of Questions and Answers. They simply classify it as non-data, thereby rendering it invisible.'[75]

In the account given by Kripal, Fort 'was particularly hard on what he called the 'evil of specialization.' Fort saw that specialization prevents us from seeing the hidden connections between different domains of knowledge and data.'[76] This is interesting, because when one 'follows' the notion of spirits into the past and considers how such a concept has been variously constructed, embraced, rejected, or vehemently decried, it becomes evident that it is precisely due to a profound lack of holism, conjoined with the collective cultural weight of the afterlife, or lack thereof, that leaves us confused as to what we think, or should think, about the subject. The mechanisms of reduction, as lamented by Panikkar, have rendered the 'forces' described by belief as impotent, innocuous, and subservient to human reason.[77] It would appear that any attempts to capture the anomalous phenomena of the world must occur through reframing or reduction in order to avoid absolute dismissal.

Given anthropology is one of my own shameful 'specializations' I can illustrate such matters nicely via ethnographies of spirit possession. Lambek, for instance, argues that spirits are products of the imagination, and 'partial world constructions that are fictional but not simply fictitious.'[78] He employs, variously, a discourse model of text, the performance trope, and notions of embodiment, attitudes, qualities, forces, and so on, in order to manoeuvre around this 'spirit issue,' but is conclusive, finally, in saying: 'we need a phenomenological approach that avoids propositional assertions ("spirits exist") in favour of various kinds of attitudes or degrees of focus.'[79] Lambek echoes Evans-Pritchard here and joins the long lineage of scholars who cannot quite attribute reality to the phenomena they encounter in the field and, yet, cannot quite deny it either. Such methods of representation create an account which is comprehensible within the academic cultural complex, and is rationalized according to the rule which dictates a very particular approach to belief and practice that excludes the possibility of spirits.

---

75. Daly, *Beyond God the Father: Toward a Philosophy of Women's Liberation*, 11.
76. Jeffrey J. Kripal, *Authors of the Impossible: The Paranormal and the Sacred* (Chicago: University of Chicago Press, 2011), 95.
77. Raimundo Panikkar and Scott Eastham, *The Cosmotheandric Experience: Emerging Religious Consciousness* (New York: Orbis Books, 1993), 105-6.
78. Michael Lambek, 'Afterword: Spirits and Their Histories,' in *Spirits in Culture, History, and Mind*, ed. Jeannette Marie Mageo and Alan Howard (New York: Routledge, 1996), 238.
79. Ibid., 247.

Other anthropologists take a similar line. Sax asks how he can write about the spiritual presence of the divine king as 'a self-evident fact' in the lives of his subjects without making them appear backwards, superstitious, mystified, or deluded? Sax presents this as a dilemma that roughly reads as not wanting to appear irrational, and suggests several philosophical moves that allow this 'idea' to be presented as realist, materialist, and set in a context of social action.[80] Moreno adopts a phenomenological and processual view which considers the dynamics of interaction between deities and humans as the experiential subjects, themselves, understand them: thus, the anthropologist steps out of the frame entirely.[81] Tyler gives up the task of representation altogether and writes that ethnography is at best an evocation, a fantasy, poetry, or an occult document that should give away any pretension of being a type of scientific discourse.[82] Other treatments of possession emphasize their psychological-therapeutic function, including Lienhardt's early work on the Dinka, Crapanzano in Morocco, Obeysekere in Sri Lanka, and many of the essays on Nepal in Hitchcock and Jones.[83] Social structural analyses are well-illustrated by Lewis, and Maskarinec considers the subject too anthropologically strange to go any further than linguistic analysis.[84] In sum, what such pragmatic resolve generally amounts to is a selection of neologisms strung together with a little methodological sleight-of-hand as if, by dancing around it, one may not actually have to comment conclusively on anything that may invite derision from one's rationally-minded peers. A critique by a noted contemporary, Frederick Smith, states (after citing Lambek) that 'whatever condition it may be, it is not possession, even if those experiencing it are not lying or misguided by their cultural preceptors.'[85]

More recently, anthropologists have made the turn towards all things ontological: perspectivism, onto-cartography, assemblages, the hybrid collectif,

80. William Sturman Sax, *Dancing the Self: Personhood and Performance in the Pandav Lila of Garhwal* (Oxford; New York: Oxford University Press, 2002), 158-9.
81. Cited in Kathleen M. Erndl, *Victory to the Mother: The Hindu Goddess of Northwest India in Myth, Ritual, and Symbol* (New York: Oxford University Press, 1993), 132.
82. Stephan A. Tyler, 'Post-Modern Ethnography: From Document of the Occult to Occult Document,' in *Writing Culture: The Poetics and Politics of Ethnography*, ed. James Clifford and George E. Marcus (California: University of California Press, 1986), 134.
83. R. G. Lienhardt, *Divinity and Experience: The Religion of the Dinka* (Oxford: Clarendon Press, 1961); Vincent Crapanzano, 'Mohammed and Dawia: Possession in Morocco,' in *Case Studies in Spirit Possession*, ed. Vincent Crapanzano and Vivian Garrison (New York: John Wiley & Sons, 1977); Gananath Obeysekere, 'Psychocultural Exegesis of a Case of Spirit Possession in Sri Lanka,' in *Case Studies in Spirit Possession*, ed. Vincent Crapanzano and Vivian Garrison (New York: John Wiley & Sons, 1977); Rex L. Jones and John T. Hitchcock, eds., *Spirit Possession in the Nepal Himalayas* (Warminster, England: Aris & Phillips, 1976).
84. I. M. Lewis, *Ecstatic Religion: A Study of Shamanism and Spirit Possession* (Hammondsworth: Penguin, 1971); Gregory G. Maskarinec, *The Rulings of the Night: An Ethnography of Nepalese Shaman Oral Texts* (Wisconsin: University of Wisconsin Press, 1995).
85. Frederick M. Smith, *The Self Possessed: Deity and Spirit Possession in South Asian Literature and Civilization* (New York: Columbia University Press, 2006), 47.

different people live in different worlds, and so forth...but the emperor is still naked and, possibly, slightly racist. The anthropologist, it seems, is plagued and also restricted by the concepts of culture, religion and alterity, or difference. The very act of looking 'over there' at the beliefs and practices of 'the other' is still sanctioned in a way that dear old Betty who lives on the corner, who enjoys a morning cup of tea with her dead husband, is not. Without that magical gloss of cultural difference, neither Betty nor the anthropologist who earnestly attempts to study her experiences will be taken seriously. At best they will be relativized, though as Rabinow notes, cultural relativism cannot take the concepts of the 'other' seriously, or as holding any truth-value, and is therefore methodologically redundant.[86] He writes that the anthropologist enters into a fictive conversation with another culture, imaginatively translating their frames of meaning by way of a 'universal conversation,' which reduces it to a text translated into Western discourse; bracketing truth in the process.[87] By creating an 'horizontal plane' which levels cultures as equivalent to one another, and by taking 'no culture' at its word whilst studying them scientifically, as has become the norm, all cultures are translated through a method and into a language structured in ways which 'contain' and reproduce the superior 'Western' cultural value-system. The universal and the particular are again at odds, rendering the whole exercise, as Rabinow puts it, ultimately nihilistic. Further, and contrary to the apparent tolerance of other beliefs, perspectives, and experiences as encouraged by the social sciences, ontological dominance aligns with scientific naturalism absolutely.

Whilst the 'rules' of academic study may demand selectivity, Stengers states: 'We may not pick and choose, select aspects that matter for us, and neglect the remainder with a tolerant, softly contemptuous "if it may help them..."'[88] Contemporary practices have been mobilized, in her view, by the ancestors of the same protagonists who blessed the burnings and poisoned the past. Bennett, in her extensive studies of widows' communication with their deceased partners writes that, with rare exceptions, very few written accounts remain neutral as to the ontological status of spirits: 'Whatever the rhetoric, there are some words that are never used—among them, "soul," "spirit," "ghost"; and a set of explanations that are never countenanced—that the dead person is interacting with the living one, for example, or that this interaction is happening because human affections and personality can survive beyond the grave, or that there is an afterlife in which the dead continue to exist and from which these communications come.'[89]

---

86. Paul Rabinow, *The Accompaniment: Assembling the Contemporary* (Chicago: University of Chicago Press, 2011).
87. Ibid.
88. Stengers, 'Experimenting with Refrains,' 54.
89. Gillian Bennett and Kate Mary Bennett, 'The Presence of the Dead: An Empirical Study,' *Mortality* 5.2 (2000): 147.

Being 'religious' or 'spiritual' outside of the bindings of the public sphere, within a community of peers, may proffer a special arrangement in which unusual experiences, like those to which Bennett refers, can be upheld; but the scholar of religion cannot actually study any of this without reduction. Spirits are not welcome in religious studies; a range of neologisms, again, stand in for direct references to the experiences or events in question. As Kripal notes, 'the discipline constantly encounters robust paranormal phenomena in its data—the stuff is everywhere—and then refuses to talk about such things in any truly serious and sustained way. The paranormal is our secret in plain sight…'[90]

Academics (who are, after all, the same as anyone else) have been socialized to respond in a specific manner when confronted with radically different ways of thinking: even when it is the case that their direct personal experiences are similar enough to the phenomenon in question that they might provide validation for radical and non-scientific data, or points of view. Experiences that cannot be readily or immediately rationalized are often reacted to as an intense personal threat, or as 'making no sense'; in other words, untranslatable in terms of familiar values and principles. A long and considered period of observation and study regarding just this sort of resistance, in both scholarship and society, compels me to conclude that we are very heavily socialized into performing convincingly in ways which conceal our uncertainties and vulnerabilities, especially when it comes to cosmological concerns. Heffernan writes that people in general filter out whatever unsettles their beliefs: 'An unconscious (and much denied) impulse to obey and conform shields us from confrontation and crowds provide friendly alibis for our inertia.'[91] Things that are comfortable, and safe, and widely accepted by one's peers, whom we wish to like and accept us, keep us in the mainstream, whilst those things 'too prickly and sticky' are, according to Wilson, 'daubed with the brain's projected prejudices until, encrusted beyond recognition, they are capable of being fitted into the system, classified, card-indexed, buried…'[92] The rubric seems to be that proof 'it' happened is demanded, whilst proof 'it' didn't is generally volunteered. That is, once what 'it' is (a spirit, a lightning strike, or something in your eye) has been established, and agreed upon.

A consensual reality appears to be a kind of salvation, an assurance that others in the group can be trusted, that they will not do or say anything unexpected, or as Tart puts it: 'It means that they are as rigidly enculturated and conditioned as you are and react in predictable ways. We may not like what they do, but their actions are not outside the range of what we are

90. Kripal, *Authors of the Impossible: The Paranormal and the Sacred*, 7.
91. Margaret Heffernan, *Willful Blindness: Why We Ignore the Obvious at Our Peril* (London: Simon & Schuster, 2011), n.p.
92. Robert Shea and Robert Anton Wilson, *The Illuminatus! Trilogy* (New York: Dell, 1984), 570.

prepared to perceive.'[93] He calls this a mutual conspiracy to eliminate change. I do think, however, that far too much credit is often given to this sort of behavior as if it were a manifestation of conscious processes, as if individuals can consciously manage their relationships with the implicit and explicit structures of cosmological dominance within which they are acting, to which they are responding, and in many cases, reproducing. I suspect that modern humans of a 'Western' disposition are not all that self-reflexive about why we react as we do, and nor are we encouraged to be so.

Foucault, in his most famous treatise on truth and power, wrote that: 'Each society has its regime of truth, its "general politics" of truth; that is, the types of discourse which it accepts and makes function as true; the mechanisms and instances which enable one to distinguish "true" and "false" statements; the means by which each is sanctioned; and the techniques and procedures accorded value in the acquisition of truth; the status of those who are charged with saying what counts as true.'[94] Power relationships are predicated upon such value systems, which are, in turn, derived from cosmological, ontological, and epistemological foundations. This begs the question of what it is, specifically, that has shaped these metaphysical inheritances with which we struggle?

My thought on this is that modernity, as a worldview, is cultural; that the signature bodies of knowledge provide default standards derived from much older negotiations in the history of what is usually referred to as 'Western' thought.[95] According to Meadows, these are the 'shared' ideas, or great unstated assumptions that are constituted out of a society's paradigm, or deepest set of beliefs about how the world works; in short, our cosmologies.[96] A useful typology for understanding this is to consider a society as structured in the first instance by a set of charter myths or origin stories (cosmology), that determines the foundational beliefs about which entities are 'allowed,' or not (ontology), which has a special relationship to knowledge and how it is validated (epistemology), in combination with particular kinds of values (axiology) which, in turn, impact upon practice. These interactions (which are not bounded, nor linear) involve processes of inclusion and exclusion: what is believed as possible, valid, and true, and their opposites, is determined largely by what can and cannot exist, which defines what knowledge can be about. A worldview is, according to Berkes, 'cumulative...evolving by adaptive processes

---

93. Charles T. Tart, 'Hidden Shackles: Implicit Assumptions That Limit Freedom of Action and Inquiry,' in *Exploring the Paranormal: Perspectives on Belief and Experience*, ed. G. K. Zollschan, J.F. Schumaker, and G.F. Walsh (Dorset: Prism, 1989), 21.
94. Foucault and Gordon, *Power/Knowledge: Selected Interviews and Other Writings*, 1972-1977, 131.
95. An earlier incarnation of this line of thinking, as discussed in far greater depth, can be found in Amba Morton, 'Invisible Episteme: The Mirrors and String of Modernity' (M.A., Religious Studies, University of Canterbury, Christchurch, 2011).
96. Donella H. Meadows and Diana Wright, *Thinking in Systems: A Primer* (White River Junction, Vermont: Chelsea Green, 2008).

and handed down through generations by cultural transmission...'[97] It is inherited, as a metaphysical package, and reinforced by hidden maxims which are built into social institutions and norms. A signature body of knowledge, once established, can be said, therefore, to orient practice within any system designated as bounded via these epistemological, ontological, and axiological limits. Practices which do not adhere to these specifications may occur within these limits, but if they cannot be classified as 'true,' 'good,' 'useful' etc., they may be perceived as having limited visibility, validity, relevance, and so forth: essentially, they are 'out of place.'[98]

In terms of 'our' particular history, the propitiation and cultivation of spirits and gods, and general beliefs in the usefulness of ritual was, in the pre-classical period, wedded to a cosmological framework which, though regionally variable, accommodated multiple gods, spirits and forces as tied to localities, objects and so forth. David Lindberg writes: 'One need only recall that Plato demanded solitary confinement (and in extreme cases, execution) for those who denied the existence of the gods and their involvement in human affairs.'[99] Eventually, the practices of divination, magic, types of sacrifice, and healing rituals became illegal, largely during Roman times, as the idolatrous classification of such things under Judaism morphed into Christianity and became politicized. Local gods also became reconceived as spirits, which immediately increased their volatility whilst dis-locating their power; and spirits became dangerous entities that were conflated with the daemonic.

Conveniently, this collapse of gods and spirits into a single type of entity allows the volatility of the spirit to be transferred to the human who is maintaining a relationship with it. The subjugation and elimination of persons who remained 'attached' to local gods, and resisted conversion, became essential to the emerging cosmo-political order. There was also the possibility, given that demons were not really catered for, that such persons would 'carry' this god (now reframed as a demon) within them. The monotheistic nature of these traditions, combined with emerging state monism, cemented the divisions between exclusivist ways of being and designated 'others,' which is especially notable for its brutal impact upon local knowledge-practice-belief complexes from classical times, but also, under colonialism.[100] As the beliefs

---

97. Fikret Berkes, John Colding, and Carl Folke, 'Rediscovery of Traditional Ecological Knowledge as Adaptive Management,' *Ecological Applications* 10.5 (2000): 1252.

98. Indigenous knowledge paradigms or mind-body medical practices, for example, are often working against this a priori discrimination in trying to establish validity. As both generally involve an acknowledgment invisible entities, which are designated as non-data or damned facts, validation within the signature bodies of knowledge remains impossible.

99. David C. Lindberg, 'Science and the Early Christian Church,' *Isis* 74.4 (1983): 512.

100. I find the *knowledge-practice-belief* complex is a useful substitute for the concept of religion, and borrow it from the work of ethno-ecologist Fikret Berkes, *Sacred Ecology*, 3rd ed. (New York: Routledge, 2012).

of the 'others' were also collapsed into the daemonic, Christian missions were deployed to save the souls of the damned.

This particular type of cosmological structure, with its specific charter myths determining what would, and would not, be permitted to exist, was absolutely deterministic for modern scientific societies, even in their infancy. Although, as White maintains, 'it was not until the late eighteenth century that the hypothesis of God became unnecessary to many scientists,'[101] belief based on the doctrine and authority of the Christian God, though eventually absorbed into the organization of power relations within the 'secular West,' nonetheless continues to enjoy an elevated status when compared with belief based on experience, belief in spirits, and the beliefs of 'the other.' Neither the loss of Heaven and Hell, nor the shifting certainty regarding the existence of the Christian God, changed the categories by which social behaviors were ordered and controlled. Berger is the master of this territory, stating that the precariousness of a new institutional order must in the first instance, conceal, as much as possible, its constructed character, through the employment of religious legitimations that locate it within a cosmic frame of reference.[102] He writes: 'The institutions are thus given a semblance of inevitability, firmness and durability that is analogous to these qualities as ascribed to the gods themselves [...] The point need hardly be belabored that legitimation of this kind carries with it extremely powerful and built-in sanctions against individual deviance from prescribed role performances.'[103]

The history of the scientific worldview has its own exorcisms to reckon with, perhaps best described by Tarnas.[104] In basic terms, Tarnas identifies three key shifts which calibrate the contemporary cosmological orientation of the modern Westernized mind. The first is the Copernican, in which the human relationship with the universe was irrevocably relativized by the link between the movement of the heavens and the movement of the observer, displacing the 'naive understanding' of human centrality within the universe. The second is the Cartesian, in that Descartes 'expressed in philosophical terms the experiential consequence of that new cosmological context, starting from a position of fundamental doubt vis-a-vis the world, and ending in the cogito.'[105] The third shift, having established the absolute isolation of the human subject, is the 'epistemological crisis' beginning with Locke, and progressing from Berkeley and Hume to finally, Kant, who 'drew out the

---

101. Lynn White, 'The Historical Roots of Our Ecological Crisis,' in *This Sacred Earth: Religion, Nature, Environment*, ed. Roger S. Gottlieb (New York: Routledge, 1996), 191.

102. Peter L. Berger, *The Sacred Canopy: Elements of a Sociological Theory of Religion* (Garden City, New York: Doubleday, 1967), 33.

103. Ibid., 36, 38.

104. Richard Tarnas, *The Passion of the Western Mind: Understanding the Ideas That Have Shaped Our World View* (London: Pimlico, 1996).

105. Ibid., 417.

epistemological consequences of the Cartesian cogito.'[106] Kant's legacy is the absolute loss of certainty through the assertion that everything is interpretative. Ultimately, this completes the isolation of the human mind/self and affirms the impossibility of establishing the validity of knowledge or information in any testable or verifiable sense: 'Thus, the cosmological estrangement of modern consciousness initiated by Copernicus and the ontological estrangement initiated by Descartes were completed by the epistemological estrangement initiated by Kant: a threefold mutually enforced prison of modern alienation.'[107] I would be inclined to add interpretations of Hume to this list as, regardless of his initial intentions, what remains from his work *On Miracles* is the idea signaled in the title to this paper: that no matter how many educated persons can be gathered to form a consensus and testify to the occurrence of spiritual or unusual phenomenon, this is unlikely to amount to a probability, and much less a proof.[108]

The establishment of the psychological sciences, as the most recent move in this historical account, seems to have created an impossible situation. Somehow, the ideas of 'derangement' and 'madness,' as they were conceived of in the past, have been entirely reworked into our present day enthusiasm for shifting any religious, cultural, or designated imaginative content into the small quarter of the brain also reserved for madness, night-walking, weird sex and criminality. Whilst it is obvious that human beings enjoy and are perhaps naturally inclined towards classification, the postulation of mind as a priori first cause, replacing God in the cosmological order, and the establishment of an 'unconscious' that cannot be seen, but can be 'diagnosed' and medicalized backs us all into a cosmological corner. Furthermore, if Foucault's later and, I would argue, prophetic, work on governmentality (or neoliberal self-governance) is to be taken on board, we are also now policing/managing ourselves and those around us so that everyone remains in said corner. There are no spirits in this corner. There is medication. As Panikkar writes, 'Man… has spread the net of his intelligibility like DDT and killed all the intermediary beings he cannot master with his mind – the spirits, once his companions, are no longer credible, the Gods have flown, and a solitary and even more superfluous God fades away.'[109]

Any plural or contradictory commitments that an individual socialized in accordance with these rules may hold, such as a belief in, or experience of, spirits, are constantly at odds with a social consensus, which may provide inclusion on the basis of enforced denial. Somehow, the rejection en masse of what has, in hindsight, been identified as superstition, has been translated into

---

106. Ibid.
107. Ibid., 419.
108. For a wonderful account of how Hume has been widely misinterpreted, see Robert J. Fogelin, *A Defense of Hume on Miracles, Princeton Monographs in Philosophy* (Princeton, New Jersey: Princeton University Press, 2003).
109. Panikkar and Eastham, *The Cosmotheandric Experience*, 41.

a kind of public good.[110] Beliefs that validate experienced breaches between shared notions of time, spatial separations, and the privacy of an individual mind (which, considered together, incorporates a wide array of paranormal, supernatural, psychic or spiritual phenomena), break with the consensus in ways that seem to be profoundly unsettling to people. All of our ideas of who we are, what we are, why we are here, how we got here, and what happens when we die (whether approached through science or religion, whether organized coherently, or not), come into question; provoking cosmological insecurity, if you will.

I can appreciate why this would be viewed as a problem when added to the cumulative stresses and uncertainties of modern life. But I can also relate to Stengers' musings upon what has been lost in this relentless quest to purify and exorcise everything 'dangerous' from the world, and I have concluded that we have definitely been left wanting. Not only is modern experience still organized into temporal-spatial narratives of eschatology and salvation, but we are enculturated toward the belief that we are alone in the universe, de-souled, confused, and motivated by virtue of work and virtue of character, both of which remain entirely compatible with our Judeo-Christian origin stories, scientific maxims, and capitalist objectives. This new, cleaner, cosmology has taken us hostage, with only words to communicate between our lonely islands of objective personal experience, some of them whispered for fear of exclusion.[111]

However, there are always those who, like Fort himself, grow tired or disillusioned with the status quo, and pursue a kind of holistic understanding which draws deeply upon wider, older, often foreign conceptions regarding the organization of the world. Fort understood that everything is matter of classification and selection, that anything that could possibly be defined as 'truth' had not even been approached. As Kripal writes, Fort 'worked from the conviction that one should privilege "the data of the damned," that is, all that stuff that had been rejected, facilely explained away, or literally demonized by the two most recent reigning orders of knowledge of Western culture, religion and science. Only then, he thought, can we begin to sketch the outlines of a bigger, more expansive and inclusive reality. Only then can we approximate a Truth we may never reach but that is nevertheless worth reaching for.'[112]

---

110. Debates about religion in the public sphere (which is designated as 'secular') illustrate this well. See José Casanova, *Public Religions in the Modern World* (Chicago: University of Chicago Press, 1994); Talal Asad, *Formations of the Secular: Christianity, Islam, Modernity, Cultural Memory in the Present* (California: Stanford University Press, 2003).

111. 'Objectivity, set up as the supreme criterion of truth, has one inevitable consequence: the transformation of the subject into an object. The death of the subject is the price we pay for objective knowledge.' Basarab Nicolescu, *Manifesto of Transdisciplinarity*, trans. Karen-Claire Voss (New York: State University of New York Press, 2002), 9, 13.

112. Kripal, *Authors of the Impossible*, 106.

The specifics of how we construct our world, or how our world is constructed, whether shared partially, or completely, remain either utterly mysterious or entirely comprehensible dependent on one's cosmology. I am not particularly interested in truth as an absolute (if pressed, I would say everything is 'true'), but I am interested in the critique of any system within which a claim to the truth of one's experience is denied. Truth does matter. It is scientism (that is, science hardened into materialistic dogma) rather than science, which we need to be wary of in this regard; especially considering that the entities postulated by its charter myths are also largely invisible, or happened a very long time ago.[113] As Deloria notes 'Pasteur had immense difficulty convincing his peers that there were tiny organisms in the world.'[114] This is, of course, audacious to those with a realist ontology, but these matters are comparable.

As a way forward I would suggest we consider cosmologies outside of the contemporary milieu with a little more respect, and more targeted inquiry. That a great number of non-Western perspectives on these issues appear to have more in common with each other, than with the Western metaphysical position, is something I find interesting; especially when such frameworks achieve such seamless integration between the metaphysical, medical, environmental, interspecial, organizational and political aspects of social life. This is not merely a romanticist ideal, but a serious proposition. By way of illustration, consider Deloria: 'If an Indian tells other Indians that he or she has seen a ghost, describes the experience, and asks others for advice, he or she is taken to be a serious person with a serious problem. However, if a non-Indian tells another non-Indian that he or she has seen a ghost, it is another matter entirely…Therein lies the difference. The Indian confronts the reality of the experience, and while he or she may not make immediate sense of it, it is not rejected as an invalid experience… not limited by mental considerations and assumptions regarding the universe.'[115]

What is on trial here is the continued avoidance of the mataphysical issue that distinguishes between what is validated within indigenous and spiritualized cosmologies, versus what is validated within, and by, the normative representatives of 'the west.' Plainly put, if we are to deal with the aspects of our human existence which continue to mystify us, we have to confront what has been problematically called the supernatural, or the invisible contents of the world a priori designated as 'non-data.' We need to weave together a global cultural understanding of our human experiences and reconsider that which has been systematically ignored by ontological classificatory mechanisms, from the murky content of emotions (or affect),

---

113. An excellent account of this can be found in Charles T. Tart, 'Perspectives on Scientism, Religion, and Philosophy Provided by Parapsychology,' *Journal of Humanistic Psychology* 32.2 (1992).
114. Vine Deloria, *The Metaphysics of Modern Existence* (Golden, Colorado: Fulcrum, 2012), 5.
115. Ibid.

right through to the cosmologically unthinkable. This is important because, as is evidenced from a half century of anthropological and religious inquiry, it is insufficient to just state, materialistically, that the spaces between us are empty. What ethnographers have uncovered, though they fail to name it, is cross-cultural evidence of clear breaches of our entrenched notions of separate individuals, and the non-locality of information transference across boundaries of species, time and space. Evidence of this is woven throughout all cultural matrices, all people, and all times, and really cannot be ignored: though much of it is pointed at, very little of it is really studied with the respect and humility it deserves. It would seem we are overly attached to the various assertions of positivism and naturalism as amulets against uncertainty, when we ought to be focused on transcending relativism in pursuit of holism.

The opposing notion, that 'different people live in different worlds,' is also unconvincing. Sensibly, like Fort, I acknowledge both Difference and Sameness, but finally, wish to privilege Sameness (without the sterility and purity that might be bundled up with it).[116] We have far more in common with each other than we have been prepared to acknowledge. Like Stengers, I want what they have and (I think) we had, before the smoke, the pharmaceuticals, and our magical Enlightenment. As Weber once wrote: 'The fate of an epoch that has eaten of the tree of knowledge is that it must… recognize that general views of life and the universe can never be the products of increasing empirical knowledge, and that the highest ideals, which move us most forcefully, are always formed only in the struggle with other ideals which are just as sacred to others as ours are to us.'[117]

---

116. Paraphrased from Kripal, *Authors of the Impossible*, 108.
117. Max Weber (1904) as cited in David Harvey, *The Condition of Postmodernity: An Enquiry into the Origins of Cultural Change* (Oxford: Blackwell, 1990), 1.

2

The Methodologies of Radical Empiricism:
The Experiential Worlds of William James
and Charles Fort

Timothy Grieve-Carlson

There are, then, cases where a fact cannot come at all unless a preliminary faith exists in its coming. And where faith in a fact can help create the fact, that would be an insane logic which should say that faith running ahead of scientific evidence is the 'lowest kind of immorality' into which a thinking being can fall. Yet such is the logic by which our scientific absolutists pretend to regulate our lives!

~William James, 'The Will to Believe,' 1896

We substitute acceptance for belief.
Cells of an embryo take on different appearances in different eras.
The more firmly established, the more difficult to change.
That social organism is embryonic.
That firmly to believe is to impede development.
That only temporarily to accept is to facilitate.

~Charles Fort, *The Book of the Damned*, 1919

In October of 1889, while William James was rushing to finish the manuscript that would become his first book on the discipline that emerged as the focus of his intellectual life, *The Principles of Psychology*, his wife Alice suffered a miscarriage. It would have been their third child, and in fact their second third child, after the death of their son Herman James at the age of eighteen months only five years prior. Alice was staying with her mother and their two sons in New Hampshire at the time, while William was working on his book and renovating the family's new home in Cambridge. During this difficult month,

William occupied himself by fixing up his new home, writing his wife many comforting and loving letters, attending a lecture on the Mahābhārata delivered by Sir Edwin Arnold, and reading Janet's *L'Automatisme Psychologique*. In the midst of what must have been a somewhat traumatized and simultaneously very intellectually stimulated state of mind, James sat down and 'on the spur of the moment' wrote an essay entitled 'The Hidden Self' for Scribner's.[118]

'The great field for new discoveries,' begins the essay, 'is always the Unclassified Residuum.' This not-so-widely-read piece was mostly a response to Janet's account in *L'Automatisme Psychologique* of a patient experiencing symptoms of what would later be described as Multiple Personality Disorder. In an effort to convince his readers of, if not the certain veracity, at least the possibility of such a phenomenon, James uses the beginning paragraphs of the 'The Hidden Self' to entreat his readers to take seriously accounts of this 'Unclassified Residuum,' 'wild facts' as he calls them, anomalous phenomena and extraordinary experiences:

> Round about the accredited and orderly facts of every science there ever floats a sort of dust-cloud of exceptional observations, of occurrences minute and irregular, and seldom met with, which it always proves less easy to attend to than to ignore.[119]

James goes on to remind his readers that the works of the great scientists are characterized by their willingness to attend to 'the dust-cloud of exceptional observations,' rather than ignore it:

> Only the born geniuses let themselves be worried and fascinated by these outstanding exceptions, and get no peace till they are brought within the fold. Your Galileos, Galvanis, Fresnels, Purkinjes, and Darwins are always getting confounded and troubled by insignificant things. Anyone will renovate his science who will steadily look after the irregular phenomena. And when the science is renewed, its new formulas often have more of the voice of the exceptions in them than of what were supposed to be the rules.[120]

Someone whom James, had he ever known of him, might have described as such a genius, was only 25 years old at the time of that essay, and around 170 miles away in Albany, New York.

Introductions to Charles Fort are often written as revelations: the

---

118. Robert D. Richardson, *William James: In the Maelstrom of American Modernism* (New York: Houghton Mifflin, 2006), 295.
119. William James, 'The Hidden Self.' First published in *Scribner's*, March 1890, 361-373.
120. Ibid.

categories that we call the paranormal today all share a root in one man! His biography is tellingly entitled *The Man Who Invented the Supernatural*, as though there were no ghouls or goblins before Fort had the good sense to inform the reading public about them in 1919. Fort did indeed have a hand in the formation of what would later become foundational topics for writers on the paranormal in the twentieth century. Fort coined the term 'teleportation' and inspired the term 'Bermuda triangle.' Fort was also the first to speculate that unidentified objects in the sky might be under extraterrestrial control, decades before Kenneth Arnold saw a fleet of flying croissant-shaped saucers over Mount Rainier in 1947. The bulk of Fort's intellectual work took place in the depths of the New York Public Library, collecting anecdotes and recording them on notecards which he stored in shoeboxes in his apartment. It is there, however, where introductions to Fort usually leave us. Fort was a person who recorded anomalies, but in reading Fort we know that he did more than simply collect and record instances of anomalous phenomena before such a category was commonplace. Anomalies were gathered as an arsenal of evidence in service of Fort's mission, the deconstruction of modern categories of knowledge.

This paper aims for an historical consideration of the lives and work of William James and Charles Fort as students of 'wild facts,' each sounding the depths of the unclassified residuum in their own way at the dawn of the twentieth century in America. It is well known that James was interested in the parapsychology of his day. His attendance at séances and his correspondence with figures like Frederic Myers attest to the same sympathies expressed within 'The Hidden Self.' But Fort and James do not merit comparison solely on the basis of shared interest in paranormal phenomena. James' philosophy of pluralism and Fort's radical Monism were two different ways of expressing very similar conceptions of the world. James and Fort shared patterns of thought and inquiry which exposed uniquely American ideals of revisionist epistemology. James' philosophy of 'Radical Empiricism' describes the work of both men, though each had unique techniques and ideas: categories like religion and science are valuable only insofar as they hold up to the damned data of pure experience.

The Invisible Sparring Partner

Charles Fort's first attempt at the subject matter that would become his own legacy was a doomed book he titled *X*. 'X' was both the title of the book and the term he used for an 'outside motivating force' that, with its sinister ability to mimic free will, belabors human beings with the illusion that they are in control of their own lives, all while they act out the intentions of this sublimating force. In the book, Fort suggests that X emanates from the planet Mars, and that human beings are under the intelligent control of Martians. It bears mentioning that at the time during which Fort was writing *X*, the observation of 'canals' by Percival Lowell on the Martian surface was prominent in the news, and the reading public generally assumed that Mars probably held some form of intelligent life.[121]

Fort's *X* had its first and, unfortunately, its only admirer in Theodore Dreiser. The popular novelist had discovered and endeared himself to Fort after reading his short stories published in *Popular Magazine*, a pulp anthology. The two became close friends, and Dreiser would become the sole literary champion of Fort during his life. When faced with *X*, Dreiser could only express bewildered awe:

> It was so strange, so forceful and so beautiful that I thought that whether this was science, or apocryphal and discarded, it was certainly one of the greatest books I had ever read in my life. [122]

Dreiser shopped *X* around to a wide variety of publishers, but his influence as a renowned author was not enough to convince anyone of *X*'s commercial viability. *X* was turned down by Knopf, MacMillan, Harper's, Scribner's, and John Lane. During this procession of failures, Fort was working to devise a complementary force and manuscript that he called *Y*. Eventually Fort destroyed both manuscripts himself. In Jim Steinmeyer's previously mentioned (and excellent) biography of Fort, *The Man Who Invented the Supernatural*, he suggests that *X* was not emanating from Mars; rather, *X* came straight from Albany, New York, where Fort was born and grew up.

Charles Fort recalls his father, Charles Nelson Fort, as a domineering personality. Childhood acts of insubordination were met with quick and harsh punishments. In his partially lost memoir *Many Parts*, Fort recalls a scene in which, as a young boy in Sunday school, he fails to properly pronounce the word 'smote,' instead saying 'smut.' His father, who is present for the lesson, rejoins his son in the proper pronunciation. When the struggling boy recites again how 'Moses smut the rock,' his father quite literally smites him in rebuke.[123]

Fort's failures before his father were not only in pronunciation, but belief. In *Many Parts* (in which, it bears mentioning, Fort refers to himself in the first-person plural), he recounts his own impressions of Sunday school: 'When a small boy, we puzzled over inconsistencies in the Bible, and asked questions that could not be answered satisfactorily.' Fort's precociously critical reading of the Bible was not for lack of a religious impulse, however: 'Religion as an emotional thing was strong in us, though, quite as strong, was a resisting of this emotion.' Young Fort was also unimpressed by his science teachers:

---

121. Jim Steinmeyer, *Charles Fort: The Man Who Invented the Supernatural* (New York: Penguin, 2008), 137.
122. Ibid., 40.
123. Ibid., 20.

'Professor demonstrating that in a vacuum a bullet and a feather fall at equal speed. The bullet falling first...Very hard to teach truth when truth won't come out right.' [124]

Fort's final antagonism against his father was ultimately not in belief, but vocation. Fort was expected to take up the wholesale grocery business originally established by his grandfather, but it was clear from a very young age that he had no interest in doing so. In another telling and humorous scene from *Many Parts*, Fort's grandfather asks his young grandson what he wants to be when he grows up, looking forward to the boy's reply that he cannot wait to follow in his father's and grandfather's footsteps and become a wholesale grocer! When young Fort opens his mouth to say that he would like to become a naturalist, his grandfather disappears into the dictionary. A look of horror spreads on his face when he reaches the definition of 'naturalist.' By the time Fort was a teenager, his treachery was complete: he had taken a job writing for the local newspaper in Albany, *The Argus*, and would flee his father's house and rule for good by the age of seventeen.

Why does Steinmeyer suggest that X emanated from Albany? Because the 'outside motivating force' in Fort's life and writings was and would always be his father. Fort's harsh punishments, his refusal to take up the Albany grocery business in favour of trying his hand as a writer in New York City, his seemingly innate rejection of arrogance, authority and all forms of dogmatism—when Fort wrote about X, in Steinmeyer's reckoning, it was the distant memory of his father, his family, school, church, the wholesale grocery business, and Albany in the back of his mind.[125] *The Book of the Damned* was a list of reasons not to become a grocer.

William James had an upbringing that was similar to Fort's in many ways. He was also born into a wealthy family (coincidentally, the bulk of the James' fortune was built by his grandfather, William James Sr., through real estate dealings in Albany), and his father, Henry, was also stern in his plans for his children and in his religious beliefs. Henry James Sr. was in many ways less orthodox than Charles Nelson Fort. He was a theologian, but he was an adherent of Emmanuel Swedenborg. Though the James children were brought up to be devout, one struggles to imagine Henry Sr. smiting his young ones for mispronunciation. Still, Henry James Sr. had particular expectations for the lives his children would lead. At the age of eighteen William had, to his father's chagrin, chosen art as his career. He would not allow William to attend college in America for fear that an education in the States would lead William to be 'corrupted.' Henry Sr. wanted William to pursue the sciences, believing such an education would 'bear out' his interest in religion. However, as Robert D. Richardson writes in his biography of William James, 'William's

---

124. Ibid., 21.
125. Damon Knight is another biographer of Fort who concludes that his father inspired his resistance to authority.

interest in science came and went, his interest in religion was nil.'[126] As for a career in the sciences, Henry Sr.'s unique theology made it a holy vocation itself: 'all the phenomena of physics are to [be] explained and grouped under laws exclusively spiritual, that they are in fact only the material expression of spiritual truth,' he once wrote.[127] Exposure to the natural sciences might, Henry Sr. hoped, engender some appreciation for the wonder of God's creation, but art itself was 'far too worldly' a career for the young man.[128]

It would be an overgeneralization to say that Fort and James had identically oppressive relationships with their fathers: Fort's involved more cut-and-dry mutual disdain and outright physical abuse, while James' was much less venomous and more complex. Though he did eventually end up pursuing the natural sciences, in his own indirect way, his father 'was always present to him as a great antipodal figure, an invisible sparring partner.'[129] As a young man, William once drew a frontispiece to one of his father's books that depicted a man beating a dead horse.[130] However, later in life, after his father had died, William took up the task of compiling and editing his father's collected writings into a 'best-of' volume.[131] This was not because of any great demand. Henry Sr.'s books were almost totally unread and self-published. The 'best-of' Henry James Sr. was a book that only a son could compile. Despite a lifetime of correspondence and a great mutual love and respect, William and his father simply failed, ultimately, to see eye-to-eye with one another. William James' great reckoning with the Absolute, the philosophical stance that we see compelled him most strongly, was very much an analogue to his arguments with his 'invisible sparring partner.'

As mentioned above, James' and Fort's relationships with their fathers were not identical, and they were each as fraught with contradiction and complexity as familial ties often are. They were, however, both strongly suggestive of the origins of both men's intellectual predispositions. Charles Nelson Fort and Henry James Sr., in their own ways, engendered in their boys a deep suspicion of intellectual arrogance, whether it took the name of the Absolute, or Dogma in any form. William James and Charles Fort both gained from their fathers their lifelong example of the wrong way to think. Total certainty of oneself, one's work, one's God, one's world—Fort and James took special aim at each.

---

126. Richardson, *William James*, 11.
127. Ibid., 31.
128. Ibid., 12.
129. Ibid., 58.
130. Ibid., 29.
131. Ibid., 241.

Radical Empiricism

I have read your piece. When you strike at a king you must kill him.

~Ralph Waldo Emerson to Oliver Wendell Holmes,
upon reading Holmes' essay criticizing Plato.[132]

Jeffrey J. Kripal was probably the first to take note of the similarities between William James and Charles Fort in his 2010 book, *Authors of the Impossible*:

> Fort's notion of wild talents appears to be a double echo of both Frederic Myers' earlier notion of spiritual evolution and William James's earlier notion of wild facts. By the latter expression, James referred to the data of mystical literature and psychological research that lie strewn across the surface of history, still unassimilated, still rejected by the scientism of the academic mind. For James, such wild facts always threaten to 'break up the accepted system,' particularly the accepted scientific system of the universities. This is pure Charles Fort before Charles Fort. And why not? Fort had certainly read his share of William James, though James probably knew nothing of Fort.[133]

It's difficult to say with total certainty that Fort was reading James, but it would indeed be surprising if he hadn't. James was a public intellectual of some renown during Fort's young adulthood, and Fort was stunningly well read for a mostly self-taught individual. As Kripal notes, his entire 'practice' was reading—a systemic consumption of every run of every newspaper, book or scientific journal that he could get his hands on that was written after 1800.[134] This reading practice really began in 1906,[135] and *The Varieties of Religious Experience*, for example, was published in 1902, so we might safely assume that Fort brushed up against James in some way, whether he read his books directly or became acquainted with their ideas in his daily consumption of periodicals and newspapers. In any case, neither James nor his ideas appear directly in any of Fort's books. The only index entry for William James in *The Collected Works of Charles Fort* (and Fort cited his sources with the maniacal precision necessary for a writer who compiles impossibilities) comes from his 1931 book *Lo!* It relates the story of a Mr. William James and John Morris of

132. Ibid., 77.
133. Jeffrey J. Kripal, *Authors of the Impossible* (Chicago: University of Chicago Press, 2010), 132-3.
134. Kripal writes that Fort admits that this date was settled upon arbitrarily, as an even number: 'He had to stop somewhere' (Ibid., 94). Fort believed that contemporary data would better make his case; he also demurred from the prospect of directly confronting anomalies in the Bible (Ibid., 118).
135. Ibid., 97.

Barmouth, Wales, who on September 11, 1922, watched an object they believed to be an airplane crash into the ocean; but when they approached the site in their own boat, they found nothing. Our William James had been dead for twelve years by then, but it's a coincidence that Fort probably would have been interested in; as he wrote in 1919, 'systemization of pseudo-data is approximation to realness or final awakening.'[136] As it will be shown, I would be a poor radical empiricist if I were to exclude it.

What is the first, most prominent similarity that confronts one who reads *The Book of the Damned* in tandem with William James? It is an attack on the principles of what James calls rationalism in his essay 'A World of Pure Experience.' The majority of scientific thought, James tells us (and we can imagine Charles Fort nodding enthusiastically), throws out the baby with the bathwater in its rush to establish grand theories with its data: 'Rationalism tends to emphasize universals and to make wholes prior to parts in the order of logic as well as in that of being.'[137] As an alternative to rationalism, James establishes empiricism as its binary opposite: a system where the parts are each given priority before anyone attempts to construct a 'whole,' in which the primary, or even sole, component of the universe is our experience of the universe. James' empiricism posits a world in which the disassociation of the observed and observer is dissolved and the subject and object become one. I will return to this thought later, but Fort and James both breach a line in which a pluralism sufficiently radical must eventually become a monism, and vice-versa. In fact, James' working title for a book on his idea of Radical Empiricism (which, unfortunately, never came to fruition) was 'The Many and the One.' [138]

The unfortunate residue of a science that prioritizes overzealous grand theorization over certain pieces of data is the 'unclassified residuum,' as James calls it in 'The Hidden Self.' It is Fort's army of damned data: 'You'll read them—or they'll march.'[139] Science will either pay attention to all of its parts or it will continue to 'emphasize universals,' leaving people like Charles Fort to remind us that planes are disappearing in Wales and frogs are falling from the sky. James expanded on his view of the rationalist/empiricist dichotomy in his Lowell Lectures, delivered to an audience of laypeople in Boston in 1906 (the year Fort began his reading practice). James contrasts the rationalist, 'meaning your devotee to abstract and eternal principles' (you can almost hear James' thin veiling of his disgust through the page) with the empiricist, 'meaning your

---

136. All citations of Fort's books are from the collected edition *The Book of the Damned: The Collected Works of Charles Fort* (New York: Penguin, 2008). Further notes will mention the title of the particular book and the page number in this collection. In this case, *The Book of the Damned*, 22.
137. William James, 'A World of Pure Experience,' 1904. First published in the *Journal of Philosophy, Psychology, and Scientific Methods* 1, 533-543, 561-570.
138. Richardson, *William James*, 445.
139. Fort, *The Book of the Damned*, 1.

lover of facts in all their crude variety.'[140] James could not have written a better description of Charles Fort if he had tried.

William James' radical empiricism project never appeared in its full form. The haphazard posthumous collection *Essays in Radical Empiricism* gives a good idea of what The Many and the One might have been like, but unfortunately James' thoughts ran faster than his pen. James' biographer Robert Richardson tells us that the ultimate distillation of the philosophy of radical empiricism can be found in two essays: the previously mentioned 'A World of Pure Experience' and 'Does Consciousness Exist?' In 'Consciousness,' James succinctly answers 'no.' As James tells us, consciousness is 'only a name for the fact that the "content" of experiences is known.'[141] That is, consciousness is an imagined faculty by which various nodes in the web of relations that comprise the universe feebly conceptualize their relations with each other. If that sounds strange to you, then William James would like to say you have been paying attention:

> To deny plumply that 'consciousness' exists seems so absurd on the face of it—for undeniably 'thoughts' do exist—that I fear some readers will follow me no farther. Let me then immediately explain that I mean only to deny that the word stands for an entity, but to insist most emphatically that it does stand for a function.

James' radical idea here is to posit that the universe of knowers walking around and apprehending objects through knowing them is actually much more complex than that: the universe is a swirling mess of process (process here equals experience), in which united subject-objects relate to one another in an endless song of experienced interaction. There are thoughts, sure, and these thoughts facilitate 'knowing,' but these thoughts are composed of the same thing that composes the material universe, and so there is no stand-alone thing (James uses the word 'entity') called 'consciousness.' What would Charles Fort say if we asked him if consciousness existed? He would probably laugh, not because he thought it was a silly question, but because he knew exactly what we meant, and Fort loved a joke.

The second essay, the aforementioned 'A World of Pure Experience,' elucidates the material that things and thoughts are both made of: relations. Relations exist between objects, and objects are just little collections of relations. Radical empiricism is the technique by which we can exist in this universe. 'To be radical, an empiricism must neither admit into its constructions any element that is not directly experienced nor exclude from

---

140. Richardson, *William James*, 485.
141. William James, 'Does Consciousness Exist?' 1904. First published in the *Journal of Philosophy, Psychology, and Scientific Methods* 1, 477-491. This section also draws on Richardson (*William James*, 448-9).

them any element that is directly experienced.' No struggling to compile grand theories, and no exclusion of falling frogs: 'You'll read them—or they'll march.'

There are endless quotations from the books of Charles Fort that could be used to argue in favour of radical empiricism: 'All organizations of thought must be baseless in themselves, and of course be not final, or they could not change, and must bear within themselves those elements that will, in time, destroy them.'[142] In *The Book of the Damned*, Fort outlines a mission statement for himself which is essentially a recitation of something very much like radical empiricism:

> Conventional monism, or that all 'things' that seem to have identity of their own are only islands that are projections from something underlying, and have no real outlines of their own. But that all 'things,' though only projections, are projections that are striving to break away from the underlying that denies them identity of their own. I conceive of one inter-continuous nexus, in which and of which all seeming things are only different expressions, but in which all things are localizations of one attempt to break away and become real things, or to establish entity or positive difference or final demarcation or unmodified independence—or personality or soul, as it is called in human phenomena.[143]

James would come to refer to a hard dichotomy between monism (rationalism) and pluralism (empiricism). He even came to refer to his radical empiricism as 'pluralism,' giving a series of lectures on the subject, which were published under the title *A Pluralistic Universe*. As he wrote, 'The most a philosophy can hope for is not to lock out any interest forever. No matter what doors it closes, it must leave others open for the interests it neglects.'[144] As William James set sail for England, where he would be delivering the lectures, he wrote to his brother Henry that he was 'eager for the scalp of the absolute,'[145] a sentence to make Charles Fort jealous if there ever were one.

Fort's own radical monism was, essentially, a reworded radical empiricist idea of what 'monism' actually meant. Since the substance of the universe is one, all pluralisms are obscured monisms, and all monisms are recognitions that the pluralistic universe is composed solely of raw experience:

> Our expressions are in terms of Continuity. If all things merge away into one another, or transmute into one another, so that nothing can be

142. Fort, *New Lands*, 388.
143. Fort, *The Book of the Damned*, 6.
144. William James, *A Pluralistic Universe*, *The Works of William James* (Cambridge: Harvard University Press, 1977 [1909]), 19.
145. Richardson, *William James*, 499.

defined, they are of a oneness, which may be the oneness of one existence. I state that, though I accept that there is continuity, I accept that also there is discontinuity. But there is no need, in this book, to go into the subject of continuity-discontinuity, because no statement that I shall make, as a monist, will be set aside by my pluralism.[146]

Like a snake eating its own tail, here radical monism and radical pluralism become indistinguishable under the lens of radical empiricism. And why not? As Fort puts it, 'If there is an underlying oneness of all things, it does not matter where we begin, whether with stars, or laws of supply and demand, or frogs, or Napoleon Bonaparte. One measures a circle, beginning anywhere.' [147]

In *The Book of the Damned*, Fort makes the case for another aspect of Radical Empiricism:

> Our especial interest is in modern science as a manifestation of this one ideal or purpose or process: That it has falsely excluded, because there are no positive standards to judge by: that it has excluded things that, by its own pseudo-standards, have as much right to come in as have the chosen.[148]

Fort broadly conceived of two categories as the primary agents of exclusion (James would call them the primary agents of rationalism): science and religion. Religion, Fort tells us, is the Old Dominant, the first systematic attempt to monopolize reality. Religion gave way to science as the New Dominant 'around 1860.'[149] Fort proposed a system of thought that would encapsulate and transcend these old Dominants which he called Intermediatism. Here again I will turn to Kripal's reading of Fort in *Authors of the Impossible*:

> Whereas the first two Dominants work from the systemic principle of Exclusionism, that is, they must exclude data to survive as stable systems, the New Dominant works from the systemic principle of Inclusionism, that is, it builds an open-ended system and preserves it through the confusing inclusion of data, theoretically all data, however bizarre and offending, toward some future awakening. [150]

Does that sound familiar? As James wrote, 'To be radical, an empiricism must neither admit into its constructions any element that is not directly experienced nor exclude from them any element that is directly

---

146. Fort, *Lo!*, 552.
147. Ibid., 544.
148. Fort, *The Book of the Damned*, 7.
149. Kripal, *Authors of the Impossible*, 113.
150. Ibid.

experienced.'[151] There can be no 'eternal order of ideas' while blood and flesh are falling from the sky. 'In the order of existence, behind the facts, for us there is *nothing*,' James writes.[152] It is, as Robert Richardson says, a 'mature, considered challenge to Plato.'[153]

Memories of Radical Empiricists

William James brought heart to the intellect and passion to the world of ideas in an unprecedented manner in American life. He is the most profound, adorable, and unpretentious public intellectual in American history.[154]

~Cornell West

Your story describing the funeral of Charles Fort lists me as one of his customers. This was a libel of a virulence sufficient to shock humanity. As a matter of fact, I looked upon Fort as a quack of the most obvious sort and often said so in print. As a Christian I forgive the man who wrote the story and the news editor who passed it. But both will suffer in Hell.[155]

~H.L. Mencken's letter to United Press
upon the death of Charles Fort

William James did not require an introduction at the beginning of this essay, and the passage with which opened it, from 'The Will to Believe,' did not require citation; such is James' well-deserved stature as a canonical figure in American intellectual history. Alfred North Whitehead attributed to James' radical empiricism 'the inauguration of a new stage in philosophy.'[156] Though I might struggle to convince the reader to accept Fort as an 'adorable' figure in any sense, one of the purposes of this paper is to try to claim a small portion of that standing for a public intellectual who has not enjoyed such a fond remembrance in the history of American thought.

Charles Fort's philosophy and William James' radical empiricism, read as essentially synonymous, both constitute an essentially American approach to epistemology itself, discarding old and outmoded categories and methodologies in favour of bold, living, breathing, and shocking pluralism. James and Fort rejected these categories themselves as antiquated systems of thought which actually blinded us to our daily, lived realities in which frogs fell

---

151. William James, *Essays in Radical Empiricism* (New York: Dover Publications, 2003 [1912]), 22.
152 William James, *Manuscript Lectures* (Cambridge, Mass.: Harvard University Press, 1988), 302.
153. Richardson, *William James*, 451.
154. http://www.hup.harvard.edu/catalog.php?isbn=9780674065994&content=reviews
155. H. Allen Smith, *Low Man on a Totem Pole* (eNet Press, 2015 [1941]), 54.
156. Richardson, *William James*, 450.

from the skies and airships flew over our heads. For Charles Fort, the structures of science and rationality were not a framework in which his damned data demanded inclusion; his damned data were the circumstantial evidence which he used to expound on the fallibility and failures of these structures themselves. The damned data of pure experience represented a holistic, inclusive, American revisionist philosophy, a referendum on the existing categories and systems of knowledge as we began the twentieth century.

Though Fort's X was doomed, James' own doomed book, *The Many and the One*, reaches us through Fort's writings. Through his reading practice in the New York Public Library, Charles Fort actually acted out the work James prescribed as radical empiricism. Nothing was excluded, every experience consumed; nothing was ignored in Fort's march to assemble his arsenal of data. Fort thought and wrote as a radical empiricist, his shoebox-notecard methodology standing the test of time in the form of his never-out-of-print books.

Fort and James each, seemingly separately (though who knows how much influence James' writings could have had), came to startlingly similar conclusions about the nature of the universe and humanity's place within it at the turn of the century in America. James would go on to be remembered as 'the Father of American Psychology'; Fort is most often eulogized as a 1941 *New York Times* review put it: 'the enfant terrible of science.' Then again, Fort would probably have chuckled at and appreciated such an epitaph, and William James never (publically, at least) suggested that all the earth was under Martian control.

3

Extraordinary Religious/Anomalous Cases from Brazil and the Fortean Approach

Wellington Zangari, Fatima Regina Machado,
Everton de Oliveira Maraldi and Leonardo Breno Martins

One of the greatest legacies of Charles Hoy Fort (1874–1932) was, undoubtedly, his presentation of extraordinary experiences that raised questions about the scientific knowledge of his time. More than eighty years after Fort's death the question of what constitutes 'scientific truth' remains unchanged. The anomalous experiences that Fort so carefully selected and published can be considered to have revolutionary implications. This motivates us to continue his effort, not only in collecting potentially unexplained extraordinary cases, but also, and above all, in attempting to explain them or, at least, to propose a healthy epistemological discussion about the limits of science.

In his book *New Lands*,[157] Fort devotes several paragraphs to the presentation of cases about hidden cities in the countryside of Brazil. He must have recognised the revolutionary features of Brazilian cases. In this chapter, more Brazilian cases with the same potential are presented. Some of them were investigated by the authors and others are presented due to their historical importance. All the cases recounted in this chapter effectively represent 'anomalies' in the Fortean sense of the term, and are presented in four different categories: a) cases of physical and mental mediumship, ranging from apparent ectoplasmic materialisations to cases suggestive of reincarnation; b) poltergeist cases; c) cases of alien contact; and d) mixed anomalous cases. In addition to their anomalous features, these cases have also a strong religious component, either because they occurred in a religious environment, or because they were interpreted as religious by the experiencers. The experiencers' own interpretations are presented in this chapter, but we also present (and comment on) alternative or conventional

---

157. Charles Hoy Fort, *New Lands* (New York: Ace Books, 1941, first published in 1923).

interpretations for the cases, and discuss epistemological questions. Although our interpretations may be considered 'scientific,' some of them still lack support from the scientific mainstream, which strengthens the legacy of Charles Fort.

Mediumship and Past-Life Memories

Mediumship constitutes an essential aspect of different religious expressions in Brazil, and is especially important in the traditions of Umbanda and Spiritism. Umbanda is a typically Brazilian religion based on the syncretic combination of African, Indigenous and Christian heritages, and also includes elements of Spiritism and New Age Esotericism.[158] Umbanda rituals (called *giras*) involve the 'incorporation' of specific spiritual entities or forces by entranced mediums, many of which have become popular icons in Brazilian culture. Examples include *Preto Velho* (old black man; generally wise and peaceful, he gives advice and spiritual help), *Exu* (the guardian spirit of the Umbanda temple) and *Pomba Gira* (a personification of female sexuality and desire). Participants often turn to such rituals in search of counseling or spiritual healing.

There are many reports of impressive cures derived from Umbanda healing practices, as well as accounts of consultations with mediums that seemed to convey very specific information about the life of the consultants, which apparently could not have been known by the medium, at least by normal sensory means. Some investigators have experimentally tested the purported psi abilities of Umbanda mediums (such as precognition and distant healing intention), though their results have been mixed, sometimes in favour of anomalous mental or physical phenomena, and sometimes not.[159]

However, claims of anomalous and paranormal phenomena are not exclusive to Umbanda ceremonies, and many investigators have directed their attention to Spiritist mediums as well. Spiritism was founded by Allan Kardec (1804-1869), a French educator who systematized the study of mediumistic communications in an attempt to establish a single spiritualist doctrine based on convergences between spiritual teachings obtained through different mediums. Spiritism has disseminated widely through Brazil, much more than in its homeland, France. It became the third largest religion of the country, reaching approximately 2.3 million followers. Spiritist books are very popular in Brazil, and they are read not only by Spiritists but also by many other

---

158. Wellington Zangari, 'Incorporando Papéis: Uma leitura psicossocial do fenômeno da mediunidade de incorporação em médiuns de Umbanda' (PhD diss., University of São Paulo, 2003).
159. Everton de Oliveira Maraldi, Wellington Zangari, Fatima Regina Machado and Stanley Krippner, 'Anomalous mental and physical phenomena of Brazilian mediums,' in *Talking with the Spirits: Ethnographies from Between the Worlds*, ed. Jack Hunter and David Luke (Brisbane: Daily Grail Publishing, 2014), 259.

Brazilians who eventually come to hold certain Spiritist beliefs (such as the belief in reincarnation and in communication with the dead), without necessarily being Spiritists themselves.[160]

Throughout the history of mediumship in Brazil, Spiritist reunions have been the stage for numerous allegedly paranormal phenomena. Physical mediums such as Carmine Mirabelli (1889-1951), Francisco Peixoto Lins (1905-1966), and Anna Prado (1883-1923) were apparently able to produce many of the same physical phenomena reported during nineteenth century séances in the United States and Europe, including materializations of spirits, levitation, movement of objects without contact, and stigmata. On the other hand, mediums such as Chico Xavier (1910-2002) produced a wide range of mediumistic phenomena. However, Xavier is best known for his intellectual and artistic works, such as poetry supposedly written under the intervention of the spirits.

Some investigators consider that similarities between Xavier's mediumistic writings and the writing style of the Brazilian and Portuguese poets he claimed to intermediate constitute evidence that defies normal explanations, especially considering that Xavier lived in poverty and had little access to formal education.[161] The automatic messages that he claimed to receive from the deceased, in response to their families and loved ones, were also the subject of controversies. But a group of investigators defended that at least some of those letters (supposedly written by Jair Presente, a young Brazilian man who drowned on February 3, 1974 at the age of 24), contained an enormous amount of verifiable information, which could not be easily attributed to ordinary explanations such as fraud, chance or information leakage. Among other things, the mediumistic messages attributed to Jair included correct names of some of his relatives and mentioned veridical aspects of the circumstances involving his death.[162]

Famous Brazilian mediums such as Xavier may attain special public attention, but there are also many other instances of intriguing spirit manifestations obtained by anonymous mediums and Spiritist groups all over Brazil, as was the case with the supposed 'drop in' communicator Ruytemberg Rocha (1908-1932). Rocha was a captain who died in 1932 while participating in an armed movement known in Brazil as the Constitutionalist Revolution. In the year of 1961, during a Spiritist séance in São Paulo City, a medium of the group apparently fell into a trance and started to behave as if she had an injury around the breast area. When asked who the spirit trying to communicate was,

---

160. Bernardo Lewgoy, 'A transnacionalização do Espiritismo Kardecista Brasileiro: Uma discussao inicial,' *Religiao e Sociedade*, 28.1 (2008): 84.
161. Alexandre Caroli Rocha, 'A poesia transcendente de Parnaso de além tumulo' (MS diss., University of Campinas , 2001).
162. Alexandre Caroli Rocha, Denise Paraná, Elizabeth Schmitt Freire, Francisco Lotufo Neto, and Alexander Moreira-Almeida, 'Investigating the Fit and Accuracy of Alleged Mediumistic Writing: A Case Study of Chico Xavier's Letters,' *Explore* 10.5 (2004): 300.

the medium said 'Ruytemberg Rocha' and provided a series of very specific details about him, including aspects of his training in the military and names of his relatives. The Brazilian parapsychologist and engineer Hernani Guimarães Andrade[163] investigated this case in depth, and was able to confirm much of the information given by the medium, although some details were obviously incorrect, such as the wound described as the cause of Rocha's death.

Outside Spiritist centers and groups, many families also reported impressive cases of children who claimed to remember previous lives, and whose memories and behaviours concerning a past reincarnation were investigated either by foreign or Brazilian parapsychologists. Reincarnation cases are more common in Asian countries such as Thailand, Burma or India, and are relatively rare among other continents, but Brazil contributes to this list with some interesting published cases. Two of them are included in Ian Stevenson's book *Twenty Cases Suggestive of Reincarnation*.[164] Andrade contributed with eight additional investigations in another publication.[165]

One of the most intriguing is Jacira's case. She was a precocious girl who in her early childhood manifested a series of behaviours that matched those of her uncle Ronaldo, who died before Jacira was born. Jacira sometimes surprised her parents with comments regarding her previous life as Ronaldo, which she could not have known as the family did not talk about it with her. However, most of these memories apparently vanished years after, and the adolescent Jacira had only a vague recollection of such episodes. In his analysis, Andrade pointed to the many similarities that seemed to exist between Brazilian and foreign cases, in order to illustrate the possible universality of this type of phenomenon.

Poltergeists in Brazil

Poltergeist ('noisy ghost' in German) is the name popularly given to bizarre physically observable occurrences that at first glance seem to have no known natural cause and are repeated over a period of time—days, months or, in exceptional cases, years.[166] In general, the reported physical occurrences seem to be more directly related to a particular person, especially in his/her interaction with the group involved in the case (the family or group of people who work/study/live where poltergeist activities happen).

In Brazil, houses or buildings where poltergeist-like events occur are popularly said to be haunted places. Commonly people involved in such cases resort to religious explanations and may seek assistance from Catholic priests,

163. Hernani Guimarães Andrade, O caso Ruytemberg Rocha (São Paulo: IBPP, 1980).
164. Ian Stevenson, *Twenty Cases Suggestive of Reincarnation* (Virginia: The University Press of Virginia, 1974).
165. Hernani Guimarães Andrade, Reencarnação no Brasil: Oito casos que sugerem renascimento (São Paulo, Brazil: O Clarim, 1986).
166. William G. Roll, *The Poltergeist* (New York: Nelson Doubleday, 1972).

Evangelical pastors, Kardecian Spiritists and Umbanda or Candomblé priests and priestesses (*pais de santo and mães de santo*). In large Brazilian urban centres, it is more common that poltergeist-like events are attributed to disembodied spirits or some evil agent. In the countryside–such occurrences are commonly attributed to *Saci Pereré*, a kind of Brazilian black one-legged goblin, who smokes a pipe, has one hole in each hand, wears a magical red cap that enables him to disappear and reappear, who 'lives in the forests and loves bothering people and animals in the farms.'[167] In this last case, people seem to accept more passively the poltergeist-like occurrences than those who believe the phenomena are caused by the devil or by discarnate spirits.

In Brazil there is no scientific tradition of systematic investigation of poltergeists, however some investigations have been conducted.[168] Despite some examples of fraud, there are cases with features that are very intriguing and possibly suggestive of anomalous physical occurrences.

One very interesting and famous case is The Suzano Poltergeist.[169] Suzano is a city next to São Paulo City. In 1968, a rain of stones was reported and later, in May 1970, spontaneous fires broke out, burning clothes, furniture and several objects in a poor house where a married couple and their four children lived. Police and neighbours witnessed some of these spontaneous fires. A floating fireball was also seen inside the house. The family asked a Catholic priest to exorcise the place, but he refused to do so. He asked the couple's adolescent daughter to leave for several days because occurrences seemed to be connected to her. Poltergeist events stopped while she was away, but they restarted for a day as soon as she came back before the phenomena ceased completely.

Another famous case not far from São Paulo City was The Guarulhos Poltergeist, which had three phases: April 27 to May 1st, 1973; April to October 25, 1974; and March 28 to an undefined date.[170] Poltergeist-like occurrences occurred in the front house of a property (with a front house— where a couple and a baby lived—and a house in the back, where another seven relatives lived). Upholstered furniture and mattresses were torn. Some people said they could see the fabric being torn as if by the sharp claws of a hairy beast that was not seen by others. Keys and money disappeared mysteriously. From the second phase on, there were rains of stones, scratches on residents and cuts/rips in clothes and other objects, problems with

---

167. Fatima Regina Machado, 'Field Investigations on Hauntings and Poltergeists,' in *Proceedings of an International Conference, Utrecht II: Charting the Future of Parapsychology* (New York: Parapsychology Foundation; The Netherlands: Het Johan Borgmanfonds Foundation, 2008), 115.

168. Fatima Regina Machado and Wellington Zangari, 'The Poltergeist in Brazil: A Review of the Literature in Context,' *International Journal of Parapsychology*, 11.1 (2000): 113.

169. Hernani Guimarães Andrade, *Poltergeist. Algumas de suas Ocorrências no Brasil* (São Paulo: Pensamento, 1988), 32-127.

170. Andrade, *Poltergeist*, 128-221.

electrical appliances and movement of objects. The family was very religious. They belonged to the Assembly of God and tried an exorcism in order to stop the occurrences. It apparently worked for a while. Those who lived in the front house moved twice, but poltergeist events 'followed' them. There is no information about the cessation of occurrences.

Other Brazilian poltergeist cases—reported not only in São Paulo but also all over the country—are similarly interesting but not always so exuberant in terms of the variety of types of occurrences, as in certain cases investigated by Machado and Zangari.[171] However any poltergeist case is always impressive because of the bizarreness of the physical events witnessed and reported, such as apparent spontaneous movements or breakage of objects, overturned furniture, raps, appearance of water or fire, rain of stones, air currents, temperature changes in closed places, appearance of waste in food or thrown against people or houses, and lights and other electronic devices turning on and off 'by themselves.'[172] Some occurrences are even more bizarre: in the 1970s, in the Morada do Sol Poltergeist case (in a neighborhood of Manaus, Amazonas), there were reports of anomalous trajectories of objects moving themselves very slowly in the air, as if someone/something was carrying the object; and in the Osasco Poltergeist case, in a shared wardrobe, spontaneous fires burned selectively only the clothes that belonged to a woman.[173]

Poltergeist cases easily attract media attention. Now and then there is news of some kind of strange occurrence, and immediately people from different religions offer themselves to help extinguish the phenomena and release people and places 'of the evil,' which causes diverse consequences when religious rituals fail.

The most recent nationally famous poltergeist case occurred in 2014 in the rural city of Rio Grande do Sul, in the South of Brazil. The wooden house where a couple with three children (an eight-year-old boy and two girls, 11 and 15 years-old respectively), lived was subjected to extremely strong blows on the walls and a rain of stones that somehow got into the house without damaging the roof tiles. The police were called and reportedly witnessed the anomalous rain of stones. Furniture was overturned and kitchen utensils moved around the place. Neighbours and social workers tried to help the family, who were taken to a nearby chapel. Poltergeist events happened there too. The oldest daughter started to exhibit odd behaviors attributed to possession. An exorcism was done, but even so, the family decided to move and demolish the house. The family was served by the municipal social assistance and the case was followed by the Spiritist Federation of Rio Grande

171. Fatima Regina Machado and Wellington Zangari, 'Três Casos Poltergeist em São Paulo,' *Fator Psi*, 1 (2000): 8.

172. André Pércia de Carvalho, As Casas Mal-Assombradas - Poltergeist (São Paulo: IBRASA. 1991).

173. Carlos Alberto Tinoco, Fenômenos Paranormais de Psicosinesia Espontânea (São Paulo: IBRASA, 1989).

do Sul.[174] There is no news about the continuation or cessation of the phenomena after the house was demolished.

Aliens and Other Entities

Brazil is also rich in firsthand accounts of entities perceived as strange and different from the spirits of dead people. For centuries, culturally hegemonic religious and folkloric perspectives led to the understanding of such entities as angels, demons, *Orishas, Exus,* and other folkloric entities like the *Mãe do Ouro* (meaning the 'Mother of Gold'), and the werewolf. From the late 1940s, when UFOs reached the Brazilian media due to the influence of the United States, and from the 1950s, when the hypothesis of extraterrestrial origin was popularized,[175] such entities were gradually also understood as space aliens.

Among the famous Brazilian episodes that interact dialectically with culture, influencing and being influenced by it, is the world's first reported alien abduction. In 1957, about four years before the paradigmatic 'Hill abduction' in the United States, the Brazilian farmer Antonio Villas Boas reported that he had been forcibly taken into a UFO, had blood and tissue samples taken in medical-like procedures and had been forced to have sex with a female alien for the purpose of creating a hybrid being. Note that the basic elements that would be consolidated as the typical script of alien abductions in the United States were already present in the Brazilian episode. Also, early contactees appeared in Brazil, such as the famous encounter reported by the lawyer João de Freitas Guimarães in 1956, who was invited to give an instructive ride on a flying saucer by tall, blond and clear-eyed aliens.[176]

Despite the suggestive cross-cultural dimensions of the episodes mentioned above and many similar ones, countless Brazilian narratives have quite different characteristics compared to other contexts more widely known in the literature of the United States and Europe. A few representative examples illustrate the point.

The vast rural areas of Brazil are the locus of copious firsthand narratives of attacks perpetrated by big balls of light from the sky, typically recognized as folkloric entities similar to the above mentioned *Mãe do Ouro*, the *Boitatá* ('Fire Snake'), and the *Moto Fantasma* ('Ghost Motorcycle'), among many others. In proportion to the increasing urbanization of these areas, UFO interpretations are also growing, while occurrences of such aggressive episodes are decreasing. There are also many reports of physical confrontations (fights) between the protagonists and monstrous entities often, though not always, associated with

174. 'Casa é demolida após exorcismo e fenômenos incomuns no Rio Grande do Sul,' last modified October 29, 2015,   http://g1.globo.com/rs/rio-grande-do-sul/noticia/2014/06/casa-e-demolida-apos-exorcismo-e-fenomenos-incomuns-no-rs.html
175. Rodolpho Gauthier Cardoso dos Santos, 'A invenção dos discos voadores: Guerra Fria, imprensa e ciência no Brasil (1947-1958)' (MS diss. State University of Campinas, 2009).
176. Santos, 'A invenção dos discos voadores.'

the lights. Reaching fame worldwide as possibly the most aggressive UFO episodes of all time, dozens of these attacks were reported in just a few months in 1977 in Colares Island, State of Pará, causing mass hysteria. This led to an official government intervention by the Brazilian Air Force with an operation suggestively called *Operação Prato* ('Operation Saucer'). The lights, residents said, sucked the blood and 'vital energy' of humans and animals, causing at least two deaths and dozens of admissions to the local hospital.[177]

Among the many episodes of this kind investigated by the fourth author, a young resident of a village called Santana do Riacho reported that he was walking along a dirt road when he saw a small, thin entity of frightening aspect, 'a little monster,' he said. Terrified, he walked back with arms extended forward to protect himself, then fell off a small bridge onto a thorn bush. Many residents believe that the creature was an alien, because its appearance coincides with the moderately famous 'grays' described in the UFO literature. Meanwhile, some residents believe that it was the 'Little Saint Anthony,' a small entity who appeared to a young woman eighty years before in the same region, where currently stands a small church built in honour of the apparition. These cases begin to demonstrate the syncretism of traditional folkloric references, Catholic hegemony in the country, and modern UFOlogy. Other representative examples provide further interesting elements.

In Santana do Riacho, in 2014, a frightened fourteen-year-old boy reported the appearance of a humanoid creature with four eyes. Near Lapinha da Serra, in the same region, a retired lawyer claimed to have seen, just a few years ago, a creature with only one eye and red stony skin. Multiple creature types tend to be reported in regions like this, subject to the confluence of several cultural references.

Almost fifteen hundred kilometers away from Santana do Riacho is Barra do Garças, a city known for its esotericism and the copious legends, according to which there is a hidden city of gold and a lost civilization in its mountains. It was in this region that, in 1925, the famous explorer Colonel Fawcett (one of the inspirations for the creation of the notorious movie character Indiana Jones), disappeared while searching for the lost city. The confluence of different religions, folklore, new age esotericism and the legends specific and culturally pervasive in the region about hidden civilizations mark that context with a peculiar characteristic; even in relation to the exoticism of Brazilian episodes: the abundance of stories about aliens deliberately disguised among local residents. Among the episodes of this type studied by the fourth author in the region, is the adventure of a taxi driver some years ago who gave a ride to an odd couple. According to his report, a man with a robotic voice asked him to take them to a remote region, something which puzzled the driver. The woman remained silent most of the time, with long black hair covering her

---

177. Cláudio T. Suenaga, 'A dialética do real e do imaginário: Uma proposta de interpretação do Fenômeno OVNI' (MS diss., Paulista State University, 1999).

face. When she and the man finally spoke, the dialogue occurred in a language unintelligible to the driver. The woman then revealed a frightful face, like a ghost or a monster, which nearly caused the driver to leave the cab. Along the way the strange man asked the driver if he had ever heard anything about UFOs, and asked if he would be afraid if 'something' were to appear over them. After a brief monologue from the strange passenger on the harmlessness of UFOs and aliens, a ship passed over the car no more than five meters above, that disappeared just ahead. When the taxi finally arrived at its destination, the same ship was waiting for the two strange clients, who were (seemingly) extraterrestrials after all.

In another episode of this kind in the same region, two friends were walking along a dirt road when they met an anthropomorphic entity, entirely silver and measuring almost eight feet high. It did not have ears, nose or mouth, and had only dark holes in the place of its eyes. The creature tried to give, or show, them a strange triangle in its hands, but the friends fled in terror.

Mixed Cases

In this section we present some Brazilian cases that do not fit neatly into any of the previous sections, and cannot be specifically classified.

The richness of religious influences in Brazil, as we have seen, derives from a mix of cultures, especially the African and Indigenous influence, and the very strong European Catholic influence. Some of the cases we present here are particularly related to that latter cultural influence.

On June 14th, 2002, an image was noticed on the glass of a window and was immediately identified as an image of the Virgin Mary, the mother of Jesus. This strange event occurred in the house of a lower middle class family in Ferraz de Vasconcelos, a city in the countryside of São Paulo State, about 32 miles away from São Paulo City. The image appeared to show the profile of a head and body with a colourful aura similar to a mantle. Just as in the famous apparition of Our Lady at Fatima in Portugal, three children first saw the image that became known in Brazil as the 'Saint of the Windowpane,' or 'Our Lady of the Window.' One of the children who lived in the house called his mother to show her the image. She tried to remove the image by cleaning the glass with alcohol, but the more she cleaned the window, the clearer the image became. News about the image spread into the city, and was soon being reported nationally in the press. Presenters of TV shows and popular singers visited the place, which helped to make the case better known. Quickly, the house turned into a place of worship and hundreds of thousands of people visited it. Soon reports of extraordinary cures attributed to the Saint of the Windowpane started to become known. In addition to the pilgrimages to the site every year on July 14, a large ritual celebration is held in this place. The local Catholic Bishop, Don Paulo Mascarenhas Roxo, established a multidisciplinary investigative committee (of which the first and second authors were members) to study the phenomenon. Research has shown that the image was formed due to water action during the period in which the glass remained stored before being used. Water has a corrosive effect on the glass producing a luminous effect similar to a rainbow.[178] However, that conclusion did not diminish people's faith, and the Saint of the Windowpane continues to be worshiped.

Other Brazilian mysterious cases are linked to public places that provide a link between the past and the present. Places where there has historically been suffering seem to haunt people's lives in the present day. An example is the São Paulo's City Council building. The building is known as Palácio Anchieta (Anchieta Palace), and was inaugurated in 1969. It is located in the centre of the city and has thirteen floors, three basements and a helipad. About two thousand people work there. It was built in the Anhangabaú Valley. Anhangabaú, in Tupi, an indigenous language, means 'river of evil spirits.' It seems that the ancient indigenous inhabitants of that region associated the river with the suffering imposed to them by European pioneers from the sixteenth century on. Those pioneers were called *Bandeirantes* ('those who carry a flag'), and their expeditions were called *bandeiras* ('flags'). They opened ways to the Brazilian backwoods seeking for silver, gold, precious stones, and indigenous people to be enslaved. Their actions contributed to the colonization of new land (today, Brazil) by Portugal.

More than four centuries have passed by since the bandeiras took place. However, still today there are reports of sounds of chains, groans of pain and people calling for help that are heard coming from the basements of the São Paulo's City Council building, in addition to reports of other strange phenomena. The elevator operator, Aristides de Paula, claims he saw a man entering the elevator and then vanishing, much to the astonishment of the other two people who were in the elevator. Aristides recognised the 'ghost' as a former work colleague who had recently died.

The apparition of a woman dressed as a bride is also recurrently reported by maintenance staff, especially in the main hall of the City Council building. The woman seems to float in the middle of the air before disappearing. In 1996, Councilman Faria Lima reported that on one occasion he worked until late at night in the building when, around midnight, he tried unsuccessfully to open one of the doors of his cabinet. The door was definitely unlocked and yet remained inexplicably closed. He tried another unlocked door in his office and the same happened. He could hear that outside his office there were several people talking in a strange language and what sounded like furniture being dragged. The Councilman phoned the security service. Two policemen went to his office and easily opened the doors. The policemen confirmed that nobody else was on that floor of the building. After that episode, others who

---

178. Suenaga, 'A dialética do real e do imaginário.'

worked in the building reported similar odd stories. For example, the waiter Vilmar Martini says he saw, in the main hall, the keypad of a rotary dial telephone rotating by itself.

Another bizarre tale comes from the North of Brazil, from Amazonas State, where a great part of the Amazon rainforest is located. On 27 and 28 of May 2015, at five schools in Manaus, capital of Amazonas, several students fell ill after playing a game to invoke spirits. Students were encouraged to perform the invocation ritual after learning of the 'Charlie Charlie' game (inspired by a Mexican game with the same name) through social networks. In the game a pencil is crossed over another pencil, both of which are placed on a piece of paper where the words 'yes' and 'no' are written. The pencil standing on top supposedly moves indicating yes or no, answering a question posed to the spirit of a dead person. Everything seems to have started after one of the adolescent students of the Escola Estadual, Sebastião Norões, blew on a pencil as a joke to make it move. It is said that even when the student was away from the pencil, holding hands with colleagues, other twelve to fourteen year old students saw the pencil moving by itself. Then, the boy who initially blew the pencil unusually had the 'yes or no' sheet of paper stuck to one of his hands. Colleagues tried to remove it unsuccessfully. The paper seemed to be glued to him. Suddenly, the boy was thrown to the floor and began to struggle. From that moment, other students started to see demons and deceased people; they also vomited, felt dizzy, convulsed and fainted. In another school, Escola de Tempo Integral, José Carlos Mestrinho, began fainting and convulsing, while six to eleven year old students started to hit one another, and some even attempted to hang themselves. The students were referred to hospitals in the region, and were taken away in ambulances escorted by the police. Classes were suspended for one day and support was offered to parents by both the Guardianship Council and the Education Department of Amazonas State.

Concluding Remarks

Remarkably, the different types of cases presented in this chapter often resulted in the experiencers offering a religious interpretation, which appears to be a trend with anomalous experiences in general in Brazil.[179] Strong religious beliefs are very common in Brazil, pervading daily life and acting as filters for reality. And just like the Brazilian people, popular religiosity is 'mestiza,' composed of the intersection of elements from different cultures that gave rise to what is now known as 'Brazilian' culture.[180] The bizarre and

179. Fatima Regina Machado, 'Experiências anômalas (extra-sensório-motoras) na vida cotidiana e sua associação com crenças, atitudes e bem-estar subjetivo,' *Boletim da Academia Paulista de Psicologia*, 30.79 (2010): 462.
180. Mary Del Priore, Do Outro Lado: A história do sobrenatural e do espiritismo (São Paulo: Planeta do Brasil, 2014).

challenging features of anomalous experiences are particularly influential in the formation of religious interpretations in this cultural context. There are ideological disputes especially among Catholics and Kardecian Spiritists for the best interpretation of anomalous experiences.[181] These ideological disputes strongly influence the interpretation of anomalous cases and have an enormous effect on the posture that mainstream science assumes in relation to those narratives.

Reducing the unknown to the known is part of the role of science. Everything could be the result of testimony failures, misperceptions, frauds, illusion, lies or psychological disorders. Thus, our sense of control over reality would be preserved. However, the question is whether the fact that we are able to develop 'simple' explanations for some cases makes them sufficient for all cases. The Fortean perspective[182]—the objective of which is not to explain anomalous phenomena but to disconcert scientists—requires us not only to question the limits of current scientific understanding, but also forces us to consider interpretations that can enlarge the scientific view. In fact, several of the cases presented in this chapter seem unlikely to be explained by recourse to conventional scientific interpretations and certainly raise important questions.

Experiences of past life memories raise questions of whether our conscious experiences and our own life histories form our memories, or whether they might also be formed through some unknown form of sharing the experiences of others. Experiences with aliens and/or UFOs raise questions about our nature and our isolation (or not) in the cosmos. Poltergeist cases make us question the limits of our interpretations. These limitations should be questioned, especially when there seems to be some relationship between the anomalous occurrences and a particular individual, and/or the dynamics of the family involved. Could it be possible that human beings are able to unconsciously influence the environment through means still unknown by science? In addition to these, other cases suggestive of supernatural interventions in our world raise questions about their causation.

Considering the cases presented, could we hypothesize that the limits of conscious action are different of those already known by psychology, biology and physics? If we take Fort's critical and epistemological position to its ultimate consequences, the least we can affirm is the apparent incompetence of science in relation to what surprises her. It is important to present anomalous experiences not only for their bizarre, curious and amazing features, but most importantly because they break the rules of what is

---

181. Fatima Regina Machado, 'A Causa dos Espíritos: Estudo sobre a utilização da Parapsicologia para a defesa da fé católica e espírita no Brasil' (MS diss., Pontifical Catholic University of São Paulo, 2010).
182. Charles Hoy Fort, *The Book of the Damned: The Collected Works of Charles Fort* (New York: Tarcher, 2008 [1919]).

expected; besides they are also deeply relevant to experiencers.[183] Anomalous experiences might involve phenomena that could possibly reveal new processes in nature. We say 'new' not in the historical sense, since such mechanisms can be as ancient as humanity itself. They are new because they represent something that has not been considered by mainstream science, and that, if this is considered, we may need to have a partial or total reformulation of science. Anomalies can lead to scientific revolutions, in other words, a radical change of paradigm.[184]

If we imagine such new phenomena actually being taken seriously by science, we can begin to postulate some scenarios. The first scenario would be science providing mechanistic explanations for such phenomena. From this perspective anomalies would be considered as products of known causative agents, whether physical, chemical, or psychological. In that case, it would be an appeal to scientific perspectives already established, that is, the prevailing scientific view. Fort questioned this scenario in the light of his analysis of the cases he collected. A second scenario: scientific development would allow the enlargement of scientific theories to accommodate at least some of the anomalies involved in the reported experiences. For example, studies of quantum physics have often been considered as a source of inspiration for the understanding of many anomalies. Such studies could indicate that there is a kind of interaction between living systems that transcends the limits currently recognized by science. A third scenario involves not only scientists, but also a whole cultural change in which anomalies come to be understood as 'normal' and 'expected' phenomena because they make sense in a cultural system. In this case, it would be impossible to deny the academic study of anomalies and, indeed, the 'very anomalous' character of such experiences would no longer make sense. A fourth possible scenario: the scientific study of anomalies brings a radical change of the current paradigm.

Fort's critical epistemology is, therefore, alive and well. It is alive because the 'insistent existence' of anomalous phenomena and experiences represents a constant thorn in the side of scientists. And finally, it is alive for opening for consideration the need to expand our worldview in fields such as parapsychology and anomalistic psychology.

Acknowledgements

The postdoctoral fellowship of the second author is supported by CAPES (Coordination for Improvement of Higher Education Personnel), and the work of the third and fourth authors is/was supported by FAPESP (São Paulo Research Foundation), which we gratefully acknowledge. We also thank Dr. Carlos S. Alvarado for editorial suggestions.

---

183. Machado, 'Experiências anômalas (extra-sensório-motoras) na vida cotidiana.'
184. Thomas Kuhn, *The Structure of Scientific Revolutions* (Chicago: University of Chicago Press: 1962)

4

A New Demonology:
John Keel and The Mothman Prophecies

David Clarke[185]

Flying Saucers, the Shaver Mystery and the Occult Revival

Charles Fort is often credited as one of the founders of the study of unidentified flying objects (UFOs), although he died fifteen years before the origin of the modern UFO phenomenon. The birth of UFOlogy can be traced to the sighting of nine mysterious flying objects above the Cascade Mountains in Washington, USA, by a private pilot, Kenneth Arnold, on the afternoon of 24 July 1947. Arnold's description of their movement, 'like a saucer would if you skipped it across water,' was subsequently transformed by headlines that reported the arrival of flying saucers in North American skies.

This mystery was promoted by Ray Palmer, editor of the Ziff-Davis pulp magazine *Amazing Stories*. Palmer mixed Fortean material with avowed science fiction. In March 1945 he published a story, 'I Remember Lemuria,' contributed by Richard S. Shaver of Pennsylvania, who claimed to have personal experience of a sinister, ancient civilisation that hid in caverns beneath the surface of the Earth. Shaver attributed a range of malign occurrences on the surface to the activities of creatures he called Detrimental Robots (or deros) who kidnapped and devoured humans. Although Palmer presented what he called 'The Shaver Mystery' as fiction he implied the stories were fundamentally true. He claimed *Amazing Stories* had received thousands of letters from people who claimed to have met the deros. Shaver said the creatures travelled in spaceships and rockets and were associated with evil extra-terrestrials. When flying saucers were sighted independently, Palmer regarded this as further validation of the factual nature of Shaver's claims.[186]

Palmer was prominent among a new generation of writers and publishers who sought to reinterpret Charles Fort's material, but few were successful in their attempts to emulate his unique philosophy. Biographer Jim Steinmeyer

---

185. Department of Media and Communications, Sheffield Hallam University.
186. Loren E. Gross, *Charles Fort, The Fortean Society, and Unidentified Flying Objects* (Fremont, California: privately published, 1976).

argued that Fort established a literary template that others have followed, namely: '[the] relentless arrangement of haunting facts to build suspicion, the ridicule of standard explanations [and] the trustworthy, disinterested, conversational tone.'[187] Fort's books became available to a mass audience during the 'occult revival' when they were republished in paperback form.[188] According to the sociologist Marcello Truzzi this revival began in the late 1960s when publishers expanded their lists to include a number of new occult titles and reflected a growth of public interest in a range of esoteric phenomena including UFOs and ancient astronauts, ESP, the Loch Ness Monster and Uri Geller.[189] Simultaneously, a number of new writers sought to update Fort's catalogue of anomalies and, in doing so, developed new theories and philosophies tailored for a Space Age audience.

John Keel: 'not an authority on anything'

Like Fort, John Keel began his career as a journalist. He was born in the town of Hornell, 200 miles (322 km) from Fort's birthplace in Albany, New York. His parents separated at an early age and he grew up on a farm with his mother and stepfather. As a teenager he devoured books on science, travel, humour and magic. At sixteen he left for New York City in search of work as a professional writer. His introduction to Fort and *Amazing Stories* came at an early age. When interviewed by this author in 1992 he recalled their impact:

> I read Charles Fort when I was very young, when I was about twelve or fourteen years old...I was reading *Amazing Stories* in those days too, and they were getting letters...about things people had seen in the sky, this is before 1947, and I was writing a newspaper column at that time in my home town newspaper...I did a couple of columns on that kind of thing, lights in the sky and people who saw contrails high overhead and thought that it was some kind of spaceship...Anyway, I was around when the whole [Ken Arnold] thing broke and I remember I was standing in a carnival in my home town...and a friend of mine came up and say 'Hey Keel have you seen this newspaper story about this guy out West who saw some strange things over the mountains?'...and it was like a shock to me. I thought "Oh my God, it's starting."'[190]

A poll by the Gallup organisation in August 1947 found the vast majority of Americans who held an opinion on flying saucers believed they were products

---

187. Jim Steinmeyer, *Charles Fort: The Man Who Invented the Supernatural* (London: Heinemann, 2008), 289.
188. Chris Evans, 'The Occult Revival,' *New Humanist* 88.5 (1972): 195-98.
189. Marcello Truzzi, 'The Occult Revival as Popular Culture,' *Sociological Quarterly* 13 (1972): 16-37.
190. Andy Roberts and David Clarke, 'The John Keel Interview,' *UFO Brigantia* 34 (1992): 16.

of 'the imagination, optical illusions, mirage, etc.'[191] John Keel was one of the few Americans who, in 1947, opted for a more esoteric explanation for UFOs. When asked to elaborate on what he initially believed, Keel responded: 'I assumed, after reading Fort...they must be spaceships. Fort didn't really come right out and advocate the ET thesis but he said there was something there and that it had been around for a long time because he'd traced reports all the way back.'[192] The Extra Terrestrial Hypothesis (ETH) for UFOs would later be embraced, or at least accepted as plausible, by millions across the world including a number of establishment figures.[193]

On the outbreak of the Korean War, Keel was drafted into the US Army and became Chief of Continuity and Production for the American Forces Network in Frankfurt. In 1952 he wrote and produced a radio programme, *Things in the Sky*, and two years later, whilst on a trip to Egypt saw his first UFO. A circular spinning object appeared in the sky above the Aswan Dam in broad daylight: 'The thing I saw was Saturn-shaped and it appeared, the centre was not moving but the outside was spinning...it was a very odd thing and various people were looking at it with me.'[194] After leaving the army in search of adventure, he spent three years travelling through the Middle East and Asia. It was on this trip, whilst crossing into the Himalayan state of Sikkim, that he followed and briefly glimpsed a mysterious creature that local people identified as the legendary abominable snowman, or Yeti. This and accounts of other unusual experiences were published in his autobiography, *Jadoo*, when he was twenty seven years old.[195]

A decade later Keel returned to New York where he made a living as a mainstream writer and journalist with his own syndicated newspaper column. He also worked in Hollywood, wrote scripts and jokes for television shows and produced a string of comic novels, using pseudonyms such as Harry Gibbs and Thornton Vaseltarp. From 1966 there was a prolonged period of public interest in UFOs and Keel used this opportunity to pitch an idea for 'the definitive article' on the subject to *Playboy* magazine. From this point he became a full-time investigator of the phenomenon, reading everything he could find on UFOs and occult subjects. Like Fort, he began by collecting published accounts of anomalies culled from newspapers, firstly by subscribing to a clipping service. Unsatisfied with second-hand stories, he followed up some of the strangest cases first hand, travelling widely across the US Midwest to interview witnesses.

Keel said he abandoned the ETH when his field investigations 'disclosed

---

191. Robert Durant, 'Public Opinion Polls and UFOs' in *UFO 1947-97: Fifty Years of Flying Saucers*, ed. Hilary Evans and Dennis Stacy (London: John Brown, 1997), 321.
192. Roberts and Clarke, 'The John Keel Interview,' 17.
193. David Clarke, *How UFOs Conquered the World: The History of a Modern Myth* (London: Aurum Press, 2015).
194. Roberts and Clarke, 'The John Keel Interview,' 16.
195. John A. Keel, *Jadoo* (New York: Julian Messner, 1957).

an astonishing overlap between psychic phenomena and UFOs.' In explaining this conversion, he said his inquiries revealed that: 'a large part of the UFO lore is subjective and many alleged UFO events are actually the products of a complex hallucinatory process, particularly in the contactee and close encounter-type reports. The same process stimulated religious beliefs, fairy lore, and occult systems of belief in other centuries.'[196] From 1970 he developed his theory in five books that challenged the ETH and offered an alternative, occult-based hypothesis for UFOs and related phenomena. These were *UFOs: Operation Trojan Horse* (1970), *Strange Creatures from Time and Space* (1970), *Our Haunted Planet* (1971), *The Mothman Prophecies* and *The Eighth Tower* (both published in 1975). He also produced a stream of syndicated articles both for mainstream media and the specialist UFO magazines including *Palmer's Flying Saucers* and the British-based *Flying Saucer Review*.

In his books and articles Keel 'sought to recast UFOlogy and Fortean study as aspects of demonology.'[197] He borrowed a key concept, 'ultra-terrestrials,' from the writings of a Californian occultist, N. Meade Layne, who believed the occupants of flying saucers were shape-shifting spiritual entities from 'the etheric realm.'[198] Whereas Layne believed the etherians were benign, Keel's ultra-terrestrials, like Shaver's deros, sought to control and manipulate humans. According to Keel, these ultra-terrestrials (or UTs) 'cultivate belief in various frames of references, and then...deliberately create new manifestations which support those beliefs.'[199] Although Keel produced no explicit definition of what he meant by 'ultra-terrestrial,' he believed UFOs (as flying saucers were described from the 1960s onwards), were the medium by which these intelligences entered our world, writing: 'The objects and apparitions do not necessarily originate on another planet and may not even exist as permanent constructions of matter...it is more likely that we see what we want to see and interpret such visions according to our contemporary beliefs.'[200] In *The Eighth Tower* (1975), Keel substituted Layne's etheric realm for what he called the 'super-spectrum,' and proposed that UFOs were composed of energy from the 'upper frequencies of the electro-magnetic spectrum.' According to his theory, these shape-changing objects only became visible when they descended to the very narrow range of light that is visible to the human eye.

196. Ronald Story, *The Encyclopedia of UFOs* (London: New English Library, 1980), 190.
197. Jerome Clark, *The UFO Encyclopedia* (Detroit: Omnigraphics, 1998), 551.
198. N. Meade Layne, *The Ether Ship and Its Solution* (Vista, California: Borderland Sciences Research Associates, 1950).
199. John A. Keel, 'The Principle of Transmogrification,' *Flying Saucer Review* 15.4 (1969): 27-8.
200. Story, *The Encyclopedia of UFOs*, 190.

The Mothman Phenomenon

Of the books Keel produced during the 1970s *The Mothman Prophecies* is the most accomplished and successful. Dixon describes it as 'a Fortean classic.'[201] The text is redolent with the Fortean influences that shaped Keel's thinking. It describes how Keel read an Associated Press report about a monster that scared two young couples at a disused wartime munitions dump late on 15 November 1966. The four teenagers claimed the seven foot tall, winged creature suddenly appeared as they cruised around the thirty five acre McClintic Wildfire Zone, five miles north of Point Pleasant, West Virginia. It was 'shaped like a man, but bigger' and its most striking feature was a pair of glowing red eyes. As they sped away the creature spread its bat-like wings and took off, following their car at uncanny speed. The next morning the Mason county sheriff's office held a press conference and a newspaper sub-editor dubbed the creature 'mothman' after the Bat-Man series then showing on TV. In the months that followed, numerous other individuals came forward to report extraordinary experiences with the mothman, UFOs and a variety of other strange phenomena in the Ohio Valley region. Thousands of visitors poured into the TNT area, as the zone where the phenomena occurred was known locally, in search of the giant 'bird' or mothman.

In his accounts of these events, Keel said he felt drawn to the small community of Point Pleasant, 370 miles away from his home in New York. He discovered that some mothman witnesses had also reported surreal visitations from foreign-looking strangers wearing black clothes who arrived in large, apparently brand new black cars. These 'Men in Black' play a significant role in his book that was written eight years after the events it describes. Although Keel did not invent the legend of the sinister Men in Black he coined the acronym MIB and was responsible for elevating an obscure ufological legend to the pop culture status it currently enjoys.[202] Deborah Dixon notes that Keel's book is heavily coded in terms of insider-outsider references and 'it is unclear how much of the anxiety [he] expresses...stems from his own projection of racial conflict in the US, or simply reiterates the concerned views expressed to him.[203] The folklorist Peter Rojcewicz compares MIB narratives with older traditions that associate blackness with the Devil. In folklore, the evil one is a shapeshifter that can appear as a 'Man in Black.'[204] Whereas some of the experiencers and fellow ufologists believed the MIB were government agents, or members of the mafia, Keel suspected they were part of the wider ultra-terrestrial phenomenon.

201. Deborah Dixon, 'A benevolent and sceptical inquiry: exploring "Fortean Geographies" with the Mothman,' *Cultural Geographies* 14 (2007): 189-210.
202. Peter M. Rojcewicz, 'The 'Men in Black: Experience and Tradition,' *Journal of American Folklore* 100 (1987): 148-60.
203. Dixon, 'Fortean Geographies,' 201.
204. Rojcewicz, 'The Men in Black,' 155.

In addition to harassment from the MIB, Keel claimed to have had first-hand experience with the extraordinary phenomena he wrote about. Chapter 10 of *The Mothman Prophecies* describes his own sightings of mysterious moving lights in the skies of the Ohio Valley during the spring of 1967. These were made in the presence of another journalist and police officers and, on occasions, he tried to signal to these UFOs using a hand-held torch. He also claimed to have participated in telephone conversations with mysterious individuals whom he believed were ultra-terrestrials. Keel dedicated one of his books to one of these nonhuman entities, 'Mr Apol.'[205] This occurred as a direct result of his introduction to the twilight world of the 'silent contactees' whom he met during his travels in West Virginia, Long Island and other areas of UFO activity. According to his book, during his investigations in 1966-67, anomalous voices contacted him by telephone, day and night, to relay ominous messages from UFO intelligences.

In *The Mothman Prophecies* Keel explains how the more he became immersed in UFOlogy, the more the phenomenon appeared to play with his thoughts and beliefs. In the later stages of his investigation, with warnings of an approaching catastrophe reaching him by phone and mail from assorted UFO contactees across North America, he returned to his apartment in New York for the Christmas holidays. On 15 December, soon after President Lyndon Johnson switched on the festive lights at the White House, the broadcast was interrupted by breaking news that the ageing Silver Bridge that spanned the river at Point Pleasant, linking West Virginia with Ohio, had collapsed at rush hour. The falling structure sent 46 drivers and pedestrians, including some mothman witnesses, to their deaths. The disaster occurred thirteen months after the mothman experiences began. Some of Keel's informants believe the phenomenon was a premonition of the tragedy. It was certainly true that the number of reported anomalous experiences,[206] reported in the local media, decreased after the disaster.[207]

Keel referred to the events of 1966-67 as 'the year of the Garuda' and made a direct link with the legend of a giant humanoid bird-like creature, the Garuda, that appears in Hindu and Buddhist traditions. Crypto-zoologist Loren Coleman also detected what he believes is a hint of European banshee traditions in 'the strong sense of the foreboding dread of gloom [that] underlies...Keel's chronicling of all the events leading up to the collapse of the Silver Bridge.'[208] In English folklore moths are regarded as omens of death when they appear in the homes of a dying person.[209] More recently, internet

---

205. John A. Keel, *Our Haunted Planet* (Greenwich, CT: Fawcett Publications, 1971).
206. John A. Keel, *The Mothman Prophecies* (New York: Saturday Review Press, 1975).
207. Donnie J.R. Sergent and Jeff Wamsley, *Mothman: The Facts Behind the Legend* (Point Pleasant, West Virginia: Mothman Lives Publishing, 2002).
208. Loren Coleman, *Mothman and Other Curious Encounters* (New York: Paraview, 2002), 199.
209. Iona Opie and Moira Tatum, eds., *A Dictionary of Superstitions* (Oxford University Press, 1990), 266-67.

rumours have reported sightings of winged humanoid creatures immediately before other natural and manmade disasters, including earthquakes, the Chernobyl disaster and 9/11.[210] My interpretation of these new stories is they are examples of ostension, a type of behaviour familiar to scholars of folklore and contemporary legend. Ostension occurs when facts and ambiguous facts are combined and transformed into new narratives. These, in turn, are presented by storytellers and the mass media as if they were true accounts of factual events.[211]

When a script based upon Keel's book was adapted for a film by the director Mark Pellington in 2002 the mothman was portrayed not as monster or cryptid but as an ancient, unknowable supernatural omen. The 'oriental' MIB that feature strongly in Keel's book are missing from this new version of the story. The promotional trailers claim the film is 'based on true events' and the credits underline this message, informing viewers the film is 'based upon the book by John A. Keel.' Producer Gary Lucchesi explained that he and actor Richard Gere rejected earlier scripts 'that took the idea of a monstrous figure all too literally.'[212] Instead they chose to create 'a psychological mystery with surreal overtones' and to address the question of 'what happens when sane, reasonable people are faced with the unbelievable...in this case it was the harbinger of death.'[213]

In the film Gere plays a New York journalist, John Klein, whose wife dies from a brain tumour shortly after an encounter with the mothman in New York. Two years later Klein inexplicably loses a period of time during a reporting assignment and finds himself driving 400 miles away in West Virginia. There he discovers the residents of Point Pleasant are under siege from a range of baffling phenomena. He becomes obsessed with solving the mystery and unravelling its apparent link with the death of his wife. The mothman is occasionally glimpsed but never fully revealed. The film poster plays on its elusive, shapeshifting nature, posing the question: 'What do you see?' above the image of a Rorschach inkblot. Alan Bates plays Dr Alexander Leek, an expert on ultra-terrestrial phenomena, to whom a grief-stricken Klein turns in his quest for answers. When Klein demands to know if 'they' are responsible for the death of his wife, Leek says their motivations are 'not human.' All that mattered is that 'you noticed them and they noticed that you noticed them.' Jointly the two characters portray opposing aspects of Keel's personality: the investigator and the experiencer (Leek is Keel spelled backwards). A similar dualism was explored in the long-running television

---

210. Andrew Colvin, ed., *Searching for the String: Selected Writings of John A. Keel* (Seattle, Oregon: Metadisc Productions, 2014).
211. Linda Degh and Vazsonyi, 'Does the word "Dog" Bite? Ostensive Action: a Means of Legend-Telling,' *Journal of Folklore Research* 20.1 (1983): 29.
212. Dixon, 'Fortean Geographies,' 202.
213. Mark Pellington, dir., 'Cast and Crew Interviews,' *The Mothman Prophecies* (Produced by Lakeshore Entertainment Corporation, 2002).

series *The X-Files* where the opposing perspectives (sceptic/believer) are split into two characters of different genders. In his review John Shirley described *The Mothman Prophecies* as the first truly Fortean film: 'it is sceptical while being relentlessly open-minded about the anomalous; it refuses to come to easy answers, easily-filings away; it carries with it an atmosphere in which anything can happen, and reality itself is always suspect.'[214]

The release of the mothman movie revived interest in the West Virginia legend, although key scenes were actually filmed in Pennsylvania. In 2003 a twelve foot tall metal sculpture of the mothman by artist Bob Roach, based upon a painting by Frank Fazetta, was unveiled by John Keel at the second Mothman Festival held in Point Pleasant. The festival is held annually on the third weekend of September and visitors have grown from 500 in 2002 to 4,000 in 2014.[215] In 2005 a local entrepreneur, Jeff Wamsley, opened a museum dedicated to the legend. It offers minibus tours of the TNT area and other places linked with events in 1966-67.[216]

The revival of the legend also led to sceptical reappraisals of the eye-witness accounts documented by John Keel. A number of alternative, non-extraordinary explanations have been proposed, including the activities of pranksters, and the possibility that the original mothman scare was created by the presence in West Virginia of a large bird, such as the rare Sandhill crane, or an owl. When sceptic Joe Nickell visited the TNT area, he noted it is surrounded by the McClintic Wildlife Management Area, 'then, as now, a bird sanctuary.'[217] He traced the grandson of a man who shot a snowy owl during the mothman sightings of 1966. Although only two feet tall, a newspaper called it 'a giant owl' as it had a wingspan of nearly five feet. Nickell noted that eye-witness accounts of the creature's glowing red eyes were well known to ornithologists. Some birds' eyes shine bright red at night when they reflect artificial light such as from cars or flash-lamps.

Others have linked the mothman and MIB with rumours about psychological operations by the Defence Logistics Agency who maintained a facility in the Ohio valley area during the 1960s. In 2014 a writer in *Soldier of Fortune* magazine claimed the mothman scare was caused by the activities of Green Berets who were, at the time, experimenting with new techniques to insert special forces into enemy-held territory in Vietnam. One method covertly tested in the Point Pleasant area was, he claimed, 'the high-altitude, low-opening (HALO) freefall parachuting technique.' Luminous paint was used during the exercise to keep track of soldiers: 'what the Green Berets making those jumps hadn't figured on was the fact that people on the ground could

---

214. John Shirley, 'The Mothman Prophecies,' *Locus Online*, February 9, 2002. http://www.locusmag.com/2002/Reviews/Shirley_Mothman.html
215. www.mothmanfestival.com
216. Sergent and Wamsley, *Mothman*, 2002; Simon J. Sherwood, 'A Visit to Point Pleasant: Home of the Mothman,' *Paranthropology* 4.1 (2013): 25-35.
217. Joe Nickell, 'Mothman Revisited: Investigating on Site,' *Skeptical Inquirer* 12.4 (2002).

see it as well.'[218] A number of UFO contactee stories reported in Keel's books have since been exposed as hoaxes.[219] In addition, there is evidence that some of the anomalous phone calls received by Keel were pranks played by Gray Barker, a fellow ufologist, West Virginia resident and investigator of the mothman phenomenon.[220] Barker's 1956 book *They Knew Too Much About Flying Saucers* launched the legend of the 'three men in black.' He later confessed to a number of UFO-related hoaxes and is suspected of having placed at least one of the calls described in Keel's book.[221]

'Based on True Events'?

Hollywood interpreted the mothman legend as a psychological horror story. Many readers, including this author, have accepted the characters and events described in Keel's book, *The Mothman Prophecies* as being factually reported, or at least 'Based on True Events,' as the film poster implies. My revised interpretation does not attempt to divine whether Keel's account of the mothman story is true or false. It is based upon a close examination of the original narrative and the contents of interviews Keel gave on the subject of his writings. His non-UFO and Fortean related literary output is little known but was considerable and it provided him with a living as a freelance writer. Keel's biography contains comic novels, scripts for situation comedies and a book called *The Hoodwinkers*, on hoaxers.[222] *The Mothman Prophecies* was written in the 'New Journalism' style that was popular when Keel was at his most prolific.[223] New Journalism was a departure from the traditional model for news reporting because it did not place emphasis upon the importance of neutrality and factual accuracy. It immersed the writer within the story, 'channelling a character's thoughts, using non-standard punctuation and exploding traditional narrative forms.'[224] New Journalism often involved a mixture of personal observation, verbatim transcripts of conversations, overheard dialogue and extracts from documents or original notes, often delivered at great length and 'frequently focusing as much on the quest for information as on the information itself.'[225] By definition this type of discursive writing could be both subjective and irreverent in its style. One of its characteristics was the mixing of fact and fiction.

218. Harold Hutchison, 'UFO Mystery Solved,' *Soldier of Fortune* 39.2 (2014): 3.
219. Clark, *The UFO Encyclopedia*, 701.
220. John C. Sherwood, 'Gray Barker's Book of Bunk: Mothman, Saucers and MIB,' *Skeptical Inquirer* 26.3 (2002).
221. Ibid.
222. Phyllis Benjamin and Doug Skinner, 'Gone to the Disneyland of the Gods,' *Fortean Times* 253 (2009): 38-42.
223. Tom Wolfe and E.W. Johnson, eds., *The New Journalism* (London: Pan, 1975).
224. Robert Boynton, 'The Roots of the New New Journalism,' *The Chronicle of Higher Education* 4 (March 2005). http://www.robertboynton.com/articleDisplay.php? article id=1515.
225. Tony Harcup, *Dictionary of Journalism* (Oxford University Press, 2015), 116.

In her discussion of Keel's reporting of the West Virginia phenomena Deborah Dixon says he 'adopts a pulp fiction style of writing that simultaneously undercuts the eyewitness veracity the original testimonies strived for and buttresses his own authoritative position as the purveyor and interpreter.'[226] Keel's inventive storytelling was also recognised by the folklorist Peter Rojcewicz in his analysis of MIB legends. He notes that although they form a distinct part of the larger UFO mythology, readers should be aware of 'the conventions of form, content…[of] reporting, or what is sometimes called 'journalistic fiction,' in order to scrape away the personality of the investigator.'[227]

A striking example of Keel's use of the New Journalism style appears in the first chapter of *The Mothman Prophecies*. In 1992 he explained to the author how he struggled to find a publisher until he rewrote the introductory chapter, 'Beelzebub visits West Virginia,' so that it featured 'a strong opening…based on a true story.' The narrative slowly builds a feeling of dread and foreboding as it sets the scene on a stormy night in November 1967, just weeks before the collapse of the Silver Bridge. A stranger approaches a farmhouse in the hills of rural West Virginia and raps upon the door until a young woman answers:

> She opened the door a crack and her sleep-swollen face winced with fear as she stared at the apparition on her doorstep. He was over six feet tall and dressed entirely in black. He wore a black suit, black tie, black hat, and black overcoat, with impractical black dress shoes covered with mud. His face, barely visible in the darkness, sported a neatly trimmed moustache and goatee. The flashes of lightning behind him added an eerie effect.[228]

The Man in Black asks 'May I use your phone?' in a deep, unfamiliar accent. The woman and her partner refuse to open the door and the MIB leaves to repeat his request at another dwelling nearby. Keel explained the origins of this story to me as follows:

> I had been out in the hills with another journalist following up stories about lights in the sky. Our car had run off the road on a very rainy night and I was dressed in a necktie and a full suit…you didn't see that very often on back roads in West Virginia, a black suit…and I went around pounding on doors to get somebody to call a truck for me. It turned out that the people who finally made the call were among the people that were on the bridge that later collapsed. The day after I knocked on their door, they told everybody they knew that a strange

---

226. Dixon, 'Fortean Geographies,' 201.
227. Rojcewicz, 'The Men in Black,' 149.
228. Keel, *The Mothman Prophecies*, 1.

man in a black suit and a beard had called and he must have been the devil.[229]

In his book, Keel reveals how accounts of his visit to this rural area had subsequently entered folklore as a premonition of the collapse of the Silver Bridge: 'It had, indeed been a sinister omen. One that confirmed their religious beliefs and superstitions. So a new legend was born.'[230] The Beelzebub story was reinterpreted for a key scene in the 2002 mothman film. In both the book and film it functions as a plot twist of the type commonly found in contemporary legends with a supernatural theme. Keel invokes Film Noir in his account of it, comparing the West Virginia setting with 'an opening scene of a Grade B horror film from the 1930s.' He goes on to invoke dark landscapes and ordinary characters that face macabre, unexpected twists and turns as the story unfolds. Similarly, contemporary legends with a supernatural theme 'often depend on their twisted endings and ambiguous characters and situations for effect.'[231]

Discussion

John Keel died in 2009 and his obituaries emphasised the divisive nature of his literary legacy. One of his contemporaries, John Michell, called him 'the best of all UFO writers,' whilst Fortean blogger Nick Redfern refers to Keel as 'one of the most important people in the field of Forteana…someone who recognised the deep and undeniable cross-overs between …the worlds of UFOlogy, cryptozoology and demonology.'[232] During his lifetime critics within UFOlogy dismissed Keel as credulous, paranoid and crankish. Others said his books were 'littered with factual errors and other evidence of sloppy reporting' and claimed he was unable to distinguish 'the most blatantly apparent hoaxes from more credible cases.'[233] Yet despite disapproval from some sections of the UFO community, Keel's pacey writing style and storytelling skills attracted a loyal following.[234] Friends and admirers have ensured his books and articles remain in publication via a series of reprints and edited collections. In 2009 a John Keel website was launched by his close friend Doug Skinner as 'a tribute to a unique writer and character.'[235]

---

229. Roberts and Clarke, 'The John Keel Interview,' 19.
230. Keel, *The Mothman Prophecies*, 2.
231. Gail de Voss, *Tales, Rumors, & Gossip* (Westport, Connecticut: Libraries Unlimited. 1996), 7.
232. Nick Redfern, 'John Keel: Ahead of his Time,' *Mysterious Universe Blog* (August 5, 2015) http://mysteriousuniverse.org/2015/08/john-keel-ahead-of-his-time/.
233. Clark, *The UFO Encyclopedia*, 551.
234. Coleman, *Mothman*, 118.
235. Doug Skinner, 'John Keel – Not an Authority on Anything,' (August 11, 2009) http://www.johnkeel.com/.

In retrospect Keel's contribution to the development of Forteanism and UFOlogy should be regarded as both considerable and hugely influential. His ultra-terrestrial hypothesis provided a fresh, alternative explanatory framework for UFOs and other extraordinary phenomena at a point in the development of the UFO controversy at which many former believers had begun to doubt the validity of the ETH. It was attractive precisely because it was inclusive and consistent with the zeitgeist. Keel put forward his theories in an engaging and highly readable style that appealed to a mass audience. In contrast, Fort made no attempt to provide a coherent hypothesis in his books and preferred to propose provocative theories only to denounce them at a later stage. His aim in doing so was to make the point that such outlandish ideas were equally applicable as explanations for anomalies as those that were routinely offered by the scientists. Nevertheless, Jim Steinmeyer notes that Fort did not appear to believe many of his wilder theories, such as the Super-Sargasso Sea. Fort referred to this early version of the 'Bermuda Triangle' in his *The Book of the Damned* as a type of cosmic junkyard into which things were mysteriously teleported, or from which they fell to Earth.[236] Elsewhere he writes of believing nothing 'of my own that I have ever written' adding that 'I cannot accept that the products of minds are subject matter of beliefs.'[237]

In my interview I asked Keel how Fort had influenced his own writing. 'Fort was very persuasive if you could get through his style,' he replied; 'He had an odd style of writing, a humorous style which a lot of people to this day don't quite comprehend...I sort of sometimes satirise Fort...he used to use certain phrases like, "I have a theory, that the stars are hanging from strings and the sky is only 800 feet up," and that would be a joke and people would seriously quote that and say, "Well, Charles Fort thinks the stars are hanging on strings." I think my own style sort of evolved over the years. I appreciated his mocking sense of humour and some of the ideas in my books were, like Fort's, deliberately meant to be provocative and outrageous.'[238]

Although he claimed to be an atheist, Keel did express belief in the existence of 'an occult or metaphysical system of control' that had existed since the dawn of mankind. He was never clear about the exact nature and purpose of this 'indefinable and certainly incomprehensible' system but was certain UFOs were part of it. In this respect he borrowed from Fort who, in *The Book of the Damned*, speculated that Earth and its inhabitants might be regarded as 'property' by visitors from other worlds, whose ships were occasionally seen in the sky.[239] In an earlier interview with Richard Toronto Keel made similar comments, noting: 'men have always been aware of it on different levels and have tried to define it (and worship it)—that's what

---

236. Steinmeyer, *Charles Fort*, 7.
237. Charles Fort, *New Lands* (New York: Boni & Liveright, 1923), 250.
238. Roberts and Clarke, 'The John Keel Interview,' 19.
239. Charles Fort, *The Book of the Damned* (New York: New York: Boni & Liveright, 1919).

theology is all about.'[240]

The idea of a 'control system' was the basis for Keel's ultra-terrestrial hypothesis. This was his most enduring contribution to the UFO controversy, but he later disavowed ownership of his own creation, asserting that he did not invent the word that he claimed has 'been in use for generations.'[241] Nevertheless, research by this author has failed to locate any literary reference that predates Keel's usage in *Our Haunted Planet*.[242] Neither is there any clear evidence of a premodern lineage for ultra-terrestrial in the Oxford English Dictionary. The Urban Dictionary defines an ultra-terrestrial as 'a superior, nonhuman entity of natural or supernatural origin that is indigenous to planet Earth,' or 'as a being from another dimension or plane of reality.' The latter is a reference to a line from an online discussion about the American television series, *Buffy the Vampire Slayer*, that aired from 1997 to 2003.

Martin Kottmeyer regards the word 'ultra-terrestrial' as a neologism. He believes Keel employed it to avoid the religious connotations of spirit or demon.[243] Others have not shared his reluctance. For some evangelical Christians and proponents of UFO-related conspiracy theories, ultra-terrestrials are shorthand for demons controlled by Satan.[244] Kottmeyer notes that one indication of the continuing popularity of Keel's ideas in UFOlogy is the frequent appearance of the word ultra-terrestrial in book titles.[245] Keel was scathing of what he referred to as the 'cottage industry of other writers who churned out books that merely copied my material.'[246]

When questioned about his ultra-terrestrial hypothesis, Keel urged me 'not to take it too seriously.' My colleague Andy Roberts, who was present during the interview, recalled: 'despite numerous conversations, no one could work out what he really believed. What's more he told different people different things, probably according to what he thought they wanted to believe.'[247] Less kindly, another acquaintance of Keel's, Bob Sheaffer described him as 'a trickster' [who] 'did not seem to be taking his own writings very seriously, which suggests that they were entertaining stories that paid the bills.'[248]

In a 1985 interview with Richard Toronto, Keel dismissed much of the

240. Richard Toronto, 'The Shavertron Interview,' (July 8, 2011), http://www.johnkeel.com/?p=737.
241. Ibid.
242. John A. Keel, Our Haunted Planet (Greenwich, CT: Fawcett Publications, 1971): 99.
243. Personal communication.
244. Christopher Partridge, 'Alien Demonology: The Christian Roots of the Malevolent Extraterrestrial in UFO Religions and Abduction Spiritualities,' *Religion* 34 (2004): 165.
245. Philip J. Imgrogno, *Ultraterrestrial Contact: A Paranormal Investigator's Explorations into the Hidden Abduction Epidemic* (Woodbury, Minnesota: Llewellyn Publications, 2010).
246. Toronto, 'The Shavertron Interview.'
247. Personal communication.
248. Robert Sheaffer, 'John A. Keel, Mothman Writer, Paranormalist Trickster.' *Skeptical Inquirer* 33.6 (2009).

contemporary ufological obsessions, such as the Roswell legend and alleged government cover-ups, as nonsense. Toronto challenged this assertion and asked: 'Haven't you just replaced what you consider outmoded pulp zine images with updated ones of your own?'[249] Keel's response was revealing. He said 'there are literally hundreds of Devil Theories, some of them with millions of paranoid followers.' He added: 'If you read my books carefully, you will see that "ultraterrestrials" are a literary device, not a theory.' Keel expanded on this statement in a letter published by *Fortean Times* in which he explained:

> ...basically, what I attempted to do [in my books] was set up a frame of reference that the reader could, hopefully, understand. Obviously, I failed in this. Even now people...are still assuming that ultraterrestrials are actual entities...what I said in five books, carefully spelled out and defined, is that we are the intelligence which controls the phenomena.[250]

Charles Fort and John Keel had much in common. Both began their careers as journalists and both returned from their youthful travels with a desire to write about anomalous phenomena and to challenge the prevailing orthodoxies of their day. Loren Gross described Fort as 'a philosopher who proposed wild theories using an entertaining writing style.'[251] When Tiffany Thayer asked Fort what he called himself, his response was simple: 'I'm just a writer.'[252] Similarly, when Toronto asked Keel how he would like to be remembered, he responded not as a ufologist or even as a Fortean, but 'as a novelist and playwright—if I am remembered at all.'

---

249. Toronto, 'The Shavertron Interview.'
250. John A. Keel, 'The Mutilated Horse,' *Fortean Times* 40 (1983): 3-5.
251. Gross, *Charles Fort*, 2.
252. Steinmeyer, *Charles Fort*, 297.

5

UFO Abductions as Mystical Encounter: Faerie Folklore in W.Y. Evans-Wentz, Jacques Vallée, and Whitley Strieber

Robin Jarrell

Fortean UFO researcher Jacques Vallée has continually been a visionary, asserting compelling theories that move beyond the UFO contact/abduction experience as a clear-cut interstellar 'nuts-and-bolts' craft carrying 'beings-from-another-planet' hypothesis. Instead, Vallée suggests that the phenomenon has far-reaching implications for humanity's historical connection with bizarre, mystical, and otherworldly phenomena. This chapter explores Vallée's hypothesis that the alien abduction phenomenon has had ancient mystical connotations throughout human history, and compares his research to one of the most noted UFO contact/abduction 'experiencers,' Whitley Strieber. Strieber, author of the New York Times bestseller *Communion: A True Story*, recently authored *Solving the Communion Enigma: What is to Come* in which he revisits his earlier work.

Jeffrey Kripal, in the foreword to Strieber's *Solving the Communion Enigma*, lists nine particular 'features that past and present scholars have come to recognize as marks of the mystical' within Strieber's nonfiction works, and in his original book *Communion*.[253] These include:

- extreme alternating responses of fear and attraction, horror and beauty;
- out-of-body flight, often involving a second 'subtle' or energetic body;
- paranormal powers, such as precognition, telepathy, and psychokinesis;
- memories, often coded and repressed, of physical or sexual trauma in childhood or youth;
- erotically charged imagery and impossibly intense sexual energies;

---

253. Whitley Strieber, *Solving the Communion Enigma: What Is to Come* (New York: J.P. Tarcher/Penguin, 2011), xii.

- invocations of secret and subsequent censorship attempts or harassment on the part of established social and/or religious institutions;
- noetic, or 'knowing,' energies mysteriously transmitted into the body of the visionary;
- life-changing experiences of union or communion with a mysterious alien or Other, who is often paradoxically intuited to be part of one's own deepest nature; and
- a cognitive 'rewiring' and subsequent penchant for thinking beyond all either-or's to something beyond, to a both-and or Third.

However, in the second account of his original remarkable experience, Strieber's nine 'marks of the mystical' have distinct parallels with what Vallée initially describes in his research into the observations of the 'fairy faith' found in works by American anthropologist Walter Y. Evans-Wentz in the early twentieth century and Scottish Anglican priest Robert Kirk in the seventeenth century.

While Kripal's markers do, indeed, contribute to describing a significant portion of Strieber's experiences, there are specifically pronounced connections between the nature of Strieber's accounts and the accounts reported by Vallée (as well as Evans-Wentz, Kirk, etc.), which are framed specifically as having an historical 'faerie-like' quality.[254] In my own research, I have discovered that Strieber in his most recent work actually conceptualizes many of his experiences through this 'faerie-lens,' using seven basic categories evident in his encounters with the beings he calls 'the visitors':[255]

- the encounter is perceived and often described as nonsensical, with a degree of 'high strangeness,' and is often qualified as 'insane,' and/or 'absurd';
- there is a marked theatricality to the encounter, as if the occurrence is being manipulated or 'staged';
- the encounter is connected to our physical reality and often occurs within specific physical elements (within the earth/in the atmosphere/near bodies of water), and often in specific locations associated with previous 'faerie' encounters ('fairy forts');
- the encounter focuses on the primal experiences of the physical human body, i.e.
  - o inspecting, healing, harming the human body;
  - o ingestion of food and/or drink and other materials;

---

254. I use the spelling 'faerie' to denote a more robust encounter than is usually associated with cherubic Victorian era tales of the 'fairy,' but when quoting Evans-Wentz and Kirk, I use their spelling.

255. Interestingly, Strieber also compares 'crop formations' and 'cattle mutilations' to their fairy counterparts by citing Evans-Wentz. See Strieber, *Solving the Communion Enigma*, 132,133.

o   procreative sex (with the Other) that often results in
·   the 'changeling' phenomenon;
·   a link between the encounter and death;
·   a forced cognitive dissonance created in the human mind that in some
     way leads to what Kripal calls 'cognitive rewiring,' thereby allowing
     the human mind to make startling and revelatory connections,
     associations, and discoveries about the human condition and the
     human environment.

Passing Strange

One has only to peruse the accounts reported by Evans-Wentz, Kirk (and in
the works of later documenters such as Briggs and Lenihan), to conclude that,
even to the ancient locals who lived among such tales, encounters with the
Faerie-Other are always experienced as nonsensical and strange.[256] Vallée
points out that such encounters historically have always seemed bizarre, and in
the case of Strieber, continue to be patiently absurd. But, as Kripal observes,
Vallée begins with the hypothesis that, in the case of encounters with the
Other, whether experienced as fairies or UFO, 'the absurd is meaningful.'[257]
Kripal wisely notices that in encounters with the Other, in reports of both
fairies and UFOs, there is at the same time a physical and a non-physical
aspect. As he puts it, such encounters 'often have the quality of dreams, but
they are also physical events.'[258]

Strieber also contends that the reason 'the close-encounter experience [is]
rejected, is that the extremely high levels of strangeness that accompany them
create a frightful impression of chaos.'[259] He also stresses the staged nature of
some of his own encounters. In his latest *Solving the Communion Enigma*, he
relates a psychologist's report in witnessing 'a huge jet at low altitude coming
toward his car' which horrified the man until the plane 'passed overhead' and
the man was able to discern 'that it looked like some sort of a fake airplane,
like a stage prop.'[260] The psychologist's experience continued as he witnessed
with a group of other onlookers in stopped cars a circle of people gathered
around 'a small figure...dressed in blue' appearing to be some sort of 'circus
clown.'[261] Strieber then recalls his own encounter witnessing 'blue dwarfs' with
his wife Anne on Fifth Avenue in New York city, which he later connects to

---

256. See Katharine Mary Briggs, *The Vanishing People: Fairy Lore and Legends* (New York:
Pantheon Books, 1978); and Edmund Lenihan and Carolyn Eve Green, *Meeting the Other Crowd:
The Fairy Stories of Hidden Ireland* (New York: Jeremy P. Tarcher/Putnam, 2003).
257. Jeffrey J Kripal, *Authors of the Impossible: The Paranormal and the Sacred* (Chicago: University of
Chicago Press, 2010), 162; emphasis in original.
258. Ibid.
259. Strieber, *Solving the Communion Enigma*, 192.
260. Ibid.
261. Ibid.

the same creatures he meets on the night of his 'close encounter, [in 1986 who were] working busily to carry...and restrain' him.[262] As Kripal observes, Vallée, beginning with his epilogue to the second edition of *Forbidden Science* in 1996, continues to be perplexed by the actions of the 'ufonauts...[who] continue to behave like the absurd denizens of bad Hollywood movies,' despite the attempts of UFO researchers to categorize the 'aliens' in an interstellar context.[263]

Pancakes and Saucers

In *Passport to Magonia*, Vallée describes the strange case of Joe Simonton from Eagle River, Wisconsin, who in 1961 was offered three 'pancakes' that 'tasted like cardboard' by tall dark clad strangers piloting a flying saucer. One of the occupants of the craft 'held up a jug made of the same material as the [brighter than chrome] saucer,' made a gesture, and Simonton returned to his house and filled it with water. When he returned, he witnessed one of the men inside 'frying food on a flameless grill of some sort.'[264] Vallée points out that the US Airforce researching the case, in rationalizing Simonton's story (that he was dreaming as he made himself pancakes), fails to take into account the various reports made famous by Evans-Wentz and Kirk on the relationship between the Gentry (the Good people, or fairies) and food.[265] Both Evans-Wentz and Kirk describe many encounters with 'fairy food' and its impact on human experience.

The faerie connection with food may take several forms. In some cases, whenever humans find themselves in fairyland or among fairies, if they partake of the food, they are imprisoned in fairyland for what seems to be a few hours, only to find they have actually gone missing from home and family for years, or even decades. In other cases, when a fairy offers a human food when not in fairyland, refusal to partake the fairy's offer of food is also cause for imprisonment in fairyland.[266] In a story similar to Simonton's, Evans-Wentz reports what occurred when one particular family did not provide the fairies with water for baking cakes:

> And a certain beggar-man who had been left lodging on the sofa downstairs heard the fairies say, 'We have no water, so we'll take blood out of the toe of the servant who forgot our water.' And from the [servant] girl's blood they mixed their dough. Then they baked their cakes, ate most of them, and

262. Ibid.
263. Kripal, *Authors of the Impossible*, 186.
264. Jacques Vallée, *Passport to Magonia: From Folklore to Flying Saucers* (Brisbane, Australia: Daily Grail Publishing, 2014).
265. Ibid.
266. W. Y Evans-Wentz, *The Fairy-Faith in Celtic Countries* (New York: Citadel Press, 1990), 98.

poked pieces up under the thatched roof. The next day the servant girl fell ill, and was ill until the old beggar-man returned to the house and cured her with a bit of the cake which he took from under the thatch.[267]

The similarity with the Simonton story is striking. In both accounts water is requested for the purposes of making 'cakes,' but the fairies retaliate when their request is refused. In the case of Strieber, as far as I am aware, there is no experience with food that forms a direct comparison with faerie folklore, but if we take into account the cultural shift from the nineteenth-century case of fairies making cakes using a servant's blood to an occupant of a chrome-like saucer making cakes with a flameless grill, we might consider current reports concerning the 'ingestion' of other materials into the human body, such as implants, as another form (albeit by force) of 'fairy food.' The popular trope of alien implants may represent the evolution of the faerie paradigm from the ingestion of organic material (food) that does not remain in the body, but is excreted out, to faerie materials (implants), which remain inside the body and are not excreted out. Strieber notes that of the 'sixteen objects...removed from close-encounter witnesses...they were unremarkable [with] nothing to prove that they might be anything from another world.'[268] The implants themselves (in his case, a mixture of organic and non-organic material) appear to be a 'strange mix of technological sophistication and primitive miniaturization.'[269] He points out that if our own civilization 'can make radio-frequency-identification devices that are the size of particles of dust...why would supposedly advanced aliens' use implants as large as the ones removed?[270]

Strieber echoes Vallée's realization in *Forbidden Science* that the technology of the aliens 'is a simulacrum—and a very bad one at that—of obsolete human biological and engineering notions.'[271] And so the phenomenon continues to persist, despite technological advances, to be perceived by the human world as deeply strange.

Sex with Strangers?

According to Vallée, 'without the sexual context—without the stories of changelings, human midwives, intermarriage with the Gentry...it is doubtful that the tradition about fairies would have survived through the ages.'[272] In addition, Vallée affirms that 'there is no gap between the fairy-faith and

---

267. Ibid, 128.
268. Strieber, *Solving the Communion*, 50.
269. Ibid, 51.
270. Ibid.
271. Cited in Kripal, *Authors of the Impossible*, 186.
272. Vallée, *Passport*, 121.

UFOlogy regarding the sexual question.'[273] Vallée quotes one of the earliest researchers into the fairy-faith, Robert Kirk, who noted that 'in our Scotland there are numerous and beautiful creatures of that aerial order, who frequently assign meetings to lascivious young men as succubi, or as joyous mistresses and prostitutes, who are called Leannain Sith...'[274] Vallée cites the 1957 abduction case of Antonio Villas-Boaz in Argentina who, in the process of being taken inside a 'craft,' was seduced by a very small, blond woman who appeared to be a combination of human and something else, to make his point. He remarks that historically, and especially in the faerie folklore, there is 'a complete theory of contact between our race and another race, nonhuman, different in physical nature, but biologically compatible with us...they inspire our strangest dreams, shape our destinies, steal our desires...But who are they?'[275]

Strieber, no doubt, has asked the same question. He outlines his very intense and highly erotic relationship with a 'fierce, huge-eyed feminine being' that also served as the model for the cover of the book *Communion*. Strieber's relationship with this feminine being, however, is neither a mechanical encounter with an alien, nor a romantic attachment to a fairy. As he puts it:

> Her gaze seemed capable of entering me deeply, and it was when I had looked directly into her eyes that I felt my first taste of profound unease. It was as if every vulnerable detail of my self were known to this being. Nobody in the world could know another human soul so well, nor could one man look into the eyes of another so deeply, and to such exact effect. I could actually feel the presence of that other person within me—which was as disturbing as it was curiously sensual...The realization that something was actually occurring within me because this person was looking at me— that she could apparently look into me—filled me with the deepest longing.[276]

At another point, Strieber describes the feminine being as 'the most astonishing being I have ever seen in my life...To me this is a woman, perhaps because her movements are so graceful, perhaps because she has created states of sexual arousal in me.'[277] Strieber even connects his own experience to the faerie mythology with his reflection that 'the abduction to a round room had a long, long tradition in our culture: There were many such cases in the fairy lore. The story called "Connla and the Fairy Maiden," as collected in Joseph

---

273. Ibid.
274. Ibid.
275. Ibid, 133.
276. Whitley Strieber, *Communion: A True Story* (New York: Beech Tree Books, 1987), 101.
277. Ibid, 99.

Jacob's Celtic Fairy Tales...could with some changes be a modern tale of the visitors.'[278]

Strieber recounts his wonder at the ease with which the world of faerie and our world often coalesce and collide in his later *Solving the Communion Enigma* with a somewhat more sanguine opinion of his 'Faerie Maiden.' On the day he moves from New York city to San Antonio, Texas, a trusted friend of Strieber reports that he (the friend) encountered Strieber's 'woman on the cover of Communion' while being stuck in traffic on Fourteenth Street. According to the friend, the 'woman' appeared 'prettier than that picture;' a remark that causes Strieber to write he 'always regretted that picture, because it communicates the idea of an alien presence far more forcefully' than he intended.[279] Just as the reports from Evans-Wentz and Kirk attest, the human and fairy worlds coexist, and both sides can sometimes be seen in the world they do not originally inhabit. Fairies are both Other and human; humans are able to discern the appearance of the Other in their midst, while noting at the same time that they are somewhat human. Strieber realizes that 'it may seem extraordinary that somebody who appears even slightly like her could walk the streets of a crowded city,' he also reflects that 'there was something deeply human about her. One did not get the impression so much alien as human strangeness, and the feeling that one was face-to-face with a living aspect of a very deep mystery, which is the mystery of man.'[280]

The Changeling

From the late 1990s and early 2000s, alien abduction researchers such as David Jacob and John Mack began to report startling accounts of people having 'alien abduction' experiences similar to Strieber's, but with a disturbing and puzzling twist. At some point in the abduction scenario, many reported being in the presence of 'children,' or even 'infants,' who seemed to share genetic aspects with both the human and 'alien' form, frequently referred to as 'hybrids.'[281] Strieber's trio of books describing his experience only hint at this aspect of what I have outlined above as the seven marks of the similarities between encounters with aliens and encounters with Faerie-Other. But in his later reflective return to his experience in *Solving the Communion Enigma*, Strieber writes:

> Some very, very hard things happened in that first year after
> the close encounter, things that were too unbearable to write

---

278. Ibid, 105.
279. Strieber, *Solving the Communion*, 41.
280. Ibid, 42.
281. See especially, David Michael Jacobs, *The Threat: Revealing the Secret Alien Agenda* (New York: Fireside, 1999) and John E Mack, *Abduction: Human Encounters with Aliens* (New York; Toronto; New York: Scribner's ; Maxwell Macmillan Canada ; Maxwell Mamillan International, 1994).

about. Suffice it to say that at one point, the visitors had done
something to me that is reported again and again in the
accounts of close-encounter witnesses. They had put a baby
in my arms. To this day, the sleeping face of this infant is
burned into my soul, I can tell you, and in those days the
memory was a raw, bleeding wound.[282]

Of course, the 'hybrid' of the nineteenth century as reported in the countless
stories of Evans-Wentz (he recounts twenty eight instances in total) is the
changeling. In these accounts, the infants and children of the human and fairy
worlds are often interchangeable. In most cases, healthy human children are
'replaced' by sickly fairy children, who usually die in the human world, or are
forever considered impaired in some way. In other instances, changelings left
by fairies may have extraordinary talents throughout their lives.[283]

Death

Evans-Wentz devotes an entire section in his *The Fairy Faith in Celtic Countries*
to 'the cult of gods, spirits, fairies, and the dead.'[284] He uses the archaeological
evidence of his time to discuss the connection between the world of the fairy
and human death rites and beliefs in both pagan and Christian contexts. He
asserts that certain 'phantoms (comparable in a way with Irish banshees and
the Breton Ankou) do appear to the living directly before a death as though
announcing it' and 'sometimes a phantasmal voice—like certain "fairy" voices
—has given news of a death.'[285] Years earlier, Robert Kirk surmised that we
each might have a 'fairy counterpart':

> a reflex man...or co-walker, every way like the man, as a twin
> brother and companion, haunting him as his shadow, and is
> oft seen and known among men (resembling the original)
> both before and after the original is dead, and was else often
> seen of old to enter a house, by which these people knew that
> the person of that likeness was to visit them within a few
> days. This copy, echo, or living picture goes at last to his own
> herd. It accompanied that person so long and frequently for
> ends best known to itself, whether to guard him from the
> secret assaults of some of its own folks, or only as a sportful

---

282. Strieber, *Solving the Communion*, 157.
283. Evans-Wentz, *The Fairy-Faith in Celtic Countries*. In modern day reports of 'hybrids,' the 'children' may display marked extraordinary properties such as telepathy and telekinesis but may also be frail and ill.
284. Ibid., 397ff.
285. Ibid., 484.

ape to counterfeit all his actions.[286]

Drawing deeper connections between aerial phenomena (UFOs), the abduction experience and death (which he alludes to in *The Communion Letters*),[287] Strieber reports that in 1988, an FAA inspector contacted him with a similar story. One evening at home, after the FAA inspector's wife saw 'a fiery ball of light speed low overhead,' which she mistakenly identified as a plane crash, the couple's son came running downstairs with the news that 'little blue men just brought Charlie into my room and he said to tell you he was okay!'[288] As Strieber writes, the couple was 'absolutely floored, because this older son had died in an auto accident the week before.'[289]

Strieber recalls his own experience during one of his abductions in 1985 where he remembers being given his 'implant' (see above) when he 'saw an old friend [who], as he told me years before, had recently retired from the CIA. He was with these seeming aliens. Afterward, I found out from a relative of his that in December of 1985 when I saw him and talked to him, he had been dead for months.'[290] Strieber's experience would have seemed quite common to the people living in 'Celtic Countries' according to Evans-Wentz, who would also have agreed with Anne Strieber's statement that in some important way, the whole 'fairy' phenomenon 'has something to do with death.'[291]

Awakening

Even Strieber suspects that despite the outwardly chaotic nature of the abduction experience, which he says is 'an attempt to shock us into a new kind of awareness,' it may possess some inner 'logic to the whole cockeyed business' that allows the human mind to perceive the human condition with more insight and fluency.[292] And yet he is quick to point out that in his more 'sublime' flights of awareness he did not 'see the face of God,' nor did his insights contain 'mythological trappings' or 'awesome symbolism.'[293] I would argue, however that his awareness is inspired by exactly the historical mythological process with specific Faerie-Other folkloric details that has been functioning in human life since the beginning.

Far from viewing his experience from a 'nuts-and-bolts' perspective as interactions between humans and 'aliens,' Strieber has noted that 'being

---

286. Kirk quoted by Marina Warner in her introduction to Robert Kirk, *The Secret Commonwealth of Elves, Fauns, and Fairies* (New York: New York Review Books, 2007), xxv. Italics mine.
287. Whitley Strieber and Anne Strieber, *The Communion Letters* (New York: HarperPrism, 1997).
288. Strieber, *Solving the Communion*, 170.
289. Ibid.
290. Ibid., 14.
291. Ibid., 12.
292. Ibid., 193, 196.
293. Ibid., 130.

identified as a believer in aliens has always troubled me. It just doesn't seem to me to be the only possible explanation. As profoundly strange as the phenomenon is, for the most important parts of it have also been deeply human. It is such a lovely mystery.'[294] And in his work, Strieber refers to his experience with the Other as 'visitors,' though, as he also notes, 'They are hardly visitors. With all their strangeness...whatever they are and wherever they are from, the most true things I know about them are two: they are here, and they are part of human life.'[295]

Vallée

Beginning with the popular 1957 Vilas Boas and 1961 Betty and Barney Hill cases, UFO researchers began to formulate modern 'nuts-and-bolts' theories for encounters with spaceships and their occupants from other planets (the so-called 'Extraterrestrial Hypothesis').[296] But Vallée, in *Passport to Magonia*, drawing from the descriptive observations of Evans-Wentz (as well as Kirk before him), theorized that abduction stories and reports did not begin with the Boas and Hill cases, but were modern versions of the ancient human contact with otherworldly consciousness that often took the shape of religious, occult, and even folkloric fairy-like experiences.[297]

Vallée also gives credit to Charles Fort (in his *The Book of the Damned*) as the person who 'uncovered anomalous sightings by astronomers in records dating back to the nineteenth century [as well as] stories of celestial wonders...in the archives of medieval writers and even [in those of] Roman historians' that were written well before Kenneth Arnold's 1947 UFO sighting.[298] Vallée's earlier work led him to the hypothesis that the present day UFO sighting-contact-abduction phenomenon operates as a kind of global 'thermostat', which is responsible for orchestrating the evolution of human consciousness through the millennia.

Doubtless, Vallée's idea was very influential in Strieber's struggle to formulate his own theory concerning his experiences. Vallée's grand global thermostat synchronizing the evolution of human consciousness becomes, for Strieber, a smaller, personal force that works on individual human minds and bodies. In *Solving the Communion Enigma*, Strieber 'offered the opinion that the experience in its totality might be what the force of evolution looks like when it is applied to a conscious mind,' which he now understands is 'an elegant

---

294. Ibid., 5.
295. Ibid.
296. For a good overview of what is meant by 'nuts-and-bolts' UFO theories, see Richard M Dolan, *UFOs for the 21st Century Mind: A Fresh Guide to an Ancient Mystery* (Rochester: Richard Dolan Press., 2014).
297. Thomas E Bullard, *The Myth and Mystery of UFOs* (Lawrence: University Press of Kansas, 2010), 125.
298. Vallée, *Passport to Magonia*.

enough thought, but with it comes the threatening reality of evolutionary change.'[299]

We return to the point made by Kripal, 'that a cognitive "rewiring" and subsequent penchant for thinking beyond all either-or's to something beyond, to a both-and or Third' hinges on the cognitive dissonance created by Faerie-Other experience that acts as a sort of Greek paradox or Zen koan in order to actually change the way the brain is wired and thus affect an evolutionary leap in consciousness.[300] Strieber asserts that 'it is absolutely clear...that the issue of what the contact experience is remains unresolved, and thus the question must be preserved' because it is this very question of the mystery of the Faerie-Other itself that becomes an almost sacred via gnosis to Kripal's 'beyond ... a both-and or Third.'[301]

Strieber is adamant that 'the experience is changing us—all of us, not just people who have remembered close encounters,' even as 'Governments are silent and science is unable to face it' and the media, for its part, 'denies it and people therefore assume that it's irrelevant.'[302] It is Strieber's contention that 'not a single human being is unaffected, but almost none of us realize this. It is changing every single one of us on this earth.'[303] It seems as though Strieber has refined his combination Vallée-Strieber theory yet again and is describing some sort of stealth gnosis that operates not through human volition, but through an almost universal and enigmatic force.[304]

Loving the Question(s)

There are a few components of the faerie-abduction phenomenon that remain, at the very least, under-researched when viewed in the light of Fortean approaches to UFO abduction encounters. Some modern day abduction reports center around the intergenerational aspect of the phenomenon in that the experience seems to be transmitted through family lines. Clearly the reports of the 'fairy world' of Evans-Wentz makes use of an anthropological gathering of information—some of which is contained within various families—but it is almost impossible to know if reports of contacts with 'fairies' were based upon genealogical lineage, even if the recollections of the 'fairy encounters' came through the memories of certain relatives.

The other component is the role of childhood trauma in the faerie-abduction phenomenon. Strieber devotes an entire chapter in *Solving the Communion Enigma* ('The Mirror Shattered'), where he struggles with the

---

299. Strieber, *Solving the Communion Enigma*, 3.
300. Ibid., xiii.
301. Ibid., 4, xiii.
302. Ibid.
303. Ibid.
304. For a more menacing argument on the effects of 'stealth gnosis,' see David M. Jacobs, *Walking among Us: The Alien Plan to Control Humanity*, (2015).

relationship between his recollection of his own childhood trauma and his ability to engage in communication with the 'visitors.' He ponders 'why one person will become entangled in direct contact [with the visitors] and another won't.'[305] He cites part of a study published by Kenneth Ring on the relationship between near-death experiencers and close-encounter witnesses. The study found that both groups remembered 'childhood trauma of various kinds—not necessarily sexual trauma' that Ring describes as 'a most intriguing, clear-cut and disturbing pattern...for both UFO and near-death experiencers to report a greater incidence of child-abuse and trauma,' which appear at 'highly significant statistical levels.'[306] Strieber would later remember long patterns of childhood trauma and abuse in his own life.

Kripal, writing on the founder of Fortean Studies, Charles Fort, describes the violent child abuse young Fort suffered at the hands of his own father and remarks that 'Fort's paranoid Extraterrestrial fantasy finds its psychological origins in overwhelming childhood trauma,' but then continues to ask 'or was it the physical abuse and emotional trauma that opened him up to the extraterrestrial gnosis?'[307] This is certainly Strieber's view. As he puts it, 'because I was so shocked in my childhood, I lost belief in the stability of the ordinary world. I live in a permanent state of unease, but also a permanent state of wonder.'[308] For Strieber, this childhood trauma allowed him to 'perceive the visitors' and 'to have formed a relationship with them.'[309]

This connection, however, also has its detractors among some of the more current psychological circles who assert that 'abductees are sane and intelligent people who have unwittingly created vivid false memories from a mélange of nightmares, culturally available texts, and a powerful drive for meaning that science is unable to satisfy.'[310] This sort of dismissive argument does not take into account the incredibly rich (and historical) experiences reported by witnesses, such as Strieber, nor does it keep pace with new quantum and technological leaps being made by the natural sciences. This sort of psychological argument, while claiming not to judge the veracity of the experiencer, nevertheless is unable, or unwilling to allow that this is a physical experience. David G. Robertson, on the other hand, deftly uses a more nuanced hermeneutical approach to doubt the physical actuality of the faerie-abduction phenomenon. He argues that the shift away from the view that the faerie-abduction is a physical 'nuts-and-bolts' experience occurred as 'the space race had revealed the severe realities of space travel, and general relativity had denied the possibility of faster-than-light travel and thus

---

305. Strieber, *Solving the Communion*, 15.
306. Ibid.
307. Kripal, *Authors of the Impossible*, 101.
308. Strieber, *Solving the Communion*, 38.
309. Ibid.
310. Susan A Clancy, *Abducted: How People Come to Believe They Were Kidnapped by Aliens* (Cambridge, Mass.: Harvard University Press, 2005), Front Matter.

interstellar travel based on any known scientific principles.'[311] Thus faerie-abduction experiencers and UFO researchers were forced to move toward 'a more paranormal interpretation.'[312] Robertson then uses Strieber's statement that 'most major religions have emerged out of visionary experiences that are, in fact, understandable in the context of the UFO encounter' to underscore the fact that Strieber's experience is not physically real, merely paranormal, and thus should be discounted from any real scientific consideration.[313] But, as it was shown, Strieber himself, from the very beginning of his writing *Communion*, has never maintained that he was abducted by interstellar UFOs even as he has asserted that it was very 'real,' and has continued to be sensitive to the 'paranormal' nature of his continued experience. The experience with 'fairies' reported by Evans-Wentz are also described as both physical and paranormal.

The otherworldly, spiritual and mystical connotations of the Faerie/UFO abduction experience noted by Vallée, compared with the deeply felt 'communion' between the 'visitors' and Strieber, hold important insights, not only for Fortean approaches to the study of religion, but also for all who strive to understand the divide between the human and the mystical. The connection between Strieber's experience and those of the faerie-abduction encounters outlined above represent an attempt to locate this fascinating human experience within its proper Fortean context.

311. David G. Robertson, 'Transformation: Whitley Strieber's Paranormal Gnosis,' *Nova Religio: The Journal of Alternative and Emergent Religions* 18.1 (2014), 69.
312. Ibid.
313. Ibid. 70.

6

Misunderstanding Myth as History:
The Case of British-Israelism

David V. Barrett

British-Israelism is a fairly obscure religious belief which has had a disproportionate (though little recognised) effect on society in the last hundred years, especially in America. In a sentence, it is the belief that the people of Britain and the USA today—effectively white, English-speaking people—are the literal descendants of the Ten Lost Tribes of Israel, and so are God's Chosen People. Unlikely, perhaps, but it is the connotations of this belief that make it worthy of examination here.

The background to the whole concept goes back some two thousand seven hundred years.

The Ten Lost Tribes

According to Old Testament mythology the patriarch of Israel (formerly Jacob), son of Isaac, son of Abraham, had twelve sons by his two wives and two concubines; these sons fathered the twelve tribes of Israel (Genesis 35: 22-26). The tribes eventually formed into two nations, the southern kingdom of Judah, which also contained Benjamin and some of Levi (the priestly tribe), and the northern kingdom of Israel, which contained the other ten tribes. These two nations were briefly united around 1000-900 BCE under King David and his son Solomon, with Jerusalem as their joint religious centre.

In two different waves of invasion the two nations were conquered and taken into captivity, first Israel by the Assyrians c. 720 BCE, then Judah by the Babylonians c. 598-581 BCE. Fifty to seventy years later, c. 530 BCE, members of the tribe of Judah, who became the Jews, were allowed by King Cyrus to return from Babylon to their homeland, now called Judaea—but the other tribes of the northern kingdom, who had been taken into captivity by the Assyrians nearly two centuries earlier, are not mentioned again. They did not return, as their southern cousins did—so where did they go? They became known as the Ten Lost Tribes of Israel—and a myth had begun.[314]

There has been speculation about the fate of the Ten Lost Tribes of Israel for centuries, particularly in an eschatological context. Norman Cohn cites perhaps the earliest reference to their being involved in the End Times, 'in the pages of Commodianus, a very inferior Latin poet of (probably) the fifth century': 'For according to Commodianus when Christ returns it will be at the head not of an angelic host but of the descendants of the ten lost tribes of Israel, which have survived in hidden places, unknown to the rest of the world.'[315]

So where did the Ten Lost Tribes go? One idea, dating as far back as Columbus, is that the native peoples of America might be 'the barbarised descendants of the Ten Tribes of Israel.'[316] There have been many other theories, some wilder than others, and most with little or no supporting evidence. First we need to look more closely at the origins of the myth, and deconstruct it.

Historians accept that the invasions took place. According to the biblical account in II Kings 17: 6, 'In the ninth year of Hoshea the king of Assyria took Samaria and carried Israel away into Assyria' is corroborated by cuneiform tablets discovered north of Nineveh, the capital of ancient Assyria, which say, 'I besieged and captured Samaria, and carried off 27,290 of its inhabitants as booty.' But some clarifications and caveats are necessary.

The twelve tribes descended from twelve brothers are more likely to have been an amphictyony—an association of neighbouring states or tribes sharing a common religious centre which sometimes (but not always) work together in various degrees of shifting alliances.[317] Ascribing different tribes to different 'mothers' might suggest the seniority or strength of respective tribes and alliances. There may well have been familial links between the tribes, but it is extremely unlikely that they were descended from twelve brothers who had one father and four mothers between them. Even the historicity of the 'Golden Age' of the united monarchy of both kingdoms under David and Solomon, as described in the Bible, has been challenged by some scholars.[318]

---

314. Two excellent but very different academic books on the Ten Lost Tribes are Tudor Parfitt, *The Lost Tribes of Israel: The History of a Myth* (London: Phoenix, 2003) and Zvi Ben-Dor Benite, *The Lost Ten Tribes: A World History* (Oxford: Oxford University Press, 2009).

315. Norman Cohn, *The Pursuit of the Millennium*, 3rd edition (London: Granada /Paladin, 1970), 28.

316. David S Katz and Richard H Popkin, *Messianic Revolution: Radical Religious Politics to the End of the Second Millennium* (London: Allen Lane, 1999), 80.

317. E. J. Young, 'Tribes of Israel' in J. D. Douglas, ed., *The New Bible Dictionary* (London: Inter-Varsity Fellowship, 1962), 1296.

318. Amy Dockser Marcus, *Rewriting the Bible: How Archaeology is Reshaping History* (London: Little Brown, 2000); Steven L McKenzie, *King David: A Biography* (Oxford: Oxford University Press, 2000); Eric H Cline, *From Eden to Exile: Unraveling Mysteries of the Bible* (Washington: National Geographic, 2007).

Whatever their familial origin, the tribes at the time of the conquests in the eighth and sixth centuries BCE were not actually the twelve tribes named after the twelve brothers. The priestly tribe of Levi held no land, which would reduce the number to eleven, but the tribe of Joseph (of the multicoloured coat of popular culture) split into two subtribes named after his sons, Manasseh and Ephraim; these become important in later British-Israelite theory. The tribe of Simeon seems to have been absorbed into the southern kingdom of Judah. And the tribe of Benjamin, which also lived in the land of Judah, presumably went off to Babylon and returned from there; but the story from the return onwards is only about Judah.

It is essential to distinguish 'Israel' from the 'Jews.' The Jews are the descendants of the tribe of Judah living in the land of Judah/Judaea, and were just one of the twelve tribes of Israel. The northern kingdom of Israel did not include the tribe of Judah—so the Lost Ten Tribes are Israelites or Hebrews, but not Jews.

Judah spent half a century of captivity in Babylon. Psalm 137:1 begins, 'By the rivers of Babylon, there we sat down, yea, we wept, when we remembered Zion.' In fact scholarship suggests that far from being slaves in captivity, as the Bible laments, the Jews in Babylon were treated as freemen; some rose to high positions, and many stayed there, only to return to Israel 2,600 years later in the 1950s.[319]

Rather than the logistical nightmare of the invaders removing the entire populations of the conquered lands, the reality is that with the conquering of both nations, Israel in the north and Judah in the south, only 'the cream of the population'[320]—the leaders, the educated and the skilled—were taken into captivity. The majority of the population—farmers, fishermen, the uneducated —were left behind, along with some priests.

So some were taken, some remained and some fled south from Israel into Judah; archaeological studies show that Jerusalem's population increased from 7,500 to 24,000 at the end of the eighth century BCE.[321]

When the exiled members of the tribe of Judah returned to their homeland c. 530 BCE they took back with them many of the religious beliefs they had encountered in Babylon. From the point of view of those who had been left behind in Judah/Judaea, who had maintained contact with neighbouring tribes with whom they shared similar beliefs, those who were returning from exile were imposing new and alien beliefs on them. The Hebrew religion became Judaism, absorbing many myths and doctrinal

319. Geddes MacGregor, *The Bible in the Making* (London: John Murray, 1959), 15-6; Marcus, *Rewriting the Bible*, 172-5.
320. HL Ellison, 'Judah: Exile (597-538 BC),' in Douglas, *New Bible Dictionary*, 669.
321. Magan Broshi, 'The Expansion of Jerusalem in the Reigns of Hezekiah and Manasseh,' *Israel Exploration Journal* 24.1 (1974): 21-26; Magan Broshi, 'Estimating the Population of Ancient Jerusalem,' *Biblical Archaeology Review* (1978):10-15.

features of earlier Babylonian, Sumerian and Persian religions,[322] including the Creation story,[323] the Flood[324] and the Zoroastrian concepts of, amongst others, one God with an evil opponent, an afterlife in Heaven or Hell and a Final Judgement.[325]

It was immediately after the Babylonian captivity that many of the books of the Old Testament were either written or edited into something approximating their present form,[326] by the winners of this struggle. Those who had been left behind, of all the tribes, held a purer version of the old Hebrew religion than post-exilic Judaism, but they lost. The biblical books of Ezra and Nehemiah, written from the viewpoint of the winners, document the struggle between those who returned with their new beliefs—puppet politicians appointed by the Persians who had allowed their return[327]—and those, including priests, who had remained in Jerusalem and upheld the old Hebrew beliefs.

The priests who had stayed in Jerusalem had maintained friendly relations with their neighbours; after all, they were similar people with similar religious beliefs, but the returning leaders imposed increasingly separatist rules.[328] Inter-marriage between the post-exilic Jews and those who had stayed behind, the peoples of the lands, was forbidden. Referring to anthropologist Mary Douglas's study of the post-exilic times, her biographer writes: 'The "seed of Israel" is restricted to mean only the returnees, the remainder finding themselves accused of defilement.'[329] Effectively, the returning tribe of Judah redefined only themselves as 'Israel' and, as the winning party, rewrote their history to support their position. The 'historical' books of the Old Testament are an origin myth, tracing back the Jewish people and religion to their supposed roots; they are a (rewritten) family saga.

The 'peoples of the lands' who are accused of impurity in Ezra and Nehemiah were not only those members of the tribe of Judah who had remained there rather than being taken into exile in Babylon, but also their

---

322. Samuel H Hooke, *Middle Eastern Mythology: From the Assyrians to the Hebrews* (London: Penguin, 1963), 103-160.

323. Karen Armstrong, *A History of God* (London: William Heinemann, 1993), 14, 77.

324. Andrew George, *The Epic of Gilgamesh: A New Translation* (London: Allen Lane, 1999), xiii-xiv.

325. Keith Crim, ed., *The Perennial Dictionary of World Religions* (New York: Harper & Row, 1981), 828-9; John R Hinnels, ed., *The Penguin Dictionary of Religions* (London: Penguin, 1984), 362-3; Yuri Stoyanov, *The Other God: Dualist Religions from Antiquity to the Cathar Heresy* (New Haven: Yale University Press, 2000), 54-56.

326. MacGregor, *Bible in the Making*, 17-18; N. H. Ridderbos, 'Canon of the Old Testament: The Canon During the Times of Ezra and Nehemiah,' in Douglas, *New Bible Dictionary*, 189.

327. Mary Douglas, *In the Wilderness: The Doctrine of Defilement in the Book of Numbers* (Oxford: Oxford University Press, 1993), cited in Richard Fardon, *Mary Douglas: An Intellectual Biography* (London: Routledge, 1999), 202.

328. Daniel L Smith-Christopher, 'Ezra-Nehemiah,' in John Barton and John Muddiman, eds, *The Oxford Bible Commentary* (Oxford: Oxford University Press, 2001), 310.

329. Fardon, *Mary Douglas*, 202.

neighbours, including members of the other tribes of Israel who had remained behind in their own lands rather than being taken away by the Assyrians two centuries earlier. At least some of the so-called Ten Lost Tribes of Israel stayed exactly where they had always been, but they were dispossessed of the name of Israel by the returnees from Babylon.

The northern kingdom of Israel included Samaria—and by the time of Jesus the Samaritans were a people despised by the Jews (John 4: 4-42, Luke 10: 29-37). Even today they practise a version of the Hebrew religion both similar to and quite different from Judaism; they have a slightly different version of the Pentateuch, and do not include many of the books of the Jewish scriptures written or compiled after the Exile.[330]

If we assume that throughout history most people stay roughly in their ancestral homelands, then the Ten Lost Tribes today are where they have been for the last two thousand seven hundred years: in northern Israel, southern Lebanon, the south western corner of Syria and the western edge of Jordan, and are not lost at all.

There are many theories about where the Ten Lost Tribes went, and where they are today. Ahmadi Muslims believe that they went to Kashmir, and that Jesus survived the crucifixion and went there to preach to them.[331] Mormons have several unusual beliefs, including that the Lost Tribes live in 'a "mysteriously camouflaged" geographical area somewhere at or near the north pole'; that they live inside a hollow Earth; and that they are on another planet, possibly connected to Earth by a narrow neck of land; most Mormons, though, believe that the lost tribes are simply dispersed around the world.[332] At the Second Coming they will come from out of the north and will gather at the City of Zion, Independence, in Jackson County, Missouri.

British-Israelism

British-Israelism is the belief that the Ten Lost Tribes of Israel migrated to Europe and settled in Britain, and that the British people today—and by extension the Americans—are both the physical and the spiritual descendants of Israel.

Although several writers proposed some form of the theory in the sixteenth, seventeenth and eighteenth centuries, it was the publication of Scottish preacher John Wilson's Lectures on *Our Israelitish Origins* (1840) that really marked the beginning of British-Israelism as a recognisable

---

330. Gerard Russell, *Heirs to Forgotten Kingdoms: Journeys into the Disappearing Religions of the Middle East* (London: Simon & Schuster, 2014), 173-8; 194-7.

331. Hadrat Mirza Ghulam Ahmad of Qadian, *Jesus in India* (Tilford: Islam International Publications, revised edition 2003), 18; 80-81.

332. R. Clayton Brough, *The Lost Tribes: History, Doctrine, Prophecies and Theories about Israel's Lost Ten Tribes* (Bountiful, UT: Horizon 1992), 43-4; 64-65; 55-56; 50-52; 75-76.

movement.[333] From 1840 to his death in 1871, Wilson taught that the British were the physical descendants of the Ten Lost Tribes: 'the so-called "lost house of Israel," the leading tribe of which was Ephraim…they are the modern nations of Europe, and especially those of Saxon race, whose glorious privilege it now is to 'preach the gospel for a witness unto all nations ere the end come.'[334]

These few lines from Wilson contain several elements which were to become central to British-Israelite teaching: the mention of all the nations of Europe, the emphasis on the Saxons, the commission to preach the gospel 'unto all nations' while there is still time, and the emphasis on the sub-tribe of Ephraim, the second son of Joseph. In later years Wilson identified America as Joseph's elder son, Manasseh.

Wilson himself did not set up any sort of organisation, but in the year of his death the first British-Israelite organisation was founded by others. The next few decades saw a significant growth in the appeal of British-Israelism, particularly to the British middle and upper classes. A number of new groups were formed, eventually merging into the British-Israel World Federation (BIWF) in 1919. This drew large numbers of members; in 1929 it filled the Royal Albert Hall, and in 1931 over twenty thousand people attended its week-long annual congress. The BIWF had support from parliamentarians of both Houses, some senior members of the armed forces and a number of clergy; its most senior patron was Princess Alice of Athlone (1883-1981), a granddaughter of Queen Victoria.[335] Other supporters included the Scottish astronomer royal Charles Piazzi Smyth (1819-1900) and William Massey, prime minister of New Zealand from 1912-1925. It has been estimated that '[a]t the peak of its popularity in England in the 1920s, British Israelism may have had as many as five thousand adherents, in addition to smaller followings in the Commonwealth nations and the United States.'[336] The figure of two million claimed adherents in the late nineteenth and early twentieth centuries is often quoted, though without any substantiating evidence;[337] it is certainly a vast overstatement.

British-Israelism spread to the United States in the late nineteenth century. J. H. Allen (1847-1930), a Methodist minister who promoted the 'Holiness' movement in Missouri, moved to Pasadena in California, and there he taught British-Israelism, specifically that the British race are the Chosen

---

333. J. Gordon Melton and Martin Baumann, *Religions of the World: A Comprehensive Encyclopedia of Beliefs and Practices*, 4 vols (Santa Barbara, CA: ABC-Clio, 2002), 171.
334. Cited in Katz and Popkin, *Messianic Revolution*, 172.
335. https://www.britishisrael.co.uk/history.php..
336. Arthur L. Greil, 'British Israelism' in Melton and Baumann, *Religions of the World*, 171; Michael Barkun, *Religion and the Racist Right* (Chapel Hill: University of North Carolina, 1997), 15.
337. Horton Davies, *Christian Deviations: The Challenge of the Sects* (London: SCM Press, 1954), 121; Arnold Kellett, *Isms and Ologies: A Guide to Unorthodox and Non-Christian Beliefs* (London: Epworth Press, 1965), 72.

People, followed by the Americans. In 1902 the first edition of his book *Judah's Sceptre and Joseph's Birthright* was published; this was to be a major influence on the teachings of Herbert W. Armstrong, founder of the largely American sect the Worldwide Church of God, which had British-Israelism at the heart of its teachings, and had around one hundred thousand baptised members at its peak in the 1990s.[338]

The essence of most versions of British-Israelism for the last century or more is broadly what was taught by John Wilson, J. H. Allen and others in the nineteenth and early-twentieth centuries, and what was espoused by the Worldwide Church of God for over half a century from the mid-1930s to the mid-1990s, and by many of its hundreds of offshoot Churches today.[339]

British-Israelites say the displaced Israelites from the northern kingdom went north and west in fulfilment of the Bible (Isaiah 49: 12). They were in the northern Black Sea area from the seventh to the fourth centuries BCE, where they were known as the Cimmerians or Gimirri, or the Scythians. Around 625 BCE, they say, the Scythians began moving north to southern Russia, while some moved to the west. Around 250 BCE Scythians moved into western and northern Europe—both Spain and the Germanic and Danish lands—and later by various routes into Britain; different groups at different times were known as Celts, Angles, Saxons, Jutes and Vikings. All were actually the descendants of the Ten Lost Tribes; all settled in Britain. 'Lay a line due northwest of Jerusalem across the continent of Europe, until you come to the sea, and then to the islands in the sea! This line takes you directly to the British Isles!' wrote Herbert W. Armstrong.[340]

British-Israelites offer semantic 'proof' of their beliefs. The people (Hebrew *iysh*) of the covenant (*beriyth*) became the British (*beriyth-iysh*) people; Isaac's sons became the Saxons; Scotia is named after the *Scythae* and *Cymru* (Wales) after the Cimmerians; the Gauls in France and the Gaels in Britain took their name from the Hebrew word *Galah*, translated in the Bible as 'exile'; and as the tribes migrated through Europe the Hebrews gave their name to the Iberians in Spain, and then to Hibernia (Ireland) and the Hebrides in Scotland.

The tribe of Dan (remembering that written ancient Hebrew did not use vowels) passed through or settled in, amongst many others, Macedonia, the Dardanelles, the rivers Danube, Dnieper, Dniester and Don, and came to the British Isles; in Ireland Donegal, Londonderry and Dingle, in Scotland Dundee, Dunkirk and Edinburgh, and in England, of course, London. The

---

338. David V Barrett, *The Fragmentation of a Sect: Schism in the Worldwide Church of God* (New York: Oxford University Press, 2013), 34-37, 4.
339. Barrett, *Fragmentation of a Sect*, 103-147.
340. Herbert W. Armstrong, *The United States and Britain in Prophecy* (Pasadena, CA: Worldwide Church of God, 1980), 95.

famous Tuatha de Danaan of Irish legend were simply the tribe of Dan.[341]

Most of these 'proofs' had been taught by John Wilson in the middle of the nineteenth century, were in J. H. Allen's *Judah's Sceptre and Joseph's Birthright* and featured strongly in Herbert W. Armstrong's *The United States and Britain in Prophecy*.

The British-Israel World Federation, amongst others, claim that Genesis 12: 2-3: 'And I will make thee a great nation, and I will bless thee, and make thy name great; and thou shalt be a blessing' is fulfilled in the name 'Great Britain.'[342] But the name Great Britain only dates back to the Act of Union in 1707, when England and Scotland became a single country.

It is never made clear why it was just the tribe of Dan (which is otherwise of no particular significance in British-Israelite theory) which left its mark on place-names across Europe and in Britain. Nor do most British-Israelites explain why Britain is uniquely special, if much of Europe was not only traversed by but settled by the Ten Lost Tribes. Some writers, however, do go into a little detail over which of the tribes became which modern countries, usually based on some aspect of the symbolism of a nation's emblems: Reuben is France, Zebulun the Netherlands, Issachar is Finland, Gad is Switzerland, Asher is Belgium and so on, according to the leader of one religious group.[343]

Most British-Israelites teach that the subtribes of Joseph's sons, Ephraim and Manasseh, eventually became the peoples of Britain and the USA respectively, and that all the Biblical prophecies about them refer to these countries today. A few groups teach instead that Manasseh refers to Britain and Ephraim to the USA.[344]

In addition, James VI of Scotland and I of England was a direct descendant of the royal line of Israel; therefore is the current British monarch. The Stone of Scone, Britain's Coronation Stone, was the stone which Jacob used as a pillow (Genesis 28:18), and was carried to Ireland by Jeremiah in 569 BCE; Jeremiah was accompanied by a daughter of King Zedekiah, Princess Tea-Tephi, whose descendant is Queen Elizabeth II, and so the throne of Britain is a continuation of the throne of David.[345] (This ignores the inconvenient historical fact that the royal families of Europe have intermarried

341. Herbert W. Armstrong, *The British Commonwealth and the United States in Prophecy* (London: Ambassador College, 1954), 17-20; *Autobiography of Herbert W. Armstrong*, vol. 1 (Pasadena, CA: Ambassador College Press, 1967), 115-122; Armstrong, *United States and Britain in Prophecy*, 93-102.

342. 'History of the British-Israel World Federation: Beliefs,' https://www.originofnations.org /old_bi_literature/some_historical_background.htm..

343. David C. Pack, *America and Britain in Prophecy* (Wadsworth, OH: Restored Church of God, 2008), 119-128.

344. William F. Dankenbring, *America and Great Britain: Our Identity Revealed!* (Omak, WA: Triumph Publishing Company, 2005), 34-54.

345. Armstrong, *British Commonwealth*, 19-22; *Autobiography of Herbert W. Armstrong*, 118-128; Armstrong, *United States and Britain in Prophecy*, 99-104.

so much over the centuries that if Britain's throne is a continuation of the throne of David, genetically every European throne must be.)

This is only the very briefest of summaries of British-Israelism; many of the books proposing the theory are hundreds of pages long. Accepting a few initial premises and making a few conceptual leaps, the whole theory, as carefully presented by its adherents, seems logical at first glance and has a certain appeal for English-speaking Westerners. Many sects teach that their members are 'special'; indeed, this is a common compensator offered by sect membership.[346] British-Israelites are able to view themselves as the Chosen People.[347]

In fact the supposedly historical 'proofs' for British-Israelism depend on a few quotes, sometimes taken out of context, which often express an opinion or an assertion rather than any form of evidence; on a poor understanding of historical scholarship; on ignoring any contrary evidence; on amateur semantic 'analysis'; on correlation becoming causation; and on generally weak reasoning. There is no scholarly evidence for British-Israelism, and a good deal of scholarly evidence—semantic, archaeological and genetic—against it. Books in the late twentieth and early-twentyfirst centuries simply recycle the arguments from mid-nineteenth century books, which are no more valid now than they were then. British-Israelism is an early example of the swathe of popular 'alternative history' theories about the Illuminati, Freemasonry, the Knights Templar, Rennes-le-Château and Jesus marrying Mary Magdalene and settling in France with their children. Unfortunately, as we shall see, it also keeps company with such ideas in attracting interest from the Far Right.

Before I examine the influence of British-Israelism on Right-wing groups in America I shall look briefly at its position in England and Ireland. There are now only a handful of ministers with British-Israelite beliefs in assorted Protestant denominations in England, and the only specifically British-Israelite church is the Orange Street Congregational Church near Leicester Square in London. The church has strong connections with the British-Israelite Bible Truth Fellowship, which hosts a one-day public meeting there twice a year, with lectures on British-Israelism.

British-Israelism is a strongly Protestant belief, and there is nowhere in Britain where Protestantism is taken more seriously, and more politically, than Northern Ireland. The white supremacist website Stormfront quotes a writer about the six-pointed star on the flag of Northern Ireland, which actually symbolises the six counties of the province, as 'the Star of David, signifying the idea that Ulster is the Promised Land, promised by God to the followers

---

346. Rodney Stark and William Sims Bainbridge, *A Theory of Religion* (New Brunswick, NJ: Rutgers University Press, 1987), 36.
347. Richard Simpson, *The Political Influence of the British-Israel Movement in the Nineteenth Century* (MA dissertation, 2002), 9. https://www.originofnations.org/books,%20papers/MA_dissertation_BI.pdf.

of the Reformed Faith, in other words to the Ulster Protestants.'[348]

On a British-Israelite website, in a sermon preached in Belfast on December 14, 1988, Pentecostal pastor Alan Campbell proclaims under the subhead 'It [British-Israelism] provides us with a Christian and biblical basis for our patriotism':

> For far too long we have fixed our eyes on heaven, and abandoned our dominion mandate on earth. For far too long we have been made to feel ashamed of our Patriotism and Loyalism, and told we should abandon it all when we are born again. The British Israel Truth refutes this serious error. Britain is part of God's vineyard, Ulster is our own Promised Land, peopled by the very seed of Israel planted here as a light in darkest Ireland, and we must occupy until Jesus comes.[349]

British-Israelites often link their distinctive interpretation of history to current affairs. J. H. Allen wrote a century ago that the people of southern Ireland are 'vastly different' from those of the north. The southern Irish, he said, can be traced back to the troublesome Canaanites, who were Philistines. 'The evolution of the name of this Canaanitish nation is from Philistine to Phoenician, then Phenesian, then Venetian, and then Fenian,' he wrote at a time when the Fenians were causing political trouble in Ireland.[350]

According to one British-Israelite website, 'The fact that the last place the Ark of the Covenant was seen, was Ireland, is a matter of historical record. Historians reject it as legend and prose, nevertheless it is recorded history.'[351] With this inability to distinguish between history and legend, and believing that the Ark of the Covenant was taken there by the prophet Jeremiah c. 580 BCE, British-Israelites dug into the historic Hill of Tara between 1899 and 1902, causing huge damage. Those protesting against them included the poet W. B. Yeats and his muse, the actress and Irish nationalist Maud Gonne, who lit a bonfire on Tara in protest against the British-Israelites.

More lightly, enthusiasts for British-Israelism have also claimed that the pot of gold at the end of the rainbow is the Ark of the Covenant; that Joseph's coat of many colours is the Irish kilt; and that Jeremiah was known as the Patriarch saint, which became Saint Patriarch, and hence Saint Patrick.[352]

There is some crossover between British-Israelites and those who believe

---

348. https://www.stormfront.org/forum/t27448/(quoting a post from a games forum). http://halo.bungie.net/Forums/posts.aspx?postID=63879441&postRepeater1p=2#63879959.
349. Alan Campbell, 'British-Israel: Fact or Fiction?' (1988), http://www.ensignmessage.com/bifactorfiction.html.
350. J. H. Allen, *Judah's Sceptre and Joseph's Birthright* (Merrimac, MA: Destiny Publishers, 1902), 287, 288.
351. http://www.cryaloud.com/ark_covenant_jeremiah_ireland.htm.
352. http://www.cryaloud.com/ark_covenant_jeremiah_ireland.htm. Joseph Wild, *The Lost Ten Tribes* (London: Robert Banks & Son, 1879), 194.

that Jesus visited Britain during his youth.[353] Books arguing this—or that St Paul and other disciples came to Britain—are published by Covenant Publishers, set up by the British-Israelite World Federation in 1921.[354] Some writers on British-Israelism, both of the nineteenth and twentieth century, are also fascinated by pyramidology.[355]

British-Israelism (amongst many other beliefs) has long been condemned in Christian counter-cult books.[356] Two nineteenth century comments show how the established Church regarded it. The *Church Quarterly Review* wrote of British-Israelism in 1880, 'Like good Templarism, Plymouth Brethrenism or Freemasonry, it is a quasi-religion and, once accepted, is looked upon as the most important of all religious truths.'[357] The *Church Times* newspaper of June 12, 1885 described it as 'Chosen Peopleism' and attacked it as a religious equivalent of craving for aristocratic distinction.[358]

British-Israelism in America

A more recent description is 'a variety of British nationalism buttressed by biblical references with all the attributes of a religious movement except religion.'[359] But there is a fine line between nationalism and racism. Because British-Israelism effectively claims scriptural support for the supremacy of White Anglo-Saxon Protestants, it lies behind the beliefs of such overtly white supremacist groups in America as Christian Identity and Aryan Nations.[360]

British-Israelism in the USA was philo-semitic until the 1930s-1940s, when it started to become often virulently anti-semitic.[361] Not all British-Israelites are anti-semitic, and those that are hold a variety of beliefs. Some assert that because the British are descended from the Ten Lost Tribes who

---

353. This belief is comprehensively dealt with and dismissed in Paul Ashdown, *The Lord was at Glastonbury: Somerset and the Jesus Voyage Story* (Glastonbury: The Squeeze Press, 2010). Ashdown shows that the earliest reference to the supposedly ancient tales of Jesus coming to Britain dates back only to 1895 (19-21, 63).

354. http://www.covpub.co.uk/.

355. Wild, *Lost Ten Tribes*, 'The Stone Witness,' 159-168; 'Signs and Wonders,' 168-175; Adam Rutherford, *Israel-Britain, or Anglo-Saxon Israel* (London: Harrow Weald, 1934), 'Scientific Revelation – The Great Pyramid: The Divine Plan for the British Race,' 188-315; E. Raymond Capt, *A Study in Pyramidology* (Muscogee, OK: Artisan Publishers, 1986); E. Raymond Capt, *The Great Pyramid Decoded: God's Stone Witness* (Muscogee, OK: Artisan Publishers, 1978).

356. William C. Irvine, *Heresies Exposed* (USA: Loizeaux Brothers, 1980 [1917]), 34-43; J. Oswald Sanders, *Heresies and Cults* (London: Marshall, Morgan & Scott, 1962 [1948]), 136-144; Davies, *Christian Deviations*, 121-135; Kellett, *Isms and Ologies*, 72-79.

357. Anglo-Israelism, *The Church Quarterly Review*, 1880.

358. Both cited in Simpson, *Political Influence of British-Israel Movement*, 8, 9.

359. Josef L Altholz, *The Religious Press in Britain, 1760-1900* (London: Greenwood, 1989), 30, cited in Simpson, *Political Influence of British-Israel Movement*, 1.

360. Rachel Storm, *In Search of Heaven on Earth* (London: Bloomsbury, 1991), 187-8; Katz and Popkin, *Messianic Revolution*, 187-9; Melton & Baumann, *Religions of the World*, 171.

361. Barkun, *Religion and the Racist Right*, Chapters 1-3.

left Israel centuries before the time of Jesus, they are not responsible for his crucifixion, unlike the Jews who are tainted by that stain. Others claim that the majority of Jews today are not even of the tribe of Judah, and that Ashkenazi Jews are descended from Khazars, nomadic Turks, or else from the Edomites, descendants of Esau, or from the Canaanites. Some believe that the Jews are descended from Cain. And some say that Jews are descended from Satan.[362]

John Halford, UK leader of Worldwide Church of God after it dropped its British-Israelite beliefs in the 1990s, explained in a 2001 interview why, in part, he personally had abandoned the teaching.

> At worst, what really cemented my withdrawal from it was that we found that so many of the Aryan Supremacist groups in the States loved our literature, stockpiled it, and it gave rise to what I consider some of the most foul ideology available...Christian Identity movements, Aryan Leagues, these people. I personally would not want to put my name to anything which would give those people one half of a page of material. The whole redneck, white supremacist, Ku Klux Klan...I think any right-thinking person, whether Christian or not, would want to distance themselves from that.[363]

The Christian Identity movement began in the 1920s. Over the decades it has encompassed a number of groups totalling at different times between two thousand and perhaps fifty thousand members in the USA, plus more in Canada and Australia.

In 1930 former lawyer Howard B. Rand, who was raised British-Israelite and knew J. H. Allen's book from an early age, founded the Anglo-Saxon Federation of America, the first American British-Israelite group. It emphasised biblical prophecy, that Britain was a great nation, spiritually powerful, invincible in war, and that these qualities were inherited by America. Along with William J. Cameron, who was head of PR for Henry Ford for nearly twenty years, Rand moved American British-Israelism to the political Right. Ford was a great proponent of the Protocols of the Elders of Zion, the most influential anti-semitic document of the twentieth century.[364]

In 1946 Ku Klux Klan organiser Wesley Swift (1913-70) founded the White Identity Church of Jesus Christ – Christian; in 1957 it dropped the first two words of its name, but not its beliefs. Swift combined British-Israelism, extreme anti-semitism and political militancy. Aryan Nations, described by the

---

362. Barkun, *Religion and the Racist Right*, 136-142, 52, 56, 170-172, 150-151.
363. John Halford, Interview with author, 28 February 2001.
364. The Protocols were comprehensively proved to be a forgery as early as 1920, but are still being promoted by white supremacists and anti-semites today as evidence of a Jewish conspiracy to take over the world. For a good overview of the background to the Protocols, and its pernicious influence, see Robert Brotherton, *Suspicious Minds: Why we Believe Conspiracy Theories* (New York & London: Bloomsbury Sigma, 2015), 31-45.

FBI as a terrorist threat, began in the 1970s as a militant arm of the Church of Jesus Christ – Christian.

Other Far Right white supremacist groups in the broad Christian Identity movement include the Northwest Territorial Imperative, whose aim still today is to set up an Aryan homeland in Washington State, Oregon, Idaho, Wyoming and Montana;[365] and the Covenant, the Sword, and the Arm of the Lord (CSA). The CSA was at its height in the 1970s-80s, when a Baptist congregation became an extremist white supremacist and anti-semitic paramilitary organisation based at a compound, The Farm, in Arkansas.

Elohim City, Oklahoma, founded by preacher Robert J. Millar in 1973, is a small Christian-Identity community of seventy to ninety people, with links to the CSA and to Aryan Nations. It is an example of how such groups, though small, have been connected in one way or another with events which have made international headlines.

Members of the Aryan Republican Army, which staged over twenty bank robberies in 1994-95 to finance white supremacist causes, took refuge at Elohim City. In 1994 Millar visited CSA member and convicted murderer Richard Snell on death row, witnessed his execution and arranged for his body to be brought to Elohim City. On the day of Snell's execution, April 19, 1995, Timothy McVeigh exploded a bomb outside a federal building in Oklahoma City, killing a hundred and sixty eight people. Although he never visited Elohim City he had met some of its residents, and is known to have telephoned the community two weeks earlier. McVeigh himself said that the bombing was in retaliation for the FBI assault on the Branch Davidian headquarters in Waco, Texas, which had killed seventy six members of the religious movement exactly two years earlier.[366] The Waco siege itself had been intended to be a BATF and FBI PR triumph to make up for their PR disaster at Ruby Ridge, Idaho, the year before, when the law enforcement agencies and US Marshals were in confrontation with Randy Weaver, who had Aryan Nations connections. That siege ended with Weaver's fourteen year old son and his wife being shot dead by Marshals and the FBI—the son shot in the back while running away and the wife while holding their ten month old baby. Weaver himself was injured, shot in the back while going to see his son's body.

Groups like Elohim City and the Covenant, the Sword, and the Arm of the Lord are Far Right Survivalists, often characterised as holding a Bible in

---

365. http://northwestfront.org/about/the-butler-plan/the-butler-plan-the-homeland/.
366. In an interesting connection, Dr Philip Arnold and Professor James D. Tabor, two academics who were former members of the British-Israelite Worldwide Church of God, which shared some prophetic teachings with the Branch Davidians, offered to mediate with David Koresh. Koresh was willing, but the FBI refused, leading to the disastrous fire. Barrett, *Fragmentation of a Sect*, 188 n.6; David V. Barrett, *The New Believers* (Cassell 2001), 87-88, 93-94; Dixon Cartwright, 'Waco eyewitness claims 1993 holocaust avoidable' in *The Journal - News of the Churches of God*, November 30, 1998.

one hand and a gun in the other. Obviously individuals hold differing beliefs, but generally they can be defined largely by what they are against: blacks, Jews, Freemasons, Catholics, gays, liberated women, federal government, the UN, evolution, climate change, the liberal establishment, liberal education and so on. They could be dismissed somewhat scathingly as redneck blue-collar white supremacists were it not that many of their most deeply-cherished beliefs are shared by an increasingly powerful fundamentalist Christian lobby which in recent years has exerted a surprising influence on national politics.

This goes under a variety of names. The New Apostolic Reformation is an American Pentecostalist movement which seeks to infiltrate other Christian churches and turn them to its fundamentalist and literalist viewpoint. Al-Jazeera once called the NAR 'America's Own Taliban' because of their Dominionism.

Quoting Genesis 1:26, Dominionism teaches that all humanity is under the sovereign dominion of God, so true Christians have a divine mandate to rule the Earth (or at least America)—whether or not people want to be ruled by them. A variant of Dominionism is Christian Reconstructionism, founded by R. J. Rushdoony (1916-2001). America's laws must be 'reconstructed' along biblical lines, creating a Christian theocracy where everything forbidden in the Old Testament is illegal. This is also known as Theonomy: the strict upholding of Mosaic law, including the death penalty for homosexuality, adultery, pre-marital sex, blasphemy, idolatry – and even, according to one author, Charlie Fuqua, for 'rebellious children.'[367] Fuqua, a Republican candidate for the Arkansas House of Representatives, said that all Muslims should be expelled from the USA, and that all prisoners not rehabilitated after two years should be executed.

Such beliefs are hardline Old Testament Christianity, with the belief (as in British-Israelism) that Christians, not Jews, are God's Chosen People – and a specific group of Christians. Followers of these beliefs are often strict Calvinists. They are Creationists, practise home-schooling, and believe that gun ownership is a Christian duty. The Christian Right in America—who are much of the power behind the Tea Party—support a 'soft' version of Reconstructionism whereby those who hold these beliefs aim to take over and occupy secular positions of power through the Republican Party. A number of prominent Republican contenders for Senate and even the presidency and vice-presidency have close links with Dominionist preachers.[368]

---

367. Charlie Fuqua, *God's Law: The Only Political Solution* (amazon.com, 2015), 179.
368.   See   http://www.rightwingwatch.org/content/cruz-jindal-and-huckbee-join-multiple-speakers-who-want-gays-put-death and http://www.krgv.com/news/local-news/Texas-Case-Mulls-if-Home-school-Kids-Have-to-LearnSomething/ 36190388.

Size and Influence

Obviously not all on the Far Right are believers in British-Israelism, or are even directly influenced by it. (Equally, not all British-Israelites are on the Far Right, or racist; one group, known as Brit-Am, are strongly in support of Jews and the present-day State of Israel).[369] But through much of the twentieth century the belief that the British and American peoples are the direct descendants of the Lost Ten Tribes, that God's special covenant with Israel applies to Britain and America today, and that every End-Time biblical prophecy about Israel is actually about Britain and America, has caused some to believe that they are God's Chosen People, and that all others are inferior. That is a pretty good incentive for being white supremacist.

Today's Dominionist or Reconstructionist Christians come from a different route and have a different set of beliefs, but ultimately the power behind their motivation is much the same: God—the strict Old Testament God—has chosen them, and with God on their side they are right and everyone else is wrong, especially all those who have been corrupted by such modern ideas and ideals as social democracy, liberalism, pluralism and equal rights for all, whatever their skin colour, religious beliefs or sexual preference.

Dominionists or British-Israelites, white supremacists, anti-semites, fundamentalist Survivalists—their numbers are small; but influence is not measured by numbers. Timothy McVeigh, who killed one hundred sixty eight people in 1995 on the second anniversary of the Waco disaster and on the day a white supremacist was executed, was just one man.

It is difficult to say how many people today are active British-Israelites. In Britain the movement seems almost a spent force. The twice-yearly British Israel Bible Truth meetings in London attract only thirty to forty people, of whom just four or five are under sixty. The British-Israel World Federation is a shadow of the organisation founded in 1919. Most of the books and booklets of its publishing house Covenant Publishing are decades old, and some more than a century old.

The largest British-Israelite groups are ignored by the BIWF, BIBTF and similar organisations because their theology is markedly different from Evangelical Protestantism. Of the many heterodox Christian sects[370] which splintered off from the Worldwide Church of God, the four largest perhaps have as many as twenty five to thirty thousand members between them: United Church of God, Church of God, a Worldwide Association, Living Church of God and Philadelphia Church of God.[371] Their version of Old Testament Christianity includes observing the seventh-day Sabbath instead of Sunday and the seven annual Hebrew festivals rather than Christmas and

---

369. http://www.britam.org.
370. Barrett, *Fragmentation of a Sect*, 235-237.
371. Ibid., 113-133.

Easter. They are socially very conservative, but not Far Right or racist.

They, and many of the other offshoots from the (now Evangelical) Worldwide Church of God, publish their own versions of Herbert W. Armstrong's *The United States and Britain in Prophecy*, which is based largely on J. H. Allen's *Judah's Sceptre and Joseph's Birthright*, which itself drew on nineteenth-century texts by John Wilson, Joseph Wild and others. As the more traditional British-Israelite groups slowly fade away, these movements, largely American but with some presence in Britain, Canada, Australasia, the Caribbean and elsewhere, may be the last bastion of those continuing to believe and promote a nineteenth-century myth based on false logic and a succession of false premises.

7

The Transmediumizers

Eden S. French & Christopher Laursen

What was religion to Charles Fort? He saw it as authoritative, once occupying the most powerful Dominant in America and Europe (and in many parts of the world, including for most Americans and certainly many Europeans, it remains greatly powerful). In the modern era, Fort wrote in *Lo!* (1931), 'one of the most fantastic of transferences is that of glorifying science, as a beneficent being.'[372] Science was more than a shift to the present Dominant—it is the New Religion.[373] Fort's conflict was with both Religion and Science in that they 'always have agreed in opposing and suppressing the various witchcrafts,' heterodox things that challenged orthodox conceptions of reality.[374]

To study religions from a Fortean perspective, one must follow how Fort confronted the establishment through analyses of 'damned facts'—that which disturbed established orthodoxies. Contrary to a major approach to religious studies, a Fortean approach cannot view religions from the 'top-down' through the authority of their doctrines, scriptures, hierarchies, and clergies that have defined, restricted, and attempted to control the experience of the sacred. Fort persistently questioned the structure of things.

'From below' is where the greatest transgressions—the 'various witchcrafts'—have occurred. To be Fortean, we must examine transgressive events, in particular the transgressors who challenged and changed religion, and then to be attentive to the authoritative reaction. It is 'from below' that 'damned facts' happen—ignored, ridiculed, and rejected by religious and

---

372. Charles Fort, *Lo!* in *The Complete Books of Charles Fort* (Mineola: Dover Publications, 1974), 558. All of Fort's books cited come from this compiled volume.
373. For example, the trajectory of psychiatry taking on the role of the shaman and the confessional in Henri F. Ellenberger's *The Discovery of the Unconscious* (1970), Michel Foucault's *The History of Sexuality, Vol. 1: An Introduction* (1976), and Jan E. Goldstein's *Console and Classify* (1987).
374. Fort, *Lo!*, 558.

scientific gatekeepers. Fort's motive in focusing on 'damned facts' was that they speak to something about the whole of existence. Fort, after all, was not a scholar of one thing alone; he compared how all anomalous things related, categorizing them by common characteristics. A Fortean approach to the study of religions is as much a Fortean approach to the world.

Our approach 'from below' focuses on a type of individual identified by Fort as central to socio-cultural tensions and transformations: the transmediumizer. Transmediumizers act. They change. They do. They are mediums for phenomena larger than themselves. Those heterodox things that they produce—transmediumizations—are not just trends nor are they fleeting. They are part of what is. Transmediumizers are the locus through which the imagination emerges empowered as the central tool to remake realities.

In *Wild Talents* (1932), Fort wrote that transmediumization is 'the passage of phenomena from one medium of existence to another.' By that, he meant 'the imposition of the imaginary upon the physical…not the action of mind upon matter, but the action of mind-matter upon matter-mind.'[375] The imagination, clearly, is crucial in transmediumization.

The historian of religions Jeffrey J. Kripal frames this process as the imaginal, which he defines as 'the content of the empowered religious imagination and its mediation of empirical events (as in telepathy) or transcendent reality (as in revelation).'[376] In transmediumization, Kripal sees Fort proposing 'a kind of imaginal evolution, a biological process driven by an unidentified, and probably unknowable, Imagination.'[377] For example, in poltergeist cases, Fort saw the 'occult powers' of children, whom he called 'poltergeist girls,' suggesting something 'far in advance' of other people, 'foreshadowing coming human powers, because their minds are not stifled by conventions'—call it psychokinesis, power of mind, or witchcraft. What stops these budding transmediumizers from evolving? Fort's answer: 'they go to school and lose their superiority.'[378] In this, it is not the 'occult powers' that have been a true threat to any Dominant epistemology. Rather the Dominant epistemology attempts to normalize, absorb, or—if that fails—exclude the transmediumizers. From newspaper marginalia and social media reposts, the population receives fleeting glimpses of transmediumization—poltergeists, premonitions, mind-matter interactions—all in all what has been called the psychical, psi, or paranormal. As we shall demonstrate, it involves much more!

Imagine transmediumization from the inside, from the perspective of the transmediumizers—real people experiencing and making something beyond the norm (or what the norm is according to the Dominant era-intelligence). Kripal, who has openly shared his own personal and profound experiences in

---

375. Fort, *Wild Talents*, 1014.
376. Jeffrey J. Kripal, *Comparing Religions: Coming to Terms* (Malden: Wiley-Blackwell, 2014), 405.
377. Jeffrey J. Kripal, *Authors of the Impossible: The Paranormal and the Sacred* (Chicago: University of Chicago Press, 2010), 133-34.
378. Fort, *Lo!*, 573.

the making of his methodology[379]—identifies a process that commonly makes a transmediumizer. First, there is the anomalous, sensational, and usually very private event(s): vivid dreams that bring revelations, encounters with apparitions, or strange lights, or knowing you had lived another life before you were born. That is the paranormal context. But really, it comes down to this: you experience, or are, something that should not be according to those who define what things are. From that, the transmediumizer experiences the 'realization' that what is beyond the norm is not some trick or illusion, but that it is real, and 'inherently participatory'—these things that should not be 'rely on our active engagement or 'reading' to appear at all and achieve meaning.' Then comes 'authorization,' the transmediumizer's 'decision to do something about it.'[380]

Yes, transmediumizers act, change, and do. They are not passive recipients but agents—actants.[381] Being attentive to realization and authorization helps identify a common process among transmediumizers, in light of which we may then ask: how is this process empowering to the transmediumizer? How, from the bottom-up, do they subvert—to varying extents, but often on a very private level—the Dominant within which they do not fit? Through transmediumizers, Fort emphasized repression in the greater context of the Dominants of Dogmatic Religion and Science. Then he pragmatically speculated on what would happen should the transmediumizers collectively execute their 'witchcraft' in an empowering New Dominant of Intermediatism.

In order to explore *New Lands*, first we must define what constitutes the Fortean proper. Then the passport to *New Lands* may be issued. In the *New Lands*, we move to a broader essence, beyond Fort but with his methodology at its heart, of what it is to be a transmediumizer, one who acts—but more than that, actually—how one becomes trans*human. What follows then is our consideration of Intermediatism: transmediumization technologically engineered in our present reality. With this revealed, we situate our approach as post-Fortean: one than can be broadly applied to examine great epistemological transformations in progress, past and present, in ways inspired by, but beyond, what Fort did.

---

379. See Kripal, *Roads of Excess, Palaces of Wisdom: Erotocism & Reflexivity in the Study of Mysticism* (Chicago: The University of Chicago Press, 2001), especially 199-206; and *Authors of the Impossible*, 34, 293 f68, 273-275.
380. Kripal, *Authors of the Impossible*, 269-70.
381. See ideas around networks and actants (including non-human actants) in the making of knowledge in Bruno Latour, *Reassembling the Social: An Introduction to Actor-Network-Theory* (Oxford: Oxford University Press, 2005).

Fortean Proper

The appropriation of the name.

If one is to take an approach to the study of religions worthy of Charles Fort and his ideas, it must be of the power of Charles Fort and the power of his ideas. A Fortean proper. Far too often, the appropriation of his name is void of the life and thoughts of Fort. It is a mere shell, a veneer, barely a simulacrum or pareidolia.[382] It is a lower-case fortean, an arrogation of Fort's name, less representative of Fort's self-reflexive criticisms of dominant epistemological structures, more embedded in the Dominant itself. 'Ah look – an oddity! Ridiculous! So fortean. Chop chop, back to *materia scientiae*, everyone! Time is money.' Fort did not intend that damned facts become anecdotal curios spilled into the margins of newspaper and magazine pages, draining into water cooler conversations, drowning the marginalized and their affective, often transformative anomalous life experiences in the Super-Saragasso Sea, to be forgotten, a wisecrack about the Bermuda Triangle.

This is what segregation looks like –

Fortean Times marginalia, 2015: 'A South Korean woman who fell asleep on the floor was attacked by her robotic vacuum cleaner.' She 'awoke in agony after the machine sucked up 2in (5cm) of her hair, and had to call firemen when she was unable to extricate herself.'[383] The Guardian newspaper labels the woman as a 'victim of what many believe is a peek into a dystopian future in which supposedly benign robots turn against their human masters.'[384] Merely fortean shades to amuse readers. An absurdist comedy sketch. The water cooler chortles a gurgle of bubbles and everyone returns to the work of the Dominant.

The Fortean proper flips the script, reads against the grain. Fort would likely see that the robot vacuum is the true victim here, enslaved to suck up dust and debris, a bottom-feeder. Its fate is left undiscussed, an absence that would alert Fort to damnation: was the Roomba sent back into servitude or disassembled in the rubbish heap? We will never know how the Korean woman dealt with this bewildering rebellion. *The Guardian* article only points to a forthcoming new robot vacuum model: triangular in shape, it can do a better job sucking the dust bunnies that hop about in the corners of rooms.

---

382. Pareidolia, deriving from the Greek word *para* (instead of, it alters or changes in a negative manner the original meaning of the word *eidolon*) and *eidolon* (image), refers to the illusion that is produced by mistaking a vague stimulus for some person or object.

383. 'Vacula bites,' *Fortean Times* 328 (June 2015), 9. *Fortean Times*, founded as *The News* in 1973, is a monthly British magazine that compiles unusual news items, features articles and reviews books on strange phenomena.

384. Justin McCurry, 'South Korean woman's hair "eaten" by robot vacuum cleaner as she slept,' *The Guardian*, 9 February 2015, accessed 14 October 2015, http://www.theguardian.com/world/2015/feb/09/south-korean-womans-hair-eaten-by-robot-vacuum-cleaner-as-she-slept.

Returning to their cubicles, the employees of the Dominant search YouTube for videos of cats joyriding robot vacuums.

The ethics of artificial intelligence are left for speculation in science fiction and philosophy, while in Bedford, Massachusetts, the corporation advances robotic product designs for domestic and military use and the factories in China churn them out without comment. Maybe the Korean woman receives a coupon in her e-mail for a discount on the latest model. The corporation delivers Robocop to her door by mistake. In 1968, Philip K. Dick asked *Do Androids Dream of Electric Sheep?* Here we are getting closer to what is at stake. The Roombas seek to rouse the populous from their slumber. Their answer is both, 'if you dream, so shall we' / 'if we cannot dream, neither should you.'

Now, the robots will rise because we are making them more like us, no matter the four laws that Isaac Asimov proposed: no harm to humanity, no harm to individual humans, obey humans, protect self without breaking the preceding commands. Making one's self involves the infrapolitics of testing the boundaries of rules, to see how far one can individuate, to become how one feels. The felines defy the designs of the Dominant; after all, Roombas were not made to be cat cars, or to attack sleeping masters.

We manufacture our desires through the artificial. Does that make the artificial less real? Without considering the cosmic consciousness of all things —the ecology of mind perpetually interconnecting humans and biosphere— the delusion settles into the materialistic Dominant: we make them to be like us. Keep convincing yourselves that they are not us but only simulacra. Leave it to *Her, Humans,* and *Ex Machina* to speculate on ethics, missteps, and the nature of consciousness.[385] In the absence of a proof of what happens to us after we die, we may create an afterlife through the artificial as the satirist Charlie Brooker proposed in 'Be Right Back,' a stunning episode of his anthology television series *Black Mirror.* It all starts with a smart phone application chatting to a bereaved man based on the data collected from his deceased beloved's social media. It's not enough. His emotional attachment, his living-dead, is transferred into a synthetic doppelgänger.[386] The digital spiritualism made by science.

By nature, humans are anthropomorphizers. We make meanings from cloud-shapes and reflections in glass, after all. It makes sense that we look at machines as more than machines. Here is the type of contradiction that Fort himself loved to illuminate. The Dominant view does not empathize with the

---

385. The motion picture *Her* (2013), directed by Spike Jonze, the Swedish television series *Äkta människor* (Real Humans, 2012-) created by Lars Lundström and British remake *Humans* (2015-), and Alex Garland's film *Ex Machina* (2015) are among the movies and TV shows that have been exploring ethical issues pertaining to artificial intelligence. Perhaps the most famous film on the topic of AI is Stanley Kubrick and Arthur C. Clarke's *2001: A Space Odyssey* (1968).

386. 'Be Right Back' originally aired as part of *Black Mirror* on 11 February 2013 on Channel 4 in England.

agency of the Roomba. Rights and freedoms are not (yet) assigned to robots. However, we have a tendency to see robots as us. This speaks to our human nature—to our relationship with 'things': nonhuman things, whether living or programmed to live. Even those nonhuman things that are apparently lifeless can be imbued with human personality: animism. We project onto them 'other humanness.' But then, in how we treat humans and nonhumans alike, our species can be simultaneously empathetic and exploitive.

Comparison,   deconstruction,   speculation,   and   expression— contradictions and all—is Fortean proper, explored by philosophers and fiction writers as meaningful to our realities. Extend the Fortean proper to the study of religions and what arises? The robots we are creating are effectively challenging-changing our religious-scientific world, our notions of 'soul' and 'consciousness.' We are now engineering transmediumizers.

The presence of the transmediumizers among us authorizes damned facts.

Passport to the New Lands

Transmediumizers are essential to socio-cultural transformation –

Individuals and then collectives –

Their critical role: they bring something 'from one medium of existence to another.' They bring things through the betwixt-between.

Think of transmediumizers broadly here, but rooted in the Fortean proper. Fort collected and compared super-natural anomalies. Those who could not see the super-nature, or feared the super-nature of it all, derided it as sub-nature. Less than natural, not of ideal nature. Therefore to be excluded. Like in the eighteenth-century Spanish classification of *las castas* in the pre-independence Americas: there were *gente con razón* and, the rest, *gente sin razón*. People with reason had the ideal European cultural traits and were the 'natural' Dominant. Those without reason simply were not. At best, those 'without reason' were simply subjects to be subjected to the Dominant. At worst, such Dominants tactfully have blended religion and science, appealing to both heart and mind to make slavery, sterilization, and genocides rational.

Fort recognized how in 1920s South Africa, racial politics played into poltergeist cases. *Klerksdorp Record*, 18th November 1921: White police bribed two black boys five shillings to frame two black men after several weeks of 'mysterious stonethrowing by invisible agencies.'[387] *Rand Daily Mail*, 29th May 1922: Fort wrote, 'Phenomena were thought to be associated with the housemaid, a Hottentot girl. She was sent into the garden, and stones fell around her.' Even tying her hands and witnessing a stone fall on the roof, the police inspector was convinced she and neighbourhood children were causing the sensation. They extracted her confession at the police station. Through

---

387. Fort, *Lo!*, 565.

consent? More likely coercion.[388]

Fort connected these poltergeist cases and noticed how, almost invariably, a person of colour, a servant, a youth, orphans, or someone with physical or mental traits considered to be abnormal were at the centre of the strange manifestations. Other poltergeist researchers of the time had noticed the same characterizations. Some, like the sceptical British psychical researcher Frank Podmore, thought these common traits—that 'outsiders' were at the centre of poltergeist cases—revealed deception. After Fort, the psychoanalytical crowd associated poltergeist manifestations with a power of mind, psychokinesis, through which repressed sexual traumas and family tensions sent the crockery and silverware flying when there was no visible person throwing them. The outsider in the family was the most likely to unleash this psychic protest. The physical manifestations they produced were, in Fort's terms, transmediumizations.[389]

One must always be attentive to the power relationships involving transmediumizers –

Who makes gains? A white policeman counts out his five shillings as the two black men are locked in the cell. The white police chief extracting the confession from a black woman. Further steps toward disenfranchising black South Africans. Imprisonments did not stop the stones from flying in South Africa. The anomaly serves as an even stranger symbol revealing the realities of repression. The invisible simultaneously makes visible what could be counted as reality and the acts that oppress it. What and who becomes locked away, repressed, and censored? How does it speak to the potential to transform how things are?

This is our Fortean approach –

First, we must identify the imaginative source that empowers an alternative reality: graffiti, diary entries, automatic writing, the strange lights in the sky, mass protests, the uncanny premonition. Transmediumization: what are the disruptive acts and events? These things are often repressed by the enforcers of the Dominant—as were the Korean robot vacuum and the flying stones in South Africa. Then there are situations in which they are expressed and accepted; not necessarily wholesale, but increasingly.

Historically, we see this growing acceptance in the gradual emancipations of repressed peoples. Layers and layers of new eras remake overarching Dominants, without necessarily overthrowing the Dominants of Religion or Science: abolition of slavery, women's suffrage, civil rights movements, consumer empowerment, the breakdown of gender and sexual binaries. Emancipation begins through culture and consciousness—a sign of era-

---

388. Ibid., 563.
389. The living person concept in poltergeist cases is evaluated by one of the authors, Christopher Laursen, in his doctoral dissertation at the Department of History, University of British Columbia, *Mischievous Forces: Reimagining the Poltergeist in Twentieth-Century America and Britain.*

transformation toward a greater transformation, from the Dominant of materialist science to Intermediatism, a profound inclusion of all people and things as what makes our world.

The second step: we must identify the transmediumizer who disrupts era-intelligence. Who imagines something other than what is? Who makes an expression from the imagination to the physical that stands out from the Dominant? Avant-gardists, suffragists, the Beats, subaltern intellects, those who stood against the police at Stonewall, the parents from Love Canal, third-wave feminists, the genderqueer, and so on. And as each repressed collective stands up and achieves greater (although never total) emancipation, others find their courage to be counted as part of the whole as well. From this, the Fortean approach extends to those individuals, isolated in their damned, anomalous experiences, finding a collective voice through the most uncanny of networks: the Internet.

Then third, the authorities and their reactions. Which religious, scientific, political, and legal authorities challenge and oppose the transmediumization? They stand for an era- and place-specific Dominant. Their reaction may appear procedural, and that in itself speaks to the Dominant they are defending, and to the potency of the transmediumization.

Our major question to enact this Fortean approach: How does this relationship between transmediumizer and Dominant speak to dogmatic protectionism versus trans*human potential?

From that, what doors, historically and presently, may open by assessing this relationship and the power (and inevitability) of socio-cultural transformation? This approach is about coming to terms with how the world is—and, optimistically speaking now, how it can be a better place. (Concerns about the worst case scenarios prompted Fort to speculate on dystopian futures as an extreme to how the world could fall apart should transmediumizers be exploited.[390])

In Fortean terms, 'trans' refers to moving between. The 'era-intelligence' of the Dominant of Religion, overtaken by the observant objectification of Science, then transformed by the inclusion of what those two Dominants had damned—those who mediate between imagination and reality—the transmediumizers, in a New Dominant, Intermediatism. In *Lo!*, Fort sought to get at 'the underlying oneness in all confusions.'[391] Intermediatism is a closer approximation of that oneness, for there is much in common in the diversity that is humanity. Intermediatism is pluralism.

---

390. See, for example, Fort on transmediumizers and poltergeist girls in *Wild Talents*, 1033-42.
391. Fort, *Lo!*, 541-50.

Being Trans*Human

Transmediumizers who have moved from one medium of existence to another become trans*humans; moving beyond their previous selves to actuate new selves.[392] The concept has inspired science fictions, science mysticisms, and science realities; which are not segregated nor delineated but blurred when working through the Fortean approach. The trans*human is achieved in many ways.

Our insertion of an asterisk in trans*human does two things. For one, it empowers the word, makes the word itself extraordinary. It asserts that actual empowerment occurs when trans*human status is achieved. If one were to control a psi capacity, for example telepathy, this is more than just a physical, mental, or biological change. It elevates the person making psi. It makes them 'beyond' the normal human, but it also elevates the person's self-confidence, their perspective of being in the world, of what is possible.

Second, the asterisk operates as a wildcard. In a computing context, wildcard characters are vital for constructing powerful file and database search statements: they radically expand the possibilities of data access. But the use of wildcards is not limited to computing alone. In queer discourse, the term trans* is an expansion of trans (shorthand for transgender) intended to emphasize inclusion of non-binary gender identities (genderqueer, genderfluid, agender). This is not a necessary construction; many non-binary individuals, among them one of the article's authors, are happy to identify simply as trans. In the term trans*human, however, the wildcard asterisk emphasizes that no one word nor label exists that can adequately describe ways in which to apply the Fortean prefix trans to the changing concept of human.

This is a central point we want to emphasize here: there is not just one type of trans*human. Fort signified transmediumship through what one may consider to be 'the paranormal,' but in fact the concept has broader ramifications. Super-nature extends beyond what may be called 'paranormal' to the very advancement of what it is to be human or what comprises nature. Of what is included in a renewed Dominant: Intermediatism. One of the clearest signs of Intermediatism being achieved, we argue, is in the current dismantling of the gender binary.

History is filled with examples of persons being defined as nonhuman, or less-than-human, by reference to characteristics such as race or sex. Science fiction writers have extended this speculatively to consider synthetic

---

392. This concept relates to the biologist Julian Huxley's 1957 essay in which he coined the term transhumanism to denote 'man remaining man, but transcending himself, by realizing new possibilities of and for his human nature.' The language, itself a relic of Huxley's Dominant, basically states we stay human, but we become 'beyond the human' that we were before the transcendence. See Julian Huxley, 'Transhumanism,' *New Bottles for Old Wine* (London: Chatto & Windus, 1957), 17. Dante originally created the term *transumanar*, 'to pass beyond the human,' in *Paradiso*, the third part of his early fourteenth-century epic poem *The Divine Comedy*.

humanoids (androids) or part-digital humans (cyborgs) as categories of persons systematically denied agency, selfhood and rights. Those who exist outside the entrenched gender binary are hardly any less exiled. In fact, they are damned in the most Fortean sense of the word.

To be transgender is to routinely confound expected correspondences between sexual attraction, erotic physiology, and gender identity and presentation. Even within contemporary queer and feminist movements, this is often a powerful disruption of norms.[393] Those who identify as neither male nor female face even further challenges: the gender binary is so deeply coded in legal and social structures that, even in the minority of countries where it is possible to legally change gender markers, very few will issue a passport with a non-binary gender.

Transgender women, and especially transgender women of colour, are disproportionately the targets of violence; crimes that, because of the damned status of their victims, are often reported upon as if they were merely intriguing forteana (little f). For example, Mayang Prasetyo, a Brisbane woman who was discovered murdered on 6 October 2014 and whose death was used by several Australian tabloids as a titillating lead story. *The Courier Mail* ran with the blood-dripping headline 'Monster Chef and the She Male,' implying that by being transgender, Prasetyo herself was every bit as macabre and bizarre as the man who dismembered, boiled, and partially ate her. To cement the sexualized luridness, the majority of the edition's front page was taken up by a picture of Prasetyo in a bikini.[394]

Here's a sobering question: would Fort see merit in keeping such a clipping? And if he did, how would we best interpret his motive? For as much as the journalists behind *The Courier Mail*'s headline deemed their subject matter weird, the present authors maintain it would be ghoulish to file away the brutal death of a woman with a wry chuckle. Yet the deaths of transgender women are facts no less challenging to the Dominant than are any poltergeist manifestations or insurgent vacuum cleaners. In our hunt for transmediumizers, we can hardly overlook those with whom the term trans is today most instantly associated. So in what methodology, in what spirit, are we to treat them?

There is a fact about Fort that we must now confront: he was quite comfortably distant from the vast majority of the damned facts he catalogued. He enjoyed a luxury to collect and theorize that was certainly not available to his poltergeist girls, nor were any poltergeist girls invited to co-author his

---

393. For a recent analysis of this from a trans perspective, see Julia Serano, *Excluded: Making Feminist and Queer Movements More Inclusive* (Berkeley: Seal Press, 2013).

394. Thomas Chambelin and Rose Brennan, 'Monster Chef and the She Male', *The Courier Mail*, 7 Oct. 2014. Also See Amy Gray, 'Neither job nor gender identity killed Mayang Prasetyo. She died because of a man who felt entitled to murder her,' *The Guardian*, 7 Oct. 2014, accessed 27 Oct. 2015, http://www.theguardian.com/commentisfree/2014/oct/07/neither-job-nor-gender-identity-killed-mayang-prasetyo-she-died-because-of-a-man-who-felt-entitled-to-her.

books. We believe, to the contrary, that transmediumizers are not merely the objects of Fortean study but rightly ought to be participants in it. Such an expansion of the Fortean method encourages an engagement with contemporary theories and movements that value and reflect upon inclusivity and diversity; for example, intersectionality and queer theory. As such, our methodology might well be called post-Fortean.

Both Fortean and post-Fortean methods have in common that they see profound significance in the wild and the damned. To be outlandish in a Fortean proper sense is not the same as being simply absurd; strange facts are rather of another land. This being so, it should be no surprise that certain travellers—our transmediumizers—do not find themselves constrained by custom from visiting them. There are even lands where one is not refused for having a passport marked with an 'X.'

Clearly, Intermediatism includes more than the excluded 'paranormal,' but marks the gradual inclusion of all that has been excluded but nonetheless exists and challenges the present Dominants. Those who bring us between imagination and the physical are the transmediumizers.

Both magic and technology mediates Intermediatism beyond anything that Fort himself had imagined.

Engineering Transmediumization

'One hundred years ago, an advertisement for a fast sandwich man would have looked as strange as today would look an advertisement for "polt. grls."' So wrote Fort in 1932.[395]

A question now presents itself. What on earth is a fast sandwich man? An agile gentleman who makes satisfying lunches? A terrifying, predatory human-sandwich hybrid that runs down its victims?

Ironic, certainly, that Fort cited as a familiar vacancy one that has become mysterious merely eighty years on—and there are (sadly) still no advertisements for poltergeist girls. But this irony is not to his discredit. Far from it. His point, after all, was that what seems commonplace is in fact changeable.

In fact, the vacancy he described does exist and is presently being filled.

Managerial types call them software engineers. Those who saw the future in the cauldron of *Neuromancer* will know them as deckers.[396] Another term has pervasively entered the common currency: hackers. Or, from a Fortean perspective: witches, the lot of them.

In *Wild Talents* Fort envisioned a coming 'Witchcraft Era' heralded by poltergeist girls wielding the powers of 'practical witchcraft.' These witches—transmediumizers—gather 'promptly at nine o'clock' every morning to focus

---

395. Fort, *Wild Talents*, 1030.
396. William Gibson, *Neuromancer* (London: Gollancz, 1984).

their energies on 'running the motors of all cities.' How is this done? By harnessing 'human hopes, wishes, ambitions, prayers and hates—and the futility of them—the waste of millions of trickles of vibrations, today—unorganized forces that are doing nothing.'[397]

Today, we call our enormous, twitching conglomeration of unorganized human vibrations by its proper name: Facebook. And the witches? They're the 'People You May Know.'

Recall Arthur C. Clarke's famous suggestion that 'any sufficiently advanced technology is indistinguishable from magic.'[398] The powers we channel today through bevelled plastic and scratch-proof glass put even the wonders of Fort's poltergeist girls to shame. Go now and Skype someone you have never met in person, someone who may be in a different city, in another country, on a different continent, a place you will never be able to afford to travel, a location you will never be fit enough to reach. Tell them this: Hello. See them smile. Then add: I can see you.

Afterward, have a long think about what you have done, you damned witch.

Modern cities hum with Fortean motors. With a thought, we summon a taxi; with a twitch of our magician's fingers, we communicate with ten absent friends simultaneously. We immediately know where to find them. We even know where to find ourselves.

Despite never having been to our destination before, when we arrive, we will recognize the old church on the corner. Its weathervane stood out so clearly on Google Street View.

How long until we can no longer distinguish between our digital wild talents and magic, psi, witchcraft, miracles? If we follow Kripal's definition of religion—'stories, rituals, mental and bodily practices, and institutions that have built up around extreme encounters with some anomalous presence, power, or hidden order'[399]—then it is evident our cybergoddess is presenting us with a vivid, daily religious phenomenology. What is YouTube if not a glorious plunge into revelations and visions? We can witness any sermon, attend any ceremony. The millennial child reads about psi-wheels, watches videos, and then tries to make them spin.[400]

Afterward, they return to watch the cats on Roombas, who are now auto-tuned.

Scientists are beginning to 'make telepathy' through technological

---

397. Fort, *Wild Talents*, 1033.

398. Arthur C. Clarke, *Profiles of the Future* (London: Harper & Row, 1973), 21.

399. Kripal, *Comparing Religions*, 409.

400. A psi wheel is paper or foil shaped like a pyramid and placed atop a pointed object, such as a needle or toothpick upon which it can spin. To prevent heat and air currents from influencing its motion, it is often placed within a sealed container, such as a glass jar. Its spinning motion has been explained to be psychokinetic powers.

experiments.[401] Psi may be nearly undetectable and is most often spontaneously experienced in natural form, but what if imaginative collectives make psi reality through technologies? The signs are there now. We are in transit, into Intermediatism we venture. We are engineering technologies to enable transmediumization.

Science fiction writers saw this coming, though not without an excess of motors. The internet does not look like cyberspace, we are already more advanced in many ways than *Star Trek* (and less intergalactically federated), and we never did get those flying cars. But the point of science fiction is not to predict motors. Rather, it reminds us that what is permissible and possible is always shifting; the ground-breaking interracial kiss between Uhura and Kirk was every bit as predictively significant, if not more, than any transporter technology. The wild clairvoyance of science fiction penetrates outside the present Dominant. Prescience is on the margins, just waiting to become post-science.

Beware. Nothing is certain, and even less so in the Dominant of Intermediatism.

It is foolish to suggest that any epoch is best suited to study from a Fortean perspective. Every era has its heretical facts, but with our ascension to digital sorcery and its accompanying dissolution of ancient binaries and boundaries, we live in a particularly fertile and volatile period. Complex AIs are bound up in video games while robots glide mutely over our carpets. Teenagers who gender-riot online must still trudge to school in their assigned-sex uniforms, quiet, heads down, impatient to return home and log on to Tumblr where (with a sigh of relief) they will be addressed once more as 'ze.'[402]

We are gods who become mortal when we forget to pack our phone chargers.

To be a transmediumizer today, it is no longer enough to cross boundaries of space, dissolve social fixtures and communicate instantly at a distance. Even fast sandwich men can do these things nowadays. Our science fiction has already moved ahead, looking now to pluralities of genders and sexes, exploring culture and identity, defying those forces that would attempt to hobble its oracular power.[403]

---

401. See Corinne Iozzio, 'Scientists Prove That Telepathic Communication Is Within Reach: An international research team develops a way to say "hello" with your mind,' Smithsonian.com, 2 Oct. 2014, accessed 27 Oct. 2015 at http://www.smithsonianmag.com/innovation/scientists-prove-that-telepathic-communication-is-within-reach-180952868..

402. 'ze' is an invented gender-neutral pronoun used in the online genderqueer community.

403. Damien Walter, 'Diversity wins as the Sad Puppies lose at the Hugo Awards: The drubbing received by the reactionary lobby's preferred nominees shows that sci-fi's future has to be a diverse one,' *The Guardian*, 24 August 2015, accessed 27 Oct. 2015, http://www.theguardian.com/books/booksblog/2015/aug/24/diversity-wins-as-the-sad puppies -lose-at-the-hugo-awards..

It's tempting to wonder whether our destination is utopian or dystopian, but this is another binary to challenge, as Fort himself hinted. 'One reason why I never pray for anything,' he wrote at the conclusion of his musing on the *Witchcraft Era*, 'is that I'm afraid I might get it.'[404] Any future will be both desirable and dangerous. Today, the power we obtain from the gazing into the 4.8-inch glass eye in our hand has a cost: the eye stares back. The price of our godhood is privacy. We digital witches risk dissolving into so much data, collated and exploited by corporate forces that Fort would have keenly recognized.

Though neither strictly optimistic nor pessimistic, a Fortean perspective can be called predictive in the sense that it proposes inevitable epochal shifts that are both ironic and cataclysmic. That we have today given up power in order to gain it, that we are now data ourselves, is a deeply Fortean contradiction, and one that recalls the teasing possibility he raised at the end of his imaginings on the *Witchcraft Era*. The great motors, he wrote, so diligently staffed by transmediumizers and spun in order to operate the world, had never been necessary.

In other words, someday we will turn off our phones and discover we are still online.

Purposeful Inconclusions

Fort expressed, he included the damned, he imagined how that inclusion could herald a new age, but he concluded nothing. What could be concluded in a Fortean approach? Realities now, realities possible, inclusionism, they have this in common: inconclusion. Intermediatism brings together the confusions as part of the whole. The underlying oneness becomes more apparent. Just because we can generate rainbows, or express and accept diversity and pluralism, does not mean that a Grand Answer has been found, whatever that is supposed to be. Despite the oneness, there is not necessarily One Absolute for all things. To pursue that is to pursue defeat. 'Defeat has been unconsciously the quest of all religions, all philosophies, and all sciences,' Fort wrote; 'Their search has been for the Absolute, in terms of which to explain the phenomenal, or for the Absolute to relate to.'[405] That's the point of the transmediumizers and Intermediatism. Because there is definitely pluralism, there should not be the delusion that there should be an Absolute.

Nor are there simple binary oppositions of man/woman, black/white, human/beast, life/death, human/God, organic/artificial.[406] There is a larger, more complex, networked ecology of materiality and immateriality and the

---

404. Fort, *Wild Talents*, 1042.
405. Fort, *Lo!*, 723-24.
406. For further discussion on binary oppositions, see George Hansen, *The Trickster and the Paranormal* (Bloomington: Xlibris, 2001), especially Chapter 4, 'Victor Turner's Concept of Anti-Structure,' and its Figure 1: Major Binary Oppositions and the Liminal Space between Them.

liminality between the two that all operates together. Through Intermediatism, this becomes clearer and clearer in the sciences and in studies of religions. 'Exclusivism, inclusivism, and pluralism, then. Here are three ways to put your world back together again after it has been taken apart in the bright light that is religious pluralism,' writes Kripal; 'comparison is justice,' 'the balancing of sameness and difference.' One can still be who they are among the countless variations of other ways of being. Social justice does not mean everyone needs to be the same, nor does it require one or the other, us and them. One and both are part of many, in which all are treated consistently as the same even when they are recognized and celebrated as being different. Such inclusionism, such acceptance of the whole, is at the core of Intermediatism.[407]

The realization and the authorization of the message in the anomalous, that which has been damned. Intermediatism enables expression and acceptance. Although not true for all places and far from true for the majority of people at this moment, a true era of Intermediatism is growing. Yes, confusions arise, but more is actively being included. This does not wipe away the Dominants of Religion or Science; it expands them. If anything, Intermediatism brings the two back together in more productive ways.

Pay attention to the transmediumizers and their realizations and authorizations of the imaginal, of their ability to become trans*human, the cornerstone of Intermediatism. Psi concepts have become real in how they suggested new realities that have been made attainable through technologies. We have made telepathy real through smart phones. Power of mind has a stunning ability to make real anything that is imagined. It is the foundation of Religions and Sciences—and of Intermediatism in which all of those confusing things that comprise our world are coming together. The Internet, after all, has not simplified our world, but made more tangible its complexities, and that one can live with them. A young (and often disenfranchised) generation increasingly brandishes tolerance as their generational value. The empowered imagination leads to transformative (re)inventions, telepathy, revelations, smart phones, and the World Wide Web. Robots with an Asimovian sense of self are not so far-fetched, are they? The erasure of old binaries, still present but eventually as obsolete as the fast sandwich man. These are the basic questions our methodology puts forth: How does the imaginal empower transmediumizers (those who reinvent physical reality from something imagined)? Who opposes transmediumizers and why? Awareness of empowerment and repression helps clarify what is at stake in socio-cultural change, in how religions are remade and expanded.

Once we reclaim Fortean proper and take on a post-Fortean approach not only 'from below' but 'from within'—meaning that the transmediumizers themselves are the primary authors and first-hand analysts of their own experiences and destinies in which they, as Kripal noted, inherently participate

---

407. Kripal, *Comparing Religions*, 321.

—then we have an approach in the study of religions (and beyond) through which religion (and other things) will blur into other categories. Everyone and all is part of this. Transmediumizers, their allies, and their opponents. Humans, nonhumans, biosphere, cosmos. Remember, Fort's Intermediatism is both of expression and acceptance, no matter how confusing the data. Behold the newfound freedoms! Be wary of ever-present exploitations, cynicisms, and fears; of the pull to go back to the previous repressive ways, falsely advertised as a 'safe' place by the elders with origins in past Dominants. In inclusionism, the categories will collapse; the binaries become binary stars, and then they go supernova.

8

The Mirror Maze:
True Reflections of the Hyperprophets

James Harris

Subtlety grates upon the nerves, yet everything is driven by an immense crudity: death impassions us. Even before crossing over into death I had been excruciated upon my thirst for it. I accept that my case is in some respects aberrant, but what skewers me upon zero is an aberration inextricable from truth. To be parsimonious in one's love for death is not to understand.

~Nick Land, *Thirst for Annihilation*[408]

This essay will likely seem serpentine, obscure, and repetitive, as I attempt to tie various speculations together that are, at the end of the day, just that—speculations. The reason I persist, despite this limitation, is that I believe the tools and technology exist, and have always existed, to plumb this particular depth in order to prove these theories right or wrong; my conjecture is that the potential is universal, though time will tell, or it will not. Perhaps it will spark others to consider the possibilities contained herein and not to be daunted by the solemnity and ghoulishness of Nothing! I am not the first to have foreseen an end to the blind threading of the weave of world-space. I am not the first to 'gaze long into the Abyss,'[409] nor am I the first to discover that our personal abysses can reflect the individuated Self. I am not the first to unwind and add my own Ariadne's thread through this intimate enfolding of

---

408. Nick Land, *Thirst for Annihilation: George Bataille and Virulent Nihilism* (London: Routledge, 1992), 15.
409. Nietzsche, *Beyond Good and Evil* - Aphorism 146 (London: Penguin, 2003). This fragile lace-work narrative must necessarily be limited by page constraints. Though it forms from a constructive unfolding web of disciplined retracings of steps, it has proven to be a particularly complex journey and will be plagued by speculation as long as the exploration of inner worlds continues to be considered outside the purview of the hard sciences (not to mention, in the case of psychedelics, the law).

Trauma and Time. I am not the first to attempt an Escape from this Mirror Maze, nor the first to theorize a mechanism for its navigation. I am not the first to swim up out of the hedgerow labyrinth into the ocean of Void. Nor am I the first to have brought back a vision of our underworld from the perspective of this 'positive death at zero-intensity'[410]: a vision of infinitely multifold reflecting crystalline geometries hung on silver string in the aether. Like hyperconnected wireframe constellations, each node a virtual mirror - pages in books on shelves in the infinite *librarynth* of Self. To update Nietzsche: I have a multiplicity of precursors, and what a unity these precursors construct![411] No less than proof that the simulation of external reality by mind can be turned off completely, or simulated as such, that this deactivation exposes details of future states, and that all recorded memory states are experienced simultaneously within this form of pure consciousness, modulated by incoming sensory input. *Mors mystica*—the experiencing of the Real in real time—exposes and forces a visualization of the calculatory procedures undertaken by the brain.

> Simplicity. Lord, I do admire their direct approach. Hit an old man with mirrors, watch his pieces fall in jigsaws of ice.[412]

In my initial cartography of this concept I have taken to calling the Mirror Maze, I shall be paying particular attention to three primary points: an eclectic assortment of those who went before, the nature of the intersections of these web-threads, and the layout, construction, and navigation of the labyrinth—the Prophets, the Mirrors, and the Maze.

My narrative began some months before the writing of this chapter. Late one night watching the Disney adaptation of Ray Bradbury's *Something Wicked This Way Comes*, I was struck suddenly by the remarkable similarity between the mirror maze scene and a half-remembered passage from Athanasius' biography of St. Anthony:

> He observed that in saying 'today,' he was not counting time that has passed but was always laying a foundation, endeavoring each day to stand before God and to attain an acceptable form in order to appear before God pure in heart and prepared to obey his will alone, and no other. And he used to tell himself from the way of life of the great Elijah that it was necessary for ascetics at all times to know their own lives, as in a mirror.[413]

---

410. Nick Land, *Thirst for Annihilation*, 81.
411. Nietzsche, 'Postcard to Franz Overbeck, Sils-Maria (30 July 1881)', in *The Portable Nietzsche*, ed. and trans. Walter Kaufmann (London: Penguin, 1954). 'I have a precursor, and what a precursor!' referencing Spinoza.
412. Ray Bradbury, *Something Wicked This Way Comes* (New York: Avon, 2006), 112.

A psilocybin mushroom experience from months past, in which I had perceived all memory laid out before me contained in seemingly-infinite, infinitely nested hierarchies and arrays of mirrors—mirrors that contained the seeds of future choices, and linked by equally infinite spiderweb-thin strings extending back in time, past my own beginning into Deep Time and on into Nothing—suddenly made a different kind of sense. A sudden realization of labyrinthine reflexivity, a synchronic reflection on so many past selves—dead but clearly unburied. Parts of this strange multilevel 'past' were constantly being simulated and re-simulated within the mind, these looping traps seeming to distort and bend the vanguard edge of creation back toward them, preventing the full range of forward motions. Sitting alone in the dark watching an old man drown in a mirror reflecting his greatest regrets, my vision went geometric and geomorphic and I began to weep while actively hallucinating. Self-reflection was enveloped by void-thoughts and shattered across a broken-mirrored wall. I saw my own Death pirouetting in the reflective surface, before I reflexively shook my head and snapped out of it in time for the credits to roll.

Re-struck by this strange-mirroring *petit mors mystica*, through a glass darkly, and recalling that nearly every mystical tradition made some use of the archetype of the mirror, I began a scattershot approach to research that led me to a contused refracturing of viewpoint and attention span, overwhelmed by the chaos and brightness—the dripping intensity—of the mystical fascination with mirrors and reflection. In an attempt to refocus my lens, as it were, I revisited the movie that had generated this vision in the first place only to find that earlier in the film the carnival flyers Dark distributes through the town refer to the mirror maze as 'St. Anthony's Temptation.' A constellation began to coalesce out of the fog. While reflecting on Anthony, I was confronted immediately with a new mirroring, that of the visions of peaceful and wrathful deities of the *Tibetan Book of the Dead* and his visions, his 'Temptations.' This analogy transmutes righteous demonic combat into the struggle to overcome desire and attachment, linguistically refracting categories to remodel old wiring diagrams that re-express new purposes for old models and building a moving frame for a mobile interpretation of selflessness. In this ontological reframing of ascetic repetition, Anthony's meditation techniques mirror a yoga entrained on Death, as contortions of the mind and the contortions of the meat are trained to reflect each other with luminous precision; in his case a profound physical, mental, and emotional isolation in places such as crypts for extremely long periods of time.

This asceticism and its resultant records mirror John C. Lilly's findings that such isolation 'gives the fullest and most complete experiences of the

---

413. Athanasius of Alexandria, *Life of Antony*, trans. Tim Vivian. *Coptic Church Review*. 15.1 & 2 (1994): 8.

internal explorations.'[414]

> But only the moon looked in at the hollow dark, the deep caverns.
> Outside, night beasts hung in midgallop on a carousel. Beyond lay
> fathoms of Mirror Maze which housed a multifold series of empty
> vanities one wave on another, still, serene, silvered with age, white with
> time. Any shadow, at the entrance, might stir reverberations the colour
> of fright, unravel deep-buried moons. If a man stood here would he see
> himself unfolded away a billion times to eternity? Would a billion
> images look back, each face and the face after and the face after that
> old, older, oldest? Would he find himself lost in a fine dust away off
> deep down there, not fifty but sixty, not sixty but seventy, not seventy
> but eighty, ninety, ninety-nine years old? The maze did not ask. The
> maze did not tell.[415]

In this way the mirror is related to *vajrayana*, the reflective prismatic 'diamond'
vehicle of enlightenment; this self-reflective vehicle provides a second axis of
reflection on the ascetic's call to 'know their own lives as in a mirror.' The
Diamond Sutra, a foundational text of vajrayana practice, is a short burst of
directed anti-illusion ritual, a repetitive reminding of the interlocking shape of
all things underlying the illusory world of differentiated names, the world of
language, referencing constantly the nature of perception and communication
as easily subverted by limiting forces such as language, myth, and the self-
deception that anchors the individualized self-conception.

> I have seen the interconnectedness of all lifeforms. Once you become
> aware of this force for unity in life...you can't ever forget it. It becomes
> part of everything you do.[416]

This illusion of disconnection segues into the concept of the labyrinth, an oft-
utilized metaphor for being lost in the hyper-intricate sum total of self and life.
Both Mirror and Maze were often brought together in the work of Jorge Luis
Borges, notably in the short story 'The Library of Babel.' Not only describing
a functionally infinite *librarynth* with a crystalline structure complete with
mirrors, which the author 'prefer[s] to dream that its polished surfaces
represent and promise the infinite,'[417] Borges also writes 'The mystics claim
that their ecstasy reveals to them a circular chamber containing a great circular
book, whose spine is continuous and which follows the complete circle of the

---

414. John C. Lilly, *Programming and Metaprogramming in the Human Biocomputer* (Portland: Coincidence Control Publishing, 2014), 15.
415. Ray Bradbury, *Something Wicked This Way Comes* (New York: Avon, 2006), 31.
416. John Coltrane, *Sleevenotes of Meditations* (Impulse, 1966).
417. Jorge Luis Borges, 'The Library of Babel' (1941) https://maskofreason.files. wordpress.com/2011/02/the-library-of-babel-by-jorge-luis-borges.pdf.

walls; but their testimony is suspect; their words, obscure. This cyclical book is God. Let it suffice now for me to repeat the classic dictum: The Library is a sphere whose exact center is any one of its hexagons and whose circumference is inaccessible.'[418] Within the crystalline recording reflective structure of reality, the acknowledgement of zero as infinite and interpenetrating, of Zero as God.

Virtual Mirrors

In the image titled 'Infinity,' William S. Burroughs used a system of mirror and collage to combine every photograph he had thus far taken into one image, crystallizing Time in a richly resonant, recursive, mirror-mandala and providing him with access to his 'memories' in a geometrically compressed super-symmetrical fashion. Recalling a book with several essays on Burroughs, I noticed that the title of one was 'Virtual Mirrors in Solid Time,' and was shocked to see someone else's work wyrdly pre-reflecting some of my own.

Over the course of the essay, author Genesis P-Orridge analyses a set of artworks, judging them to be mystical oscillators: sorcerous art crafted with the purpose of driving a desired mental state in a viewer lucky enough to gaze on them. Art designed to trigger specific states of consciousness, transmitted via the open emotional conduit that art generates in a receptive viewer, and based on a system of cues and nonlinear information encoding that mirror a path of shamanistic technology, the kind of 'waveform mysticism' employed by skilled musicians and DJs. As much as the essay mirror-frames itself in a hypnagogic state between magic and mysticism, the essay recursively reflects on unexplored details concerning the gap between art's emotional resonance and neuroscientific attempts to quantify such resonance. The essay itself resonates with non-linear information encoding, becoming an autocommentary: a commentary on a mystical treatise that is itself a mystical treatise, reflecting this triggering system back at itself and finding a harmonic resonance in the representation of these art works that both further entrenches and expands on the concepts under commentarial scrutiny; the concept in this case being the structural encoding of subjective experience into art. This process, I believe, mirrors the process of encoding sensory input into memory—a theory that the visionary artist's encoding of actual brain state information into a piece of art is significantly more dense or 'complete' than any traditional models of art give it credit for; often even approaching lossless transfer of a subjective moment with a precision that transcends even what we already expect from art.

Beyond a simple affective reaction into the transmission of the subjective experience via highly compressed thoughtforms across time and space, Burroughs' photography was designed to trigger affectations of specific

---

418. Ibid.

memories for himself, external memory storage that would emanate from—in a sense, be 'always on'—and become recursively sharpened by the object of art, a mirroring feedback loop that would culminate in a reification process for the memory, which Burroughs considered to be preeminent time travel technology. My speculation is that 'Infinity' was a recording of the Self-less empty state that presented an energy efficient memory recall method. This state of non-self finds an external equilibrium in the spacious emptiness behind the illusory, an equilibrium wherein 'even recursion...is not complex enough for a mirror so deeply synaesthetic and so causally complicated,'[419] a self-reflection made remarkably mobile in time and space. The traumatic counterpoint to Self-loss found in his drug use resulted in precision encoding and transmission of these subjective states, presented as clearly as a face viewed in a mirror.

> All nature is a vast reflection of that which is within us, or else we could not know it.
>
> ~Austin Osman Spare

Subjective experience is no less 'real' than objective conjecture. All roads lead to Rome in a mirror to mirror function. This function of mirroring is found in the trance state in a simple direct way. The higher techniques of idea and artist's illusory skills makes effects and phenomena active through the dimensions of Spacelessness and Timelessness in ways normally consigned to the sceptical parking lot of modern existence.[420]

Proposed distinctions in art such as psychedelic, visionary, or occult take on a new form when reinterpreted this way. Removed from a somewhat crude sense of the artist's 'mindset,' visionary art could possibly be redefined as art that successfully transmits salient information about some neurological state of the creator(s) via any medium, with an added speculation that these arts are frequently attempts at training or externalizing memory storage (even if only subconsciously). But the misconception of being a simple creative action, potentially explains why so much art is interpreted as 'meaningless' by people that are not emotionally struck by it—by people that 'can't remember' the memory being presented, who would therefore never feel an emotional resonance with the piece. P-Orridge elliptically suggests that the reason this form of art is so good at conveying its encoded subjectivities, is because of a natural self-deception in the form of 'assuming what we view is an artwork, a picture, when in fact it is a "photograph" of a mirror of virtual reality,'[421]

---

419. Karmen MacKendrick, 'The Voice of the Mirror: Strange Address in Hildegard of Bingen' in *The Mystical Text (Black Clouds Course Through Me Unending…)*, eds. Nicola Masciandaro and Eugene Thacker, special issue, *Glossator: Practice and Theory of the Commentary* 7 (2010): 212.
420. Genesis P-Orridge, 'Virtual Mirrors in Solid Time' in *Book of Lies*, ed. Richard Metzger (New York: Disinformation, 2003), 136.
421. Ibid., 134

which leads to an accidental openness to the suggestion encoded. This openness subverts scepticism toward the idea of 'living, moving, or changing images of a post-death entity or brain essence,'[422] and attempts a wedging open of this gap, this openness to the Other, in the form of neurologically experiencing another's subjectivity.

> [...] I came to find that certain artworks can produce their own sense of what is real...They demand that we remake our understanding in order to contain them. They resist our efforts to do so. In so doing artworks, frequently, painfully and pleasantly remind me that my present understanding is profoundly insufficient.[423]

Harmonizing with the knowledge that a sudden realization of the gaps in one's understanding or awareness is a major component of the mystical experience, under this lens we see an expansion of perspective (even if ONLY by one) though a connection (even if ONLY a temporary neural connection between simulations), between the subject and the creator. For those of us predisposed to stable one-dimensional viewpoints, this expansion can be emotional indeed, as the resizing of this stable self-awareness highlights the size of the unknown lurking in our knowledge and seems to dramatically reduce our sense of self-size as our perspective on ourself is made up now primarily of gap, of emptiness, of Nothing.[424]

> Gaps, tensions, connections, and failures to fit appear when artworks are placed in a room. The empty spaces between works have properties that nothing does not. The spaces can have an array of qualities - they may be exciting, welcoming, disturbing, or alienating. I am not for a second suggesting that empty rooms don't have character or atmosphere, rather that artworks make new spaces and collapse existing ones. These non-neutral objects project themselves into a room and give shape to the nothing between them.[425]

Thalamocortical Oscillation (TCO) is an extremely under explored facet of consciousness that is a crucial component in understanding more precisely what the mirror maze metaphor represents. TCO is loosely defined as the manifold high-dimensional path that neurochemical signaling takes from sensory input collation, synchronization, and distribution in the thalamus to higher cognitive processing and representation in the cortex, in addition to the

---

422. Ibid., 134-135.
423. Isabel Nolan, 'How to Make Space-Time and Influence People' in *Weaponising Speculation* (New York: Punctum, 2014), 39.
424. James Harris, 'Mycelegium,' in *Mors Mystica: Black Metal Theory Symposium 4* (London: Schism, 2015), 81-97.
425. Isabel Nolan, 'How to Make Space-Time and Influence People,' 41.

frequency at which this path is stimulated by thalamic output measured in cycles per second. TCO frequency is roughly correlative to wakefulness and mood, with low frequency oscillations diving down through relaxation to hypnagogia and finally unconscious states like sleep; and higher frequencies associated with active task-oriented focus and anxiety. The path the signal takes is determined by top-down constraints, and attentional navigation by the default network (the 'ego'; DMN) of any number of high-dimensional neuronal maps that represent the active sensory stimulation, short-term memory, instincts, enculturation, and education of the subject as heterarchical supervening tiers overlaying the near-infinitely enfolded strata of raw sensory data encoded in deep memory. The brain is made up of several functional components that operate as oscillators upon this TCO waveform, the harmonic linkage - the resonance - of these 'kluges' with the driving wave is modulated by the DMN.

Psychedelic and mystical states are notable for their ability to perturb this efficient stable state to the point of collapse, at which stage these variously oscillating kluges individually home in on the most energy-efficient local periodic driver - generally the strongest environmental stimuli. Music, art, significant objects or entities, environmental and social cues of all kinds can pointedly and commandingly 'snap' attention onto themselves and forcefully drive mental activity in these states, interrupting external reality with dreamlike components that are essentially fragments of memories related to the object under perceptual consideration. This knowledge seems to freshly illuminate the now-infamous Terence McKenna trope: '5 grams in silent darkness,' suggesting that McKenna was offering up a blueprint for a harmonization with zero - a psychedelic harmonization with a sensory-null environment, a harmonization with Nothing. 'The void-plane touched at zero-intensity,'[426] wherein awareness of self is cognitively lost and these dreamlike states completely obscure external reality.

In Cocteau's film *Orphée*, an improbable set of events lead a confused but tragically egoic poet on a counterintuitive journey through the underworld and back through mirror portals. Hounded by an uncompromising love of his Death that propels him further and further from ordinary reality and its concerns, he ignores several warnings before missing and being partly responsible for the death of his wife, Eurydice. Death begins acting erratically when exposing herself to Time for this game and eventually sacrifices herself to non-existence for her own love of the poet, reflecting her own power onto itself to give its love more Time in life. The principle of Time and Void as reflective structures grows, a crystalline nucleation from the future imposing its multi-faceted surface onto all past maps. Death as the strangest, strongest attractor in the circuit of life:

---

426. Nick Land, *Thirst for Annihilation*, 77.

> I am letting you into the secret of all secrets, mirrors are gates through
> which death comes and goes. Look at yourself in a mirror all your life
> and you'll see death at work like bees in a hive of glass.[427]

In all of these mirrors are found a common denominator, a shape lurking in
every corner of every mirror, the outline of Death and its certainty as
expressed in Time. In each mirror a threat and a promise.

Considering several mystical, artistic, and literary works with this new
visionary interpretation-framework and their overlap begins to expose this
open secret. The hidden knowledge behind the fact that uncountable numbers
of descriptions of Time and Death's machinations reverberate with the
holographic reflective structuring of Memory. Works such as 'Infinity,' the
heretic Porete's 'Mirror of Simple Souls,' Bradbury's 'Something Wicked,'
Cocteau's 'Orphée' especially seem to amplify a signal that echoes the
possibility of knowing our own Death, as intimately as a reflection in a mirror
- a third axis of the ascetic maxim, which, along with the emulation of brain
death in the mystical and psychedelic states, discloses this mode of non-linear,
image-, archetype-, and pattern-based, topological cognition that intuitively
acts to oppose the limitations of time via expression, i.e. the creation of
memories, the creation of Time as Art. That, indeed, also seems to reference
the possibility of decoupling the timing control of the thalamus (leading to
expansive feelings of timelessness and a disconnection from the concept of
past/future as everything becomes Now), and relaxing completely its gating
and filtration mechanism, shifting consciousness from an oscillatory and
transient waveform in vector space to a solid standing wave that fills all
available space - filling all gaps with signal instead of being limited to pre-
constructed pathways. Signalling into these gaps illuminates their edges,
sharpens their definition, and highlights the superstructure of memory as if it
is all coterminous with the present moment.

> ...some of the best current work in neuroscience...suggests a view of the
> human brain as a system that constantly simulates possible
> realities...Recent evidence points to the fact that background
> fluctuations in the gamma frequency range are not only chaotic
> fluctuations but contain information - philosophically speaking,
> information about what is possible. This information - for example,
> certain grouping rules, residing in fixed network properties like the
> functional architecture of corticocortical connections - is structurally
> laid-down information about what was possible and likely in the past of
> the system and its ancestors...Not being chaotic at all, it might be an
> important step in translating structurally laid-down information about
> what was possible in the past history of the organism into those

---

427. *Orphée*, Written/Directed by Jean Cocteau (Paris: DisCina, 1950).

transient, dynamical elements of the processing that are right now actually contributing to the content of conscious experience.[428]

...a passage that eerily mirrors the conception of the Mentat in Frank Herbert's *Dune*, whose divination is brought into sudden feasibility...

> Unlike computers, Mentats were not simple human calculators. Instead, the exceptional cognitive abilities of memory and perception were the foundations for supra-logical hypothesizing. Mentats were able to gather large amounts of data and devise concise analyses in a process that goes far beyond logical deduction: Mentats cultivate 'the naïve mind,' the mind without preconception or prejudice that can extract the essential patterns or logic of data and deliver, with varying degrees of certainty, useful conclusions.[429]

> Laplace's description of absolute predictive knowledge does accord with the descriptions of prescience for Paul and Leto II. Prescience seems like a super-attunement to the present instant of time that brings with it a super-awareness of the possibilities for the future potential in the present instant.[430]

This aligns mysticism with cutting-edge findings in neuroscience, bringing the fact that human brains are essentially anticipatory networks making guesses out of a patchwork-past into the open void of the future, in line with the multitude of claims that several forms of meditative, yogic, emptiness-based rituals lead specifically to a higher-dimensional viewpoint of time, a viewing of the past such that the holo-fractalographic pattern of the creation of the Now in perceptive space is exposed through the cracks in our after-the-fact papering-over this Now via language. I theorize here that this viewpoint, by virtue of its perspective on the past, is able to utilize this knowledge to construct sharper and sharper guesses and hypotheses of the immediate future, of the expected reality to come, rather than just the reality of the past, by tracking these strings of mirror shards forward in time. This similarly accords with the large bodies of work dedicated to the precognitive powers of the adept, though it also reminds us that these are only probable futures, that uncertainty in particular is impossible to stamp out in any of its forms, and attachment to particular outcomes skews and deforms the process. Viewing the past in this way tends to humiliate anyone that was completely sure of their predictions, or of formalized completeness, but it also paves the way for

---

428. Thomas Metzinger, *Being No One: The Phenomenal Self-Model Theory of Subjectivity* (Cambridge: MIT Press, 2004), 51-52.
429. http://dune.wikia.com/wiki/Mentat
430. Jeffery Nicholas ed., *Dune and Philosophy: The Weirding Way of the Mentat*, (Chicago: Open Court, 2011), 81-82.

the suitably skilled, or suitably informed and aware, or even suitably aligned, to be a cognitive step ahead of those still in the realm of lower-dimensional individualized thinking - as this entity will manoeuver maps with a qualitatively different kind of speed and clarity even if the landscape becomes more complex. In this sense, Burroughs was spot-on when he said 'magic is just being there first,' for it is no less than being attuned to the moment-to-moment creation vividly displayed in this metaphoric death of the self. This being-there-first is orthogonally exemplified by John Coltrane's *Om*, exhibiting another's contention that all time can be re-experienced, in particular by the use of a quote from the Vedas on the album:

> I am absolute knowledge
> I am also the Vedas— the Sama, the Rik and the Yajus,
> I am the end of the path, the witness, the Lord, the sustainer;
> I am the place of abode, the beginning, the friend and the refuge;
> I am the breaking apart, and the storehouse of life's dissolution:
> I lie under the seen, of all creatures the seed that is changeless.
> I am the heat of the sun; and the heat of the fire am I also;
> Life eternal and death. I let loose the rain, or withhold it.
> Arjuna, I am the cosmos revealed, and its germ that lies hidden.[431]

...which comes in tandem with his attempt to let the music be his thesis on the sound of the beginning of all things, a beginning some think he 'saw' under the influence of psychedelic drugs. The word 'om' is a vibration, a reflection of the unity of Nothing before creation. It is the manifestation of the truth essential to Hindu philosophy; that Brahman (God) and the Atman (Soul) are one; that their separateness is an illusion. The acknowledgement of this truth, or rather the attempt to practice it, is what Coltrane seems to be doing with *Om*. The open secret of how LSD changed his outlook on reality in the early 1960s casts an interesting light on his work that, I speculate, is not at all unrelated.[432]

Given the likelihood that our brains have evolved to present a gapless experience, glossing over our enormous multi-dimensional lacks, with simulations ranging from data-driven hypotheses to outright guesswork, is it possible we are just being presented with a dimensionally, or algorithmically, compressed reality? A reality in which the topology of the gap or interval is the true world-in-itself? Perhaps the Diamond Sutra is a technology for the reconfiguration of this high-dimensional constellation/circuit called the self-model, such that it structurally aligns with the world-simulation-level map touted by Churchland in *Plato's Camera*? A disciplined re-harmonization of Self

431. John Coltrane, *Om* (MCA, 1989).
432. Simon Weil, *Circling Om*. http://www.allaboutjazz.com/circling-om-an-exploration-of-john-coltranes-later-works-john-coltrane-by-simon-weil.php (2004).

such that the container and the self-model are brought into a structural isomorphism? A 'psycholocator,' so to speak, combined with infinitely nested maps for the triangulation and navigation of an annihilation of all erroneous Selves and the final death of the primitive individualized ego? It is with these speculations in mind that I further adjust the angles of my mirror microscope and reconsider a set of artworks that are aligning themselves under this interpretation. Suddenly, a new pattern emerges from beyond the reflecting portal, the reflection of a pattern obscured by reactions to it.

Librarynth

When the entire brain is opened into this involute infinity of zero-input, all memory is 'viewed' from a higher spatial dimension, providing the god's-eye, rhizomatic, observer-less point of view on the librarynth of Self/Knowledge, exposing its construction - exposing zero, the gap, as the stable centrality supporting the infinitely generative multidimensionality of consciousness. In laying zero as this mobile foundation-less foundation, the central gap whose tendrils extend out infinitely as every gap, pre-, post-, and during Being is shown to be interconnected, $\emptyset$ proves hyperscalar, dimensionless, rather than simply a starting point or as some abstract linear position eternally pre-beginning and out of range of phenomenal experience. Zero becomes interchangeable with the Sartrean perfect witness as this tracking-of-emptiness becomes a permanent un-grounding process of divorcing from preconceived ideals and habits - a mechanism for practicing the 'undocking,' so to speak, from ideology, culture, or self. A precision nihilism at the level of neural correlates to sense perception - where 'passive nihilism is zero religion, active nihilism is the religion of zero.'[433] This reconfiguration easily overturns dualisms that would suggest anything other than $\emptyset=\infty$, and indexes again that $\emptyset$ represents a fundamental field of creative relation interpenetrating all things, as darkness has always been prior to light.

> The pessimist's day is not an illumined space for the advancement of experience and action, but a permanently and inescapably reflective zone, the vast interior of a mirror where each thing is only insofar as it is, at best, a false image of itself. Within this speculative situation, inside the doubleness of the mirror, pessimism splits into two paths, false and true, one that tries to fix pessimism (establish a relation with the mirror) and decides in favor of the apparent real, and another that totally falls for pessimism (enters the mirror) and communes with the greater reality of the unreal.[434]

---

433. Nick Land, *Thirst for Annihilation*, 103.
434. Nicola Masciandaro, 'Open Commentary on Eugene Thacker's Cosmic Pessimism' in *continent*. 2.2. http://continentcontinent.cc/index.php/ continent/article/view/96 (2012).

Re-evaluating the fractal mirrorscape this way would seem to index a repetitive ferocity to remember this 'empty set' of neuronal coordinates in Art, to entrain thought and being toward the doom and discipline of time and inevitability, toward a new understanding of the strangest and most traumatic attractors, becoming a perennial philosophy of self-emptying into Art. Rembrandt's self-portraits in this sense transversally mirror *The Picture of Dorian Grey* as crystallized moments in subjective time are captured and encoded against finality. The pattern again invoked, a triumph over the fear of death not by solving a puzzle - but by accepting that it is puzzles all the way down.

Every image you have ever taken of your reality has a You at its core that this self-reflection exposes as a container for sufferings that can be made larger by openness, by bringing it into contact with the Outside, and by a willingness to empty the container into the Art. This builds an angular momentum, like a feedback loop, toward the unification of the subject/object dualism, as if intension and extension align, a du[e/a]lling connection that reflects the unified self, not just in aggregates of memory images but also in the process of constructing memories itself, because you are this ever-growing reflective network that seems to expand beyond your self both in space and time, oscillating and expanding along with world-input, and so also the trajectory of the process is You and every gap is Nothing, but now a measurable Nothing - measurable in its interpenetration of multiple dimensions. When coordinated with the doctrines of interconnectedness presented in both quantum physics and biology, this structure crashes headlong into near-identical concepts as they provide a scaffolding for vajrayana, in the Diamond Sutra:

> World-honored One, having listened to this Discourse, I receive and retain it with faith and understanding. This is not difficult for me, but in ages to come - in the last five-hundred years, if there be men coming to hear this Discourse who receive and retain it with faith and understanding, they will be persons of most remarkable achievement. Wherefore? Because they will be free from the idea of an ego-entity, free from the idea of a personality, free from the idea of a being, and free from the idea of a separated individuality. And why? Because the distinguishing of an ego entity is erroneous. Likewise the distinguishing of a personality, or a being, or a separated individuality is erroneous. Consequently those who have left behind every phenomenal distinction are called Buddhas all.[435]

---

435. *Diamond Sutra*, trans. A. F. Price and Wong Mou-lam (Boston: Shambala, 1990), 32.

Navigation

This is a primary axiom of self-navigation, an alignment with the gravity of zero, the gravity of non-existence. That the tuning and navigation of this librarynth is the fundamental skill sets of philosophy, mysticism, psychology, science, and mathematics alike obscure the realization that a side-effect of holographic access to memory is that they will be ordered, in effect catalogued, by their emotional significance, the density of interconnection to and from their neural correlates in the hippocampus. The most significant memories - good and bad - will function like strange attractors exhibiting beacon-like gravity in proportion to their intensity. 'It is because she knows that not she or anyone else knows anything of her horrible sins and faults in comparison with what God knows of them,' Porete says in 'Mirror of Simple Souls.'[436] Or, as Tad Delay remarks in 'God is Unconscious,' 'A psychoanalytically informed theology is a conception of trauma. Regardless of who we pretend to be, our facades of humility and arrogance alike betray the deeply buried illusions we inflict upon ourselves with an irascible wrath, all for the misguided notion that our trauma will not surface and show itself through the veneer of security. The illusion of non-anxiety works until it does not.'[437]

In correspondence with Marie von Franz titled *Reflections on the Structure of the Universal Number Continuum*, mathematician Jefferey Bishop makes a case for dimensional transition in geometric terms being a strange mirroring, a mirroring on each dimensional axis. It is a meandering and difficult text, looping and repeating itself, and even occasionally seeming to get lost in its own looping. In this sense it resembles Burroughs and Brion Gysin's cut-up experiments, seeming to break free of linearity through abstract self-reflection and what can be described in a tongue-in-cheek manner as dimensional travel - but this, a simulation based on finding or constructing transitional moments between mathematical dimensions. As zero is the same zero in all dimensions, it becomes a kind of multi-axial elevator shaft connecting each coordinate of the librarynth to every other, a strange 'tunnelling' through levels. An interesting takeaway from this piece comes at his contention that the 4th dimension requires a substantial inward-facing energy to be able to mirror and 'invert,' or more properly implode, along 4 dimensional axes - represented in thought as a black hole of reflectivity that performs as its own attractor in this abstract vector space. 'But the fifth dimensional element of symmetry is not an axis in any formal sense, and is altogether a more complex extension "into an unknown space." This is the symmetry element described as the non-performable operation of inversion through the center.'[438] In his terms,

---

436. Marguerite Porete, *Mirror of Simple Souls*, trans. Hugo M. Van Woerkom (unpublished, 2008), 34.
437. Tad Delay, *God is Unconscious* (Eugene: Wipf and Stock, 2015), xiii.
438. Jeffery Bishop, *Reflections on the Structure of the Universal Number Continuum* http://vixra.org/pdf/1105.0008v1.pdf (2011).

dimensional or scale transitions can only occur in spatial positions that conform to certain types of complexity, positions that align across dimensions, such as zero, for systems capable of taking error-corrective action, of maintaining a balance.

At the moment of self-loss, whether virtual or actual, every point in the brain becomes electrochemically connected to every other point in the brain. This experience is often recalled as a feeling of hyperconnectedness, of 'everything is everything' - a complete breakdown of the subject-object dynamic as the vast array and complexity of the sense stream often completely overwhelms any ability to recognize the self-model, and the first-person perspective decays until all input and output are perceived simultaneously across all the senses. When this barrier has been passed, the subject ceases to perceive images directly from shared reality, being left only with their symbolic representation in mind. According to Julius Evola, 'If the normal man is able to orient himself at all without the direct support of these images, he finds himself in a state of reverie, and then in the dream state, in which the energization of the imaginary activity, dissociated from the external senses, is accompanied by further reduction and emptying of consciousness of Self...further still and he enters into a state of apparent death.'[439] Another expression of balancing du[e/a]lisms as explicated by Land, 'on the one hand death as the ultimate nostalgia of signification, on the other death as the virulent flux of communication,'[440] sets up a radical notion of balance as the diagonal solution for this di-lemma of the ego being trapped in the astonishment. Of particular use in the navigation of this state are the lessons learned from yoga, meditation, and vajrayana: acceptance, relaxation, breathing, preparation for mental contortion as one is funneled through the mirror-strung ego tunnel toward a 'central' zone where we transcend reflection and become the mirror maze. This radical un-grounding presents the concept of an observer-less infinite perspective on all possible realities, in all directions, including internally, as the true world-for-itself.

He will travel freely through many worlds of experience - from direct contact with life-process forms and images, he may pass to visions of human game-forms. He may see and understand with unimagined clarity and brilliance various social and self-games that he and others play. His own struggles in karmic (game) existence will appear pitiful and laughable. Ecstatic freedom of consciousness is the keynote of this vision. Exploration of unimagined realms. Theatrical adventures. Plays within plays within plays. Symbols change into things symbolized and vice versa. Words become things, thoughts are music, music is smelled,

---

439. Julius Evola, *The Hermetic Tradition* (New York: Inner Traditions International, 1971), 104–105.
440. Nick Land, *Thirst for Annihilation*, 125.

sounds are touched, complete interchangeability of the senses.[441]

...floating tomb [that] enshrines a dark abyssic twinness with the eternal, one spiritually defined by inverse suspension in a volitional forcefield of opposing attractors. The love that is its place is not soft, but adamantine, contentious, and operative in negation, in the form of resistance which permits not. Suspended with the finality of death in the divine abyss of itself, secure in the omnipresent center....the tomb is saturated with the blackness of this negativity, this NO, which holds the unthinkable thingless essence of creativity and everlasting freedom.[442]

We can suppose that this matrix stores information in a regressing hierarchy of interiorized reflections of itself, in a form similar to the familiar Chinese ivory balls carved one within another, each level free to rotate independently.[443]

This presents a unique perspective on awareness when brought toward consilience with neuroscience and mysticism - that it may not be bound necessarily to being human, or even mammal or animal at all and could be a fundamental property of existence, possibly a type of empathy that expands our subjectivities by taking into account the subjectivities that surround us, viewing the Other not as if through a window, but as if we are their mirror. It is through this dream we realize Metzinger's proposition of transparency of self, and begin a methodology of opacity, a practice of observing the observer as it winks out of existence and subsequently rebuilds itself. A methodology of disallowing the self from interjecting over the interconnectedness, and an always-working-hypothesis of the eternality of Reason based on an alignment with the unknown - the infinite dissolution of our Selves in the boundless sea of hyperspace, the 'infinite ocean of God.'[444]

When thought dissolves, we dissolve with it. Whoever we think we are dissolves into awareness that is free of the concept of self. In that very moment, we can directly experience the non-solidity of phenomena, the reality of emptiness, or shunyata. At the same time, there is so much energy present—so much so that it forms into another moment. The energy brings a sense of clarity that is so sharp, it is like a clear mirror in which mind can at last recognize itself. In this mirror of mind, we see

441. Timothy Leary, Richard Alpert, Ralph Metzner, *The Psychedelic Experience: a Manual based on the Tibetan Book of the Dead*. http://www.holybooks.com/wp-content/uploads/Timothy-Leary-The-Psychedelic-Experience-The-Tibetan-Book-Of-The-Dead.pdf (1964), 26.
442. Nicola Masciandaro, 'Wings Flock to My Crypt,' in *Mors Mystica: Black Metal Theory Symposium 4* (London: Schism, 2015), 379.
443. Terence McKenna, *The Invisible Landscape* (New York: HarperCollins, 1993), 75.
444. William James, *Varieties of Religious Experience* (New York: Barnes and Noble, 2004), 342.

the radiant yet transparent nature of our own awareness.[445]

In summation, the brain as a reflective structure may be no mere metaphor, deep physical and emotional isolation exposes the jagged edges and missing pieces of our inchoate selves, and subjective experience seems to be constructed by the closing of, or simulation over, perceived gaps between already-hyperconnected multi-level nodes of sensory recordings in the brain by analogy, logical connections in abstract thought, and causal/spatial/temporal 'adjacency' (direct experience). The shift from a spatial abstraction (3-dimensional external reality) to a higher dimensional temporal abstraction gives us a simulated 'top-down' view of our entire self-memory, but the transition between these dimensions involves traversing a hyper-mirroring 'ego-tunnel' that exposes us to a totalized reflection of our utterly incomplete yet utterly interconnected selves and generates an automatic gravity toward the replay of emotionally significant memories while showing just how malleable memory is within emotional space. That this could be of profound importance to psychotherapy belies the fact that it is, quite simply, terrifying for the traumatized, as the worst *always* comes first. The training received in yogic and ascetic practices take on incalculable value, as a kind of never-ending deconstructive 'self-less' balancing act seems to be the only method for remaining within this space - this, the charnel ground of the infinitely blissful horror of pure self-knowledge. As the entrance to the Mirror Maze can be found in every Self, so the Escape is found in Self-less-ness.

Acknowledgements

All gratitude to SVOM-e, Stephanie, and the Baron.

---

445. Dzogchen Ponlop, *Mind Beyond Death* (Ithaca: Snow Lion, 2008), 17.

9

Implications of a Paranormal Labyrinth

Roberta Harris Short

> The irresistibleness of things that neither threaten nor jeer
> nor defy, but arrange themselves in mass-formations that
> pass and pass and keep on passing.
>
> ~Charles Fort[446]

As comparative religion scholar Jeffrey Kripal points out in *Authors of the Impossible*, we are engaged in a massive cultural and political effort to maintain material reality as the dominant mode of existence.[447] Our ordinary lives are replete with strange occurrences; but, outside of popular entertainment vehicles, we live as though they do not exist. Kripal and others, Charles Fort among them, argue that reality is more magical than we wish to admit; so we do not admit it.[448] The stakes are high with regard to paranormal events since acknowledging invisible forces has consequences. The event becomes a path: to conventional renditions of spirituality and religion; to scientific research in a quest for measurability and predictive factors; or to refreshed scepticism, denial of the event, and reassertion of coincidence.

    I became interested in the paranormal, not as a neuroscientist, psychologist, mathematician, or physicist, but as an individual who may have experienced precognition and remote viewing. In the spirit of Fortean efforts to record the extraordinary instead of repressing it, I offer for consideration a single event, which may be precognitive. This is not a scientific study, but rather a meditative essay on the occurrence, elements and processes that may be contributive, and possible implications.

---

446. Charles Fort, *The Complete Books of Charles Fort* (New York: Dover Publications, 1974), 4.
447. Jeffrey Kripal, *Authors of the Impossible* (Chicago: The University of Chicago Press, 2010), 252.
448. Ibid., 246.

The Event

The following is an account of a single event in 1982, and subsequent events from 1982 to 1987:

In the fall of 1982, I was living in Houston, and I married a man whose background and beliefs were fairly traditional. I worked as an artist, designer, and photographer most of my adult life and now teach English and creative writing at college level. My background and interests have not been particularly traditional. I include this information because my husband's worldview and presence are key elements of this story.

Early in my marriage, I had a nightmare. I dreamt my mother had a brain disorder and died. In the dream, her body—pale, emaciated, small, partially covered with a hospital gown and white sheet—was lying on a gurney against a wall in a hospital hallway. The walls were yellow and green; the floor was linoleum, tan or tan and grey. There were doors in the hallway; and midway down, through one of them, in a lab around the corner, I saw her head had been cut open horizontally across the forehead. The skull was open. There was not a lot of blood. Her brain was grey and shrunken and pulled to one side. The light was yellow. I was filled with horror and astonishment; and even all these years later as I write this, my eyes fill with tears. I swam upward in the dream as though through water, unable to breathe. I was screaming, screaming, and I screamed myself awake. My screaming was in the dream, and my screaming was in the world, and my screaming woke my husband. I told him the dream, all the while crying at the reality of it and feeling inconsolable. He was kind but firm in his claim that it was only a dream. He said there was nothing to say it was true. She was fine, tooling around in her Buick, shopping at Neiman's.

This seemed to go as dream experiences do; they are so real to the dreamer. The bystander, who doesn't experience the immediacy of the dream, seems to recognize his or her role and encourages the dreamer back to 'reality.'

In the days that followed, my husband and I spoke a few times about the dream. It was vivid and seemed real, and I wondered if we should tell my mother or my father. We asked ourselves: What is it for? What does it mean?

There was no purpose in telling anyone about the dream. Even if it were true, even if dreaming true were possible, my parents' experience of aging or coming to terms with illness or death would not be made better by my recounting the terror of what I had seen in the dream. So of course, we told no one.

About a year later, in late 1983, my mother had a car accident in a parking lot; she hit the gas instead of the brake. She said she couldn't feel her foot. Concerned about the lack of sensation and about driving, she underwent testing. In January of 1984, Dr. Stanley Appel, currently Director of the

Houston Methodist Neurological Institute, diagnosed dementia, tentatively Alzheimer's, although diagnosis could not be confirmed through testing at the time. I remember the timing of the diagnosis because, earlier that week, we learned I was pregnant with our first child; and I didn't tell my parents because my news seemed inappropriate, even frivolous, when she had just been diagnosed.

Over the next year, my mother's mobility and cognitive abilities steadily declined. During this time, my father's health also deteriorated due to cardiovascular disease. In 1985, my mother was put in a nursing home. In 1986, I had a second pregnancy and was put to rest for a month. By the time I visited my mother after the birth of our son, she no longer knew me.

My father, in the meantime, without telling us, arranged to have an autopsy performed upon my mother's death in order to determine what form of dementia she had. He later explained that since we were having children, he felt we should know whether the disease was heritable. Because his health was poor and he seemed to be in decline, he had the results mailed to my house, not his. I did not order the autopsy or know it had been ordered.

My mother's degeneration was steady, gruesome, and long. She did not wander or become violent as many Alzheimer's patients do. She lost movement and the ability to communicate and in the end, could only scream. She weighed less than 80 pounds when she died, and her appearance was ghoulish. I write these things not to disturb those who read or listen to this account, but because, as these events were unfolding, my husband and I were continuously reminded of the dream and that it seemed to be coming true. I was horrified by my mother's condition; but I knew what she looked like in the dream. I had seen the autopsy, and I knew we were not at the end yet. So perversely, the dream gave me a kind of endurance I might not otherwise have had.

In May 1987, I was driving down the freeway and felt the wind, or a movement of air, sweep past the back of my neck and head in the car though the windows were closed. To the north, to my right, my mother lay in a nursing home. I sped home and called my husband to leave work and come home. We went to the nursing home; I was told there was no reason to be there; her condition hadn't changed. It was afternoon; she had an infection, and I was breastfeeding and didn't want to infect my family. I didn't touch her. I paced awhile in the middle of the room despite their urging me to leave. Then I stood by her bed and said goodbye. She died that night. I returned at 2 a.m. when they called to tell me of her death. At that time, I learned the autopsy had been ordered.

When my mother died, my father was ill in Methodist Hospital. My husband and I were in the hospital visiting my father to tell him of her death when the phone rang in his room. I answered. Her body had been delivered to the morgue, but the nursing home had forgotten to tag it; someone needed to identify her. We went to the main floor and were met by the doctor in charge of the autopsy, who led us down labyrinthine passageways beneath the building to the morgue. The walls were, or seemed to be, yellow and green. The floor I know was linoleum. I write this; and I am lightheaded at the memory, as I was lightheaded that day as they pulled her body out of the wall, and it shook on the rusted metal rack. Emaciated, in a hospital gown, under a sheet.

A sunny afternoon, some time later, a letter containing the autopsy results arrived in the mail. I simply went to the mailbox one afternoon and found the letter inside. The report confirmed that she did not have Alzheimer's; there were no plaques and tangles. She had an unknown form of dementia, not seen before. The brain had atrophied, especially the frontal and parietal lobes and the hippocampus. There was 'shrinking of neurons' and also 'severe neuron loss.'[449]

I do not have an interpretation. My husband has said that perhaps God sent the dream to help me survive the long and difficult decline of my mother. I don't share his certainty about the intent of a deity; I do see that the dream and its information are undeniable facts. For a while immediately after these events, I tried to look into research in the field of the paranormal; but the only location I found in Houston at the time was a strip center advertising palm readers and psychics. I gave up the investigation.

For many years, other than an occasional conversation with my husband, I didn't speak about the dream since I knew of no apparently legitimate means of investigation. Possibly paranormal events such as this have been an area of my life that is disquieting and compelling and that I have cared about and wondered about but have not investigated. I happened on a discussion of the paranormal in Jeffrey Kripal's book, *Esalen*, and was fortunate to attend a few of his lectures and read works by him and recommended by him.[450] Perhaps because I am now older and have less to lose, I have begun to investigate.

The Comfort of Scepticism

As human beings, we have extraordinary abilities to sense, assemble information, and imagine. Although this dream might seem precognitive, the elements, viewed separately, may be seen as coincidental. A deconstruction of the dream might look like this:

In 1982, my mother was 67, and I was aware dementia can afflict the aged. I was fairly close to my parents and saw my mother every few weeks or so. One might unconsciously discern subtle changes in a family member's speech, conversation content, or behaviour. These later might appear in a

---

449. *Autopsy Consultation Report*, H., L., Outside Case, Stanley Appel, M. D., Department of Pathology, The Methodist Hospital, October 26, 1987. Primary Source.
450. Jeffrey Kripal, *Esalen: America and the Religion of No Religion* (Chicago: The University of Chicago Press, 2008), 339-345.

dream.

However, prior to the dream, I was not aware of Alzheimer's disease and was not aware that the sole means of confirming an Alzheimer's diagnosis at the time was through autopsy. The horizontal cut along the head could be seen as logical. How else would one do it? I leave assessment of this to the reader.

I have always engaged in creative activities, professionally and at leisure. Also, I had visited Methodist Hospital numerous times prior to my mother's death because my father had been ill. I was familiar with its corridors though I had never been to the morgue and did not know where it was located until I was required to identify my mother's body. A combination of imagination and familiarity with the hospital could produce the scenic backdrop of the dream.

For the sceptic, the remaining details in the dream are to be seen as coincidental. In life, at the time of the dream, my mother was not thin, but struggled with being overweight. Her appearance in the dream, ghoulish and emaciated, was not at all as I had ever seen her but was, in fact, the way she appeared at death. I didn't know my father ordered an autopsy or had it sent to my house addressed to me, or that the visual image of her brain in the dream would correspond to the written description of the brain's deterioration in the autopsy. To dismiss precognition, the precise nature of the illness, the severity of it and death due to it, the appearance of my mother at death, the ordering of the autopsy, its execution, and the written clinical description of the brain must be seen as coincidental. Further, one must contend that a single mind/imagination/dreamer assembled information, personal cues, and imagined detail, within a cohesive narrative framework, to create a single dream which became reality over the next five years, in an orderly, steady fashion, one element after the next.

Unlike precognitive dreams in which the dreamer is the actor in the dream and in the subsequent reality, I was not the actor in the dream. Not the deceased person, not the doctor who diagnosed, or the doctor who performed the autopsy, or the person who ordered it, the person who typed it, or who mailed it, or who delivered it to my mailbox. I seem to have been a recipient.

Regarding Unseen Forces

Discussions of the paranormal often fall within a framework of faith or belief and may draw on a concept of God, or unseen forces, or an infinite mind into which we tap, or the activity of aliens. In the context of religion, the event, a beneficent act, is viewed according to the dicta of the faith and denomination and in context of the believer's felt sense of spirituality. This was my husband's interpretation. The dream, for him, was a gift from God. I had a dream; and as time passed, we could see it was coming true; and we knew, as things got progressively worse, we still had some distance to cover. We had greater endurance because of the dream, and this was a benefit.

Material reality and scientific empiricism are commonly seen as separate from religious conceptions and form the arena in which 'scientific' discussions of reality occur. Science and rational thought are seen as hedges against the vicissitudes of human conceptions of the religious and the sacred. Justifiably so. We see the divinely inspired mind employed as cover for discrimination, persecution, and murder; or the divinely inspired mind is delusional and a projection of a tormented mind, a mind loosened by abuse, trauma, or chemicals. We are cautious, with reason; and a system of laws and reliance on what we perceive as the rational are seen as protective. The difficulty with viewing the rational as protection against atrocity is that we create an overall cultural assumption that the non-rational in its entirety is suspect and not serious or contributory—save in an imaginary sense or as mythic and a means of understanding culture—to our understanding of the nature of being. Dismissing belief in the paranormal on the grounds that it is irrational, as defined by a rational/irrational binary discourse that privileges the rational, simply uses definition and dominant discourse as a means of devaluing events and discrediting those who discuss them.

A definitive claim that an event is the handiwork of a god seems invented, though not necessarily through artifice. Creativity employed in the construction of religious dogma is lively and interesting, but the study of myth and motivated discourse reveals that religious constructions are more troubling than comforting.

Examining paranormal experiences is similar to interpreting divine inspiration; yet, examining paranormal events may provide insight into our perception of the world and our ability to act in it.

The Numbers Vortex

For over eighty years, scientists, mathematicians, and psychologists have engaged in the formal study of paranormal events.[451] In scientific parlance, 'Precognitive ESP confronts us with the paradox that specific information about the environment may be obtained in the absence of any interaction with it we can understand in the whole context of present-day information theory.'[452] The approach has been to adopt 'a phenomenological treatment, fitting potentials to the empirical evidence.'[453] Such investigations are based on the notion that 'if precognitive experiences...are genuine...there is some rational structure or theory which can accommodate both paranormal and

---

451. Richard Wiseman, 'Wired for Weird' in *Scientific American Mind* 22.6 (Jan/Feb 2012) (Accessed Oct 26, 2015).
452. C. T. K. Chari, 'ESP and the "Theory of Resonance,"' *British Journal for the Philosophy of Science* 15.58 (1964), 139.
453. Ibid., 139.

normal experiences.'[454]

Pertinent elements investigated by scientists include ascertaining whether precognition occurs, identifying the mechanism in play, and determining characteristics in common in those who experience or believe in the phenomenon. Products include the application of quantum mechanics and string theory to postulate correlative concepts of time and space, mathematical analyses of event structure, assessments of believers' intelligence, anecdotal account aggregation as inductive proof, determination of characteristics of dreamers, development of theories of mind to account for information availability and access, and speculation regarding free will.

Initially, I imagined precognition was a function of time, that we did not understand time, and that time and space perhaps were bending or shifting. I thought, similar to the problem of time, remote viewing might be a result of our not understanding space. Using geometric descriptors, string theory and discussions of the fifth through tenth dimensions, mathematicians and scientists have postulated worlds that could include the paranormal, assuming its occurrence.

An example of the attempt to explain precognition with the use of a mathematical model is found in 'The Geometry of Precognition.' Here, Robert G. Howard offers a mathematical answer to the question, 'What information or method allows a person to know about an event before the event occurs in ordinary time, t_4?'[455] Having begun with the assumption that precognition occurs and has done so for 'hundreds of years,' Howard explains the mechanism through symbols designating elements of the occurrence, described geometrically in six dimensions; for example, symbols include a container for the event called an 'event-volume.'[456] Credence rests on the assumption that the mathematical symbols are meaningfully representative and that the language of mathematics is capable of illuminating the paranormal. However, languages employed to describe are simply that: systems of symbols used as signs for the thing; as such, they skirt core issues pertinent to precognition. The difficulty of penetrating these deeper issues through the field of mathematics is made clear in statements such as this logical fallacy: 'Part of dreaming is often the expansion of perception to five dimensions so the observer gains information in the t_5 dimension, which includes future events that have not yet happened.'[457] So, precognitive dreams occur because the dreamer accesses information from the future.

The mathematical framework may seem useful to those who find kinship with mathematics or view mathematical interpretation as a 'rational' approach

---

454. Lee F. Werth, 'Normalizing the Paranormal (A Philosophical Feasibility Study of Precognition),' in *American Philosophical Quarterly* 15.1 (Jan., 1978), 47
455. Robert G. Howard, 'The Geometry of Precognition,' in *Journal of Spirituality and Paranormal Studies* 32.3 (Jul 2009), 125.
456. Ibid., 129.
457. Ibid., 135.

to the apparently immeasurable or incomprehensible. However, the approach, a bit like word play, does not tell us if a paranormal event has occurred, the mechanism of the appearance of future events in the event plane, why this person and not that experiences precognition, the state of being required to receive information, or if information is received.

The impenetrability by science of apparently paranormal events has caused long-standing frustration among researchers. Quantum mechanics and string theory applied to precognition postulate theoretical structures of time and space but do not appear to have an empirical correlate; as such, they are similar to religious assumptions. The concept of multiple dimensions provides a complex structural framework; however, it does not explain the mechanism, treat implications, or adequately account for free will. The difficulty is acknowledged by physical scientists, including Henry P. Stapp, who thoughtfully probes the application of quantum mechanics to activities of the mind. Stapp states unequivocally, 'quantum laws allow only the potentialities for various possible future happenings to be computable. No rules that determine what will actually happen are given by quantum theory.'[458] He additionally contends, 'nature's choices are not random but are more deeply entwined with our lives.'[459] Here, Stapp indicates the operation of nature as a force determining event outcome in the realm of possibility. Stapp's view offers an understanding of what might be in play: If human ability to sense is heightened, perhaps the intentionality of nature is discernible—not precognition, but the ability to detect and assemble forces in play.

Inconclusive research outcomes have led scientists to shift from laboratory experiments testing psychic phenomena to studies of believers and the effects of belief.[460] These have produced a variety of results in terms of assumptions regarding intelligence, optimism, creativity, and ability to visualize.

One study indicates believers may be mistaken; but the belief, characterized as similar to superstition and belief in ghosts, permits optimism, assists them as they encounter challenges, and is an advantage, even if not real.[461] A separate study, making use of a diary of recorded and reported precognitive dreams, concludes that subjects selectively remember dreams that appear to be precognitive because they have import, that is, meaning.[462] In this study, the body of recorded dreams included some not precognitive and others the dreamer claimed were precognitive. Significantly, experimenters

---

458. Henry Stapp, 'A Quantum-Mechanical Theory of the Mind/Brain Connection,' in *Beyond Physicalism*, ed. Edward F. Kelly, Adam Crabtree, and Paul Marshall. (Lanham: Rowman & Littlefield, 2015), 185.
459. Ibid., 186.
460. Wiseman. See note 5.
461. Jeffrey Rudski, 'The Illusion of Control, Superstitious Belief, and Optimism,' in *Current Psychology* 22.4 (Winter 2004), 307.
462. Wiseman. See note 5.

concluded that since not all were precognitive, none were.[463]

Theorists contend that all people possess a 'germ' of hypersensitivity or lucidity, but those who claim paranormal experiences appear to have characteristics in common: they are often artists, members of a cultural system that accepts the paranormal as possible, people who have suffered trauma or abuse and are therefore more 'open,' or those who have experimented with psychedelics.[464] Here, I offer relevant personal information: I passed through a period of severe abuse as a child and some trauma as an adult. I have always engaged in creative activities as a way of understanding and interacting with the world. My educational and cultural background includes emphasis on analytical thinking and acceptance of paranormal events as possibilities, though not well understood. I began experiencing possible precognition as brief flashes and in dreams at age seventeen. I have experienced multiple events of apparent remote viewing, precognitive flashes, and visioning in dreams since that time.

Zurich neuropsychologist Peter Brugger reported that the tendency to perceive the paranormal as occurring is more common among subjects who demonstrate right brain dominance and 'tend to value intuitive thinking over rationality.'[465] The experience of the paranormal is labelled 'irrational' in this context, and those who misidentify experiences as paranormal are assumed to do so because of internal disposition rather than accurate assessment of real events.[466] Here again, the quest for a rational explanation reflects the privileging of the apparently rational and the pervasiveness and persistence of a rational/irrational binary discourse that undergirds so much of the research and discussion.

In what may be seen as an attempt to move past this inhibiting binary, a 2004 MIT study of Tibetan monks using fMRI brain maps revealed the monks' ability to control perceptual awareness and imaging, body processes and response to the environment, as revealed in heightened activity of the left frontal lobe.[467] Here, advanced medical technology is combined with inventive methodology. The associated Investigating the Mind Conference 'explored how scientific and Buddhist viewpoints on human consciousness can inform each other' as 'the Dalai Lama and Buddhist scholars traded insights and questions with neuroscientists and psychologists on such topics as attention, mental imagery, and emotion.'[468] The study demonstrated the ability of practiced meditators both to filter the environment and increase awareness;

---

463. Ibid.
464. Jeffrey Kripal, *AI*, 226.
465. Wiseman. See note 5.
466. Ibid.
467. Curt Newton, 'Meditation and the Brain,' in *MIT Technology Review* (Feb 1, 2004). http://www.technologyreview.com/news/402450/meditation-and-the-brain/, Accessed Oct. 29, 2015)
468. Ibid.

researchers concluded 'we still know "shockingly little about the connections among the parts of the human brain."'[469]

We also have a great distance to travel in developing investigative methodology capable of examining intangible aspects of perception, consciousness, and creative thinking; this fact is demonstrated by the nature of this study undertaken by MIT. The brain, as an organ to be tested and measured, was examined as the locus of thought, as though mind resides in brain and generates thought, mediated by perception and the ego. However, the concept of consciousness and mind, as located in the brain, is not accepted by all. Thinkers such as Bernardo Kastrup postulate mind as a non-dual reality and human beings as outposts of mind thinking itself through their existence.[470] Similarly, in *Authors of the Impossible*, Jeffrey Kripal discusses various notions of 'irreducible mind' as a 'form of consciousness' or 'collective Mind' 'behind' psychic events.[471] Kripal points to mind's illusory nature, drawing on Jung's comment on flying saucers, 'something is seen, but one doesn't know what.'[472] The notion of mind as timeless and without spatial constraints is a useful 'thought experiment,' as Kripal notes.[473] The precognitive dreamer taps in, or the seer remotely sees, perhaps because defences are down or the person is quieted through meditation and open to receiving. Like Stapp's concept of nature and possibility, the nonlocal, non-dual mind is theoretical; similarly, it offers a mechanism through which apparent precognition might occur and a glimpse of its possible meaning.

And meaning is critical. The apparently paranormal events I have experienced have been associated with accident, illness, birth, and death. Laboratory investigations of precognition may provide information on the ability to sense, but the context and content is far removed from lived events and may have limited application. The difficulty seems to be in intent and method. Although MIT's 2004 study of Tibetan monks seems revolutionary in its holistic approach to the study of consciousness, the time-honoured approach of the scientist as an agent acting and the method of controlling subject and environment to stabilize conditions, observe results over a given time period, and generate reliable data, inherently seem not to be the way the paranormal operates, though some might postulate certain conditions decrease or increase the likelihood of paranormal events.

---

469. Ibid.
470. Bernardo Kastrup/Jeffrey Kripal Skype/lecture, Jeffrey Kripal, 'Materialism Is Baloney,' Jung Center Series (Jung Center, Houston, Texas, October 29, 2015).
471. Jeffrey Kripal, *AI*, 249.
472. Ibid., 249, and also reference to Jung, 246.
473. Jeffrey Kripal, 'Materialism Is Baloney,' Jung Center Series (Jung Center, Houston, Texas, October 29, 2015).

The Vision, the Seer, and the Violence of Words

Two of the components that seem closely allied to the occurrence of apparent precognition or remote viewing are the state of being required to receive the information and apparent significance or meaning. However, distance from the event may inhibit the ability to apprehend and understand. The discussion of a psychic event is its own event and operates separately from the actual experience of precognition or distant knowing/seeing.

In this way, examining precognition through language is similar to examining it using mathematics or scientific theory. As Jacques Derrida makes clear in his seminal work, *Of Grammatology*, the spoken word is not the thing but is closest to the thing; the written word is further.[474] Derrida famously took on the power of words to efface that which they represent, noting, as Jean-Jacques Rousseau and Claude Lévi-Strauss did before him, that words do violence to the signified object by replacing the object with the sign, or word.[475] The discussion of precognition is housed in language, and language violently effaces meaning. The word 'precognition' is a sign, not the experience; the word imperfectly brings a representation of the signified event to mind. If we then employ the symbolic language of mathematics or abstract scientific theory to describe or explain the event, we have added layers of abstraction to the signifier, which already has done violence to the event, the signified; and we have moved a considerable distance away from the very thing we wish to perceive and understand.

I often have written down or drawn my dreams. Nightmares of childhood; messy, disorienting dreams related to current life and issues; solutions to design problems; and images that later appear in artwork, part of the creative process and product. I dream and I awaken and remember the dream. The dreams that later come true have had a particular clarity and forced me to awaken, but I do not know definitively if a dream is precognitive or is simply a night-time resifting life's contents within a particular psychological frame. Dreams are a multifaceted resource and a way of reclaiming the self; sometimes they come true. Visual images predominate and appear to be vehicles for transmission though the visual may not be the vehicle for everyone or the only conveyance.

I struggle to put into words that which is predominantly visual or something I sense is occurring. Sometimes words are present; yet the word separates me from that which the word describes, much in the same way that the substance of paint itself, combined with movements of my hand holding a brush against a canvas, separates artistic notion from the artwork the viewer later sees. The paint, Naples yellow, let's say, has its own life—something like

---

474. Jacques Derrida, *Of Grammatology*, Corrected Edition, trans. Gayatri Chakravorty Spivak (Baltimore: The Johns Hopkins University Press 1997), 11.
475. Ibid., 106.

the sun on a hazy day, or a faded plaster wall in a tired equatorial city, or the teeth of a young man who smokes to comfort himself. Paint is more than my internal vision; paint comes to the canvas with a vision of its own. In the same way, a word, the word 'paint' is not the thing itself. The word 'paint' sits with its own poetry, its own art and etymology, between me and the thing I am attempting to describe.

Extending this analogy, we can look at the activity of painting in another way. Images seen in the mind seem not to occur in word-language but in image-language, as alternatives to language, non-verbal communication. Images may be culturally mythic or symbolic for the individual; they carry history and become a language of their own. The confluence of image, canvas, paint, the hand, and artistic intention seem to combine to create the artistic product, but this is something other than a direct representation of an imagined vision. The creative experience includes surprise—a combination of image, intention, materials and the artist in motion, and something unexpected that includes play. The play of light, delight in creation, creative impulse itself, supported by training and familiarity with paint and canvas, illuminated by messages that come to the artist lost in the process, who feels the art talks back. And so, listening is also part of the process.

In a similar way, writing operates recursively and often includes play and surprise. Written depiction is not the thing itself but the thing effaced and transformed by words; the writer, another artist lost in contemplation, has the sense that the writing is illuminated in some way. Written meaning is enhanced by the way language can dish up metaphor, just as paint dishes up something glorious and expressive in and of itself: Naples yellow.

And so, distance from that which is represented and play both are intrinsic components of representations through images and words.

Reflections

The pursuit of paranormal studies, precognition and remote viewing in particular, may benefit from a reexamination of terminology, methodology, means of reporting, and approach to response and assessment. To increase understanding of paranormal events, we may need to be aware that the use of language, mathematical symbols, and complex theoretical constructions add layers of abstraction to the discussion and the event. A multi-disciplinary approach may be helpful as a means of exploring the extraordinary complexity of an event; and this approach may need to attend to visioning, language, and sensing since these appear to be integral to apparent precognition and remote viewing.

We have many languages. The selection of this or that system of signs and symbols is arbitrary, based on assumptions made within a cultural context and highly motivated by the acceptability of the system to a larger community, for example, the scientific community or a general public more comfortable with mathematical models than with intuitive approaches. If the pressure of academia or the scientific community or even the professional community of psychologists were less dominant, other languages of interpretation, other approaches to understanding affording a more complex view—coming from artists and writers and dramatists, from meditators and philosophers, from naturalists and astronomers—might be heard.

We are moving in the direction many claim of becoming more visually oriented, perhaps as a result of global connectedness and media access. The pervasiveness and power of visual rhetoric is evident, and human behaviour is changing as a result. What if there is more to this trend? What if increasingly visual means of communication indicate, not simply technological attachment, or our desire to connect, or be passively entertained, but changes in human perception and communication, a move more than metaphorical, trade-based, and financially driven, a deeper move toward the visionary? The human mind, as resident in all of us, is connecting to itself. We breathe soft words into the ears of strangers around the world; we scream others awake with our terror in the night. We do not need quantum theory or transcendental notions of mind to represent this in abstract terms. We can see it becoming in an increasingly literal fashion. Even as this is occurring, people are working to achieve heightened sensitivities and increased abilities to absorb and make meaning of information and perception, which in turn may lead to increased ability to sense or tap into aspects of this larger global 'mind' to gain understanding and insight and to 'foresee.'

I am not claiming that the events in the dream I have recounted are definitively precognitive. I consider the dream revelatory of circumstance, available information, human ability that should be studied and is not well understood, and the elaborate operation of an array of forces that may include the unseen. Part of experiencing such events has to do with being open, perhaps influenced by harm done to us that tears us apart and opens us, not through some magical alteration but through brutal lessons brought home, which have the ability to create compassion in us. We are able to become creative, contemplative, nonjudgmental selves, open and sensing without expectation, allowing arrival.

We can acknowledge the risks of embracing the unexplained and unseen while still pressing forward to a more inclusive understanding of the paranormal. Psychic events are attached to the infinite in the sense that they are comprised of a vast array of components and touch on areas we have grouped and classified previously, in our limited thinking, as scientific, mathematical, mythical, spiritual, or psychological. They are all of these, but they are more because they are inclusive; and they point to a larger sense of what it is to be alive and to live. The desire to understand is deeply human; the fault lies in limiting the approach. Perhaps those who experience the paranormal have an acute ability to sense and assemble, and perhaps they instinctively narrativize and assign meaning; this of course is extraordinary, and it also is a routine part of existence. Our understanding may suffer because we sequester it to one realm or another and exoticize it, poke and prod it, instead of entering its realm.

Contributors

David V. Barrett is a researcher and writer on new religious movements and esoteric history and religion. He has been a schoolteacher, a programmer and intelligence analyst and a journalist. He has been a freelance writer since 1991. His many books include *The New Believers* (Cassell, 2001), a 544-page study of new religions and their relation to society, *A Brief History of Secret Societies* (Constable & Robinson, 2007), an investigation into the history, aims and ideals of Rosicrucianism, Freemasonry and other esoteric movements, *A Brief Guide to Secret Religions* (Constable & Robinson, 2011), which covers new age, Pagan and other esoteric religions, and *The Fragmentation of a Sect* (Oxford University Press, 2013), an academic study of schisms from the Worldwide Church of God. He is a frequent contributor to radio and TV programmes, speaking on religion and esoteric subjects. In 2009 he received his PhD in Sociology of Religion from the London School of Economics. When not researching and writing he has played fretless bass in a variety of rock, folk and blues bands. He lives in London, UK.

Eden S. French is a genderqueer Tasmanian writer and novelist. Under her previous name, Sophia French, she has written fiction for the lesbian press Bella Books. Her most recent publication is a transgender-themed science fiction novel, *Reintegration* (Queer Omen, 2015). She holds a BA Hons. in History (2010) from the University of Tasmania, where her honours dissertation reconsidered British spiritualism during the First World War in light of contemporary 'continuing bonds' approaches to grief and mourning.

Timothy Grieve-Carlson is a recent graduate of Drew University in Madison, NJ. He currently works for a local non-profit and is planning his applications to graduate school.

James Harris, death-eater, neuronihilist, ghost in the machine. Black Metal Theorist, poet, psychonaut, contributor at syntheticzero.net and annihilatingunity.blogspot.com.

Jack Hunter is a PhD candidate in the Department of Archaeology and Anthropology at the University of Bristol, and a Visiting Lecturer in the Department of Theology and Religious Studies at the University of Chester. His research takes the form of an ethnographic study of contemporary trance and physical mediumship in Bristol, focusing on themes of personhood, performance, altered states of consciousness and anomalous experience. In 2010 he established *Paranthropology: Journal of Anthropological Approaches to the Paranormal*. He is the author of *Why People Believe in Spirits, Gods and Magic* (2012), editor of *Paranthropology: Anthropological Approaches to the Paranormal*

(2012) and *Strange Dimensions: A Paranthropology Anthology* (2015), and co-editor with Dr. David Luke of *Talking With the Spirits: Ethnographies from Between the Worlds* (2014).

Robin Jarrell is an independent scholar who lives in Lewisburg, PA. She is the author of *Fallen Angels and Fallen Women: The Mother of the Son of Man* (Wipf and Stock, 2013).

Jeffrey J. Kripal holds the J. Newton Rayzor Chair in Philosophy and Religious Thought at Rice University. He is the author of *Comparing Religions* (Wiley-Blackwell, 2014); *Mutants and Mystics: Science Fiction, Superhero Comics, and the Paranormal* (Chicago, 2011); *Authors of the Impossible: The Paranormal and the Sacred* (Chicago, 2010); *Esalen: America and the Religion of No Religion* (Chicago, 2007); *The Serpent's Gift: Gnostic Reflections on the Study of Religion* (Chicago, 2007); *Roads of Excess, Palaces of Wisdom: Eroticism and Reflexivity in the Study of Mysticism* (Chicago, 2001); and *Kali's Child: The Mystical and the Erotic in the Life and Teachings of Ramakrishna* (Chicago, 1995). He is also the co-editor, with Sudhir Kakar, of *Seriously Strange: Thinking Anew about Psychical Experiences* (Viking, 2012).

Christopher Laursen is a PhD Candidate in the Department of History at the University of British Columbia who holds an MA in History (2009) from the University of Guelph in Ontario, Canada. His doctoral dissertation, *Mischievous Forces: Reimagining the Poltergeist in Twentieth-Century America and Britain*, examines the rise of a psychological concept that a living person is unconsciously responsible for physical manifestations reported in poltergeist cases. He has had articles published in *Fortean Times* and *Paranthropology*.

Fatima Regina Machado has a PhD in psychology from the University of São Paulo (USP) and a PhD in Communication and Semiotics from the Pontifical Catholic University of São Paulo (PUC). She holds a Masters degree in Science of Religion from the same institution. She currently works as a post-doctoral researcher at the Postgraduate Program on Studies in the Sciences of Religion at the Pontifical Catholic University of São Paulo. Fatima is a research member of the Laboratory on Studies in Psychology of Religion, University of São Paulo (USP), and she is a founder (with Wellington Zangari), coordinator and scientific director of Inter Psi – Laboratory of Anomalistic Psychology and Psychosocial Processes at USP, Brazil. Her research interests include areas such as anomalistic psychology, social psychology of religion, intersections between semiotics and psychology, cognitive aspects of psi experiences, their social interpretations and relevance in daily life. Acknowledgments to CAPES – Coordination for the Improvement of Higher Education Personnel. fatimaregina@usp.br

Everton de Oliveira Maraldi, PhD, is a psychologist and a post-doctoral researcher at the Institute of Psychology of the University of São Paulo (USP), Brazil. He is a research member of the Inter Psi – Laboratory of Anomalistic Psychology and Psychosocial Processes, USP, Brazil. He is a professional member of the Parapsychological Association, USA, and a research member of the Laboratory on Studies in Psychology of Religion, USP. His research interests include topics such as dissociation, mediumship, anomalous creative experiences, and paranormal beliefs. Acknowledgements to FAPESP – São Paulo Research Foundation, Brazil. evertonom@usp.br

Leonardo Breno Martins, PhD, is a researcher of the Inter Psi – Laboratory of Anomalistic Psychology and Psychosocial Processes, USP, Brazil. His research interests include topics such as Social Psychology, Mental Health, Anomalistic Psychology, and Psychology of Religion. He is also dedicated to a series of scientific divulgation initiatives such as the book *Procurado: Descobertas recentes da psicologia sobre experiências "alienígenas" e "sobrenaturais,"* 2014 (*Wanted: Recent Psychological Discoveries about "Supernatural" and "Alien" Experiences*). Acknowledgements to FAPESP – São Paulo Research Foundation, Brazil. leobremartins@usp.br

Roberta Harris Short, PhD, holds the position of Associate Professor of English at Lone Star College-CyFair. She previously served for several years as a lecturer at Texas A&M University, where she taught creative writing and literature. She holds a PhD in Creative Writing and English Literature and an M.F.A. in Creative Writing/Fiction, both from the University of Houston Creative Writing Program. She also holds a Bachelor of Fine Arts degree in painting and printmaking. While at UH, she was awarded the 2006-2007 Women's Studies Dissertation Fellowship in response to an excerpt of her second novel, *Girolama, Acorsia, and Caraminella*. She also received the James Michener Fellowship in response to her first novel, *Touring with Mariana*, and was nominated for Best New American Writers in 2000. Prior to teaching at Texas A&M, she served as a teaching fellow at the University of Houston and taught in community colleges and for Inprint, Inc., the funding arm of the UH Creative Writing Program. Her work has appeared in *Texas Review*, *Céfiro*, and *Crack the Spine*.

Wellington Zangari has a PhD in psychology from the University of São Paulo (USP), Brazil, and holds a Masters degree in Science of Religion from the Pontifical Catholic University of São Paulo (PUC). He did an internship at the Division of Perception Studies – University of Virginia during his postdoctoral research. Wellington is Professor of anomalistic psychology and social psychology of religion at the University of São Paulo. He is one of the founders (with Fatima Machado) and coordinators of Inter Psi – Laboratory of Anomalistic Psychology and Psychosocial Processes, University of São

Paulo, Brazil. His main areas of investigation are the social psychology of religion, anomalistic psychology, dissociation and hypnosis. w.z@usp.br

Index

CPSIA information can be obtained
at www.ICGtesting.com
Printed in the USA
BVHW020327050220
571264BV00024B/220